Black Power, Yellow Power,
and the Making of Revolutionary Identities

Black Power, Yellow Power, and the Making of Revolutionary Identities

Rychetta Watkins

University Press of Mississippi   Jackson

www.upress.state.ms.us

The University Press of Mississippi is a member
of the Association of American University Presses.

Copyright © 2012 by University Press of Mississippi
All rights reserved
Manufactured in the United States of America

First printing 2012

Library of Congress Cataloging-in-Publication Data

Watkins, Rychetta.
Black power, yellow power, and the making of revolutionary identities / Rychetta Watkins.
  p. cm.
  Includes bibliographical references and index.
  ISBN 978-1-61703-161-8 (cloth : alk. paper) — ISBN 978-1-61703-162-5 (ebook) 1. African Americans—Relations with Asian Americans. 2. Black power—United States—History—20th century. 3. African Americans—Politics and government—20th century. 4. Asian Americans—Politics and government—20th century. 5. American literature—African American authors—History and criticism. 6. American literature—Asian American authors—History and criticism. 7. Power (Social sciences) in literature. 8. Black power in literature. 9. African Americans—Ethnic identity. 10. Asian Americans—Ethnic identity. I. Title.
  E185.615.W3413 2012
  323.1196'0730904—dc23   2011028923

British Library Cataloging-in-Publication Data available

CONTENTS

Acknowledgments vii

Introduction
Developing a Critical Perspective on Power in Literature 3

Chapter One
Translating Fanon: Black and Yellow Power as
American Anticolonialisms 21

Chapter Two
From Gorilla to Guerilla: Defining Revolutionary Identity 53

Chapter Three
Power and the Ivory Tower: Academics as Intellectual Guerillas 82

Chapter Four
Reading Resistance: The Guerilla in Literature 114

Chapter Five
Promise vs. Praxis: The Legacies of Power 143

Notes 153

Bibliography 173

Index 187

ACKNOWLEDGMENTS

Working with words makes you acutely aware of how inadequately and incompletely they capture the fullness of human emotion. These few words can capture only the shadow of my gratitude and provide the barest hint of the depths of my esteem.

To my ancestors: Samuel Du Bois Minor, Sr., Loma Cox Minor, Julia Williams Davis, and Willie Bea Henley. I cherish every memory. To those whose names are unknown to me, those who survived the unthinkable . . . *ashé*.

To my beloved parents, Richard and Margie Watkins; my phenomenal brothers, Michael Minor and Richard Watkins; my beautiful "sisters," Lottie Minor and Marcia Moore; and my smart, funny, boisterous, warm, and loving extended family of aunts, uncles, cousins, and mo' cousins . . . thank you for your caring support and unflagging love. I heard a man say that there is a difference between family and relatives. Relatives may share a common genetic heritage, but family is bound by love and would do anything for one another. Thank you for being MY *family*! I would be nothing without you.

To my amazing friends: Colette Cummings, Laverne Deckert, Sherita Johnson, and Alveda Williams. You are the family I have chosen for myself. I feel so fortunate that you have graced my life with your presence and filled my days with laughs, hugs, wisdom, tears, and adventures (even the ones I can never remember!). Thank you for loving me for who I am (and for keeping me sane!). You are each awesome, wonderful, and inspiring in your own way.

Special thanks to James McLeod, Gerald Early, Sharon Stahl, and the Mellon Minority Undergraduate Fellowship Program at Washington University in St. Louis for setting me on this path. Thanks also for the gracious support of my friends and mentors at the University of Illinois, Robert Parker, and Canaan Baptist Church in Urbana, Illinois, my former colleagues at William Jewell College, and my colleagues at Rhodes College in Memphis, Tennessee, my hometown. Tip of the brim to my surrogate brother, Charles McKinney, and basketball buddy, Jenny Brady. Thanks to all of you who have come alongside me in community, friendship, and "sisterhood" in St. Louis, Chambana, Kansas City, and Memphis.

To my godchildren, Jennifer and Johnny: "Hold fast to dreams..."

To my creator: Psalms 27:13 and Hebrews 11:1.

Black Power, Yellow Power,
and the Making of Revolutionary Identities

INTRODUCTION

Developing a Critical Perspective on Power in Literature

Even in the growing body of work devoted to AfroAsian studies, very few scholars mention, let alone focus on, "Yellow Power." Much of this scholarship is preoccupied with black and Asian cooperation in radical political movements, in particular the nonalignment or "Third World" movement initiated at the conference of nonaligned countries held in Bandung, Indonesia, in 1955. A spate of books and anthologies, among them Bill Mullen's *Afro-Orientalism* (2004); *Everybody Was Kung Fu Fighting: Afro-Asian Connections and the Myth of Cultural Purity* (2002) by Vijay Prashad; *Writing Manhood in Black and Yellow: Ralph Ellison, Frank Chin, and the Literary Politics of Identity* (2005) by Daniel Kim; and the collections *AfroAsian Encounters: Culture, History, Politics* (2006), edited by Heike Raphael-Hernandez and Shannon Steen, and *Afro Asia: Revolutionary Political and Cultural Connections between African Americans and Asian Americans* (2006), edited by Fred Ho and Bill Mullen, are all bent on illuminating an often overlooked or misunderstood history of black and Asian cultural and political commerce. Most of these studies seek to recuperate a shared social history that challenges binaristic constructions of race, as well as the conventional wisdom that presumes a longstanding antagonism between African Americans and Asian Americans. As a result, much of this work is as intent on recovering, remembering, and recouping as, with a couple of notable exceptions, moving towards a cultural studies hermeneutic for the comparative analysis of these texts. Often, many of these works rely on a narrow range of interpretive mechanisms, evaluating AfroAsian relationships as examples of productive providence, or instances of more or less successful coalition building. This project attempts to address both gaps: providing yet another piece of the puzzle of this fascinating time in American near history and culture, while exploring the value of "Power" as a hermeneutic born of the web of social, historical, and cultural interactions, influences, and cooperations that characterize black and Asian interethnic interactions in America in order to complicate binaristic notions of race beyond black and white and provide the basis for an indigenous American comparative ethnic cultural studies.

To accomplish this goal, my work joins the work of others like Vijay Prashad, Robin D. G. Kelley, Laura Pulido, and Daryl Maeda in developing interpretive schema for cross-cultural and comparative AfroAsian analysis that account for the discursive nature of ideological and cultural productions and are based in readings of the radical political discourse of the period.[1] In *Everybody Was Kung Fu Fighting*, Prashad offers the concept of the "polycultural," which he defines as "a provisional concept grounded in antiracism rather than diversity. Polyculturalism, unlike multiculturalism, assumes that people live coherent lives that are made up of a host of lineages—the task of the historian is not to carve out the lineages but to make sense of how people live culturally dynamic lives. Polyculturalism is a ferocious engagement with the political world of culture, a painful embrace of the skin and all its contradictions"[2] (xii). His study goes on to trace a history, ancient and modern, of AfroAsian political, social, and cultural interactions that blur the boundaries between black and yellow to shake up the easy notions of contemporary "identity politics" that allow white supremacy to continue. Likewise, I locate a polyvalent sense of identity and struggle in "Power"; just as it provided a powerful organizing metaphor for African Americans, it also afforded Asian American audiences a staging ground for a panethnic identification while gesturing towards other nonwhite groups also struggling against the effects of white racism both in America and abroad.[3]

Another notable exception is Robin D. G. Kelley and Betsy Esch, who in "Black Like Mao," look to Mao and Maoism not just as an interesting historical footnote, but as one of the major influences of the development of Black Power. Drawing on the series of interactions and exchanges between Mao and early black radicals, the pair posits the idea of "black Maoism" to explain the consolidation of Black Power ideology. The authors write, "Central to Maoism is the idea that Marxism can be (must be) reshaped to the requirements of time and place, and that practical work, ideas, and leadership stem from the masses in movement and not from a theory created in the abstract or produced out of others struggles."[4] In this sense, Black Power represents a necessary adaption of the insights of Mao, Guevara, Fanon, and others in order to formulate an ideological apparatus suitable for the struggle against American racism. Likewise, I read "Yellow Power" as an effort to adapt these same political and ideological tools to address the specific effects of racism on Americans of Asian descent and their communities. Therefore, evaluations of the ideological purity or completeness of power, black or yellow, miss the point. Just as Maoism grew out of a Marxist analysis of the Chinese system, Black and Yellow Power had to grow out of the struggle against American racism; in addition, these ideologies were necessarily contingent, provisional, and highly dialectic, seeking to reconcile new strategies and challenges as each movement evolved. Just as the diffuse nature of power makes it difficult to track as a political or historical phenomenon, it also makes it difficult to pin down as an interpretive framework. However, any effort to define a cultural phenomenon must start by describing what is there.

Though Stokely Carmichael was not the first to use the term "Black Power" as a phrase, he most powerfully appropriated "Black Power" as a slogan at a rally outside of Greenville, Mississippi, during the continuation of James Meredith's March Against Fear. Stokely Carmichael and Charles Hamilton further developed the concept in the 1967 text *Black Power: The Politics of Liberation in America*. According to Carmichael and Hamilton, Black Power encompasses a political and social agenda that would enable "black self-determination and black self-identity" leading to "full participation in the decision making process affecting the lives of black people."[5] Their book-length manifesto begins with an epigraph that establishes the purpose of the work that follows: "This book represents a political framework and ideology which represents the last reasonable opportunity for this society to work out its racial problems short of prolonged destructive guerilla warfare. That such violent warfare may be unavoidable is not herein denied. But if there is the slightest chance to avoid it, the politics of Black Power as described in this book is seen as the only viable hope" (xi).

Carmichael and Hamilton then go on to do a number of things, but most relevant for this study is their attempt to delineate the concept of Black "Power." Heavily influenced by Frantz Fanon's forceful, philosophically grounded, and politically charged writings, they describe Black Power as part "political program" to bring about full inclusion and participation for Africans in America's electoral and economic systems, and part psychic prescription for black consciousness, a subjectivity grounded in "pride, rather than shame, in blackness, and an attitude of brotherly, communal responsibility among all black people for one another" (xvi). They identify the basic tenets of Black Power as: 1. redefinition or self-definition, 2. self-determination—the creation and support of community organizations and institutions (44), 3. self-defense, and 4. "political modernization" (39), a broad term that seems to include a call for greater political participation to end the economic exploitation of the black underclass, as well as the need for radical, racial consciousness—an awareness of the need for radical/revolutionary struggle to change America's racist, repressive social systems. While critics often dismiss Black Power as all rhetoric and no program, this ideology of revolutionary ethnic nationalism persists, framing discourses of African American and Asian American representation during the latter decades of the twentieth century. For this reason, it is important to understand the strength of Power's pull on our collective imagination.

In a 1996 *Callaloo* article, "'Where, By the Way, Is This Train Going?': A Case for Black (Cultural) Studies," Mae Henderson argues for an adaptation of cultural studies tools that would increase sensitivity to the historical contexts of "Black Studies."[6] Henderson points out that while the tools of British cultural studies are valuable for investigations of ethnicity and useful for opening up a range of materials for textual study, a truly Black American Cultural Studies should attend to "indigenous principles and methodologies," looking to the black experience in America for tools to investigate African American literature and culture.[7] Henderson imagines that this methodology could then be used to answer questions like "How can the paradigm of 'internal colonialism' postulated by the black theoreticians of the 1960s serve as a model for studying dominant structures of power?"[8]

By looking back to Black Power, my study represents just such an attempt. Drawing on Stokely Carmichael and Charles Hamilton, I define Power initially as a revolutionary political ideology designed to cultivate a black identified consciousness that is aware of the need to overthrow American-style colonialism using radical action. Power constitutes a new ideology of representation informed by Fanon and motivated by the principles of self-definition, self-determination, self-defense, and the need for revolutionary struggle to change America's racist, repressive hegemony. Ultimately, this study defines an aesthetic of Power, tracing how this ideology was communicated, represented, and depicted in visual and written texts from this period. While W. E. B. Du Bois, Malcolm X, Che Guevara, Mao Tse-tung, Kwame Nkrumah, Amílcar

Cabral, Léopold Senghor, and Aimé Césaire, among others, all influenced the development of radical black ethnic nationalist thought, this study centers on Frantz Fanon and his critique of colonialism largely because his work was frequently cited by activists and artists in many of the newspapers, essays, fictional works, and archival texts that I reviewed over the course of this investigation. In particular, I am interested in how the "internal colony" critique linked Black Power to contemporaneous anti-imperialist struggles, to a prior history of anticolonial struggle, and to the struggles of other ethnic groups against oppression and repression within the United States. Drawing on Black Cultural Studies, AfroAsian Studies, and New Black Power Studies, this project investigates how African Americans and Asian Americans adapted the concept of the "internal colony" to explain the sociocultural legacies of American-style colonialism in their communities and how the "internal colony" informs subsequent academic analyses of "postcolonial" black and Asian subjectivity in America. Taking all of this into account, this work proceeds from an understanding of Power as more than just rhetoric, but as an ideology of revolutionary ethnic nationalism.

Within the African American and Asian American newspapers, essays, and novels of this period, Power also informed a revolutionary aesthetic inspired by this ideology. In order to explain this movement from ideology to aesthetic, I center my inquiry on the period roughly between 1966, when Stokely Carmichael adopted the slogan, and 1981, when Elaine Brown stepped down as chair of the Black Panther Party. During what I call the Power period, there existed the political need for new modes of representation, the international templates to inspire these new identities, and the presence of sympathetic, independent media outlets to disseminate them. This period was marked by intense artistic and academic production and should, I believe, count along with Reconstruction, the Harlem Renaissance, and black naturalism and realism of the late 1940s and '50s as a period of dynamic literary production during which African American literary and cultural forms were radically redefined. One key element of the discourse of Power is the consolidation of the guerilla figure, the revolutionary subjectivity that became associated with revolutionary nationalist Power politics, during the Power period. Though Power advocates came to embrace armed resistance, they also stressed the need to be ideologically ready to pursue control of political systems and cultural representations. It is hoped that this effort to recover a sense of the related discourses of political ideology, literary innovation, and social change that defined the Power period will lead to more nuanced understandings of Power's legacies in contemporary Asian American and African American literature and literary studies.[9] Specifically, I hope that a fuller understanding of the libratory aims of these revolutionary forms will combat culturally corrosive contemporary representations of blackness and yellowness that often are attributed to this moment, but have been evacuated of political meaning. The Power era then is a pivotal moment during which these threads came together to radically reform representations of Asianness and blackness that continue to shape American popular culture today.

Though the concept of Power, as a methodology for achieving liberation, provided a space for cultural cooperation and appropriation between Africans and Asians in America, this was not the first instance of cooperation between these groups, either in America or on the global stage. While the recent history of African American and Asian American relations seems dominated by conflict and controversy—the Los Angeles riots, the Korean shopkeeper shootings, debates over access to higher education, control over the black hair care industry—there are international and national precedents for Asian and African American cooperation. Among them was the Asian-African Conference held in April of 1955 in Bandung, Indonesia.[10] Delegates from twenty-nine countries representing one-quarter of the world's landmass and two-thirds of the global population at the time came together in the midst of the cold war as representatives of independent, nonaligned, nonimperialist countries with a collective "consciousness of freedom and desire to rely upon [themselves] in co-operation with others" to secure peace.[11] As important as the discussions about the developing superpower divide was the desire to create a supportive network with other previously colonized countries moving to secure their recently realized independence. African American and Asian American activists seeking to create a revolutionary coalition to bring about change in the American context cited this legacy of global cooperation often.

In addition, Asian American activists like Grace Lee Boggs, a first-generation Chinese American activist in Detroit, Yuri Kochiyama, a nisei or first-generation Japanese American activist in New York City, and Richard Aoki, Japanese American nisei who served as field marshal and integral member of the Oakland Branch of the Black Panther Party, were involved in the Civil Rights Movement or the Black Power Movement, serving as important allies and conduits for ideology and strategy.[12] The Vietnam conflict provided yet another opportunity for black and Asian cooperation in America. African Americans protesting the racially skewed troop deployment allied with Asian Americans protesting their maltreatment in this country, struggling with the prospect of fighting against an enemy whom they in some cases resembled, while both decried the hypocrisy of America's neocolonialist aggression abroad.

The Third World College Strike at San Francisco State College in 1968 serves as yet another example of Asian American and African American cooperation. Although the strike was motivated by a disagreement over the suspension of faculty member Nathan Hare and the future of the Black Studies program, the Black Student Union was eventually joined by the Students for a Democratic Society and the Third World Liberation Front, a group of Hispanic and Asian American students. Together, the coalition demanded a School of Ethnic Studies at the then San Francisco State College.[13] Ultimately, their actions led to the organization of the college's School of Ethnic Studies, the first of its kind in the country. Though I have chosen to highlight a few instances of AfroAsian cooperation, there exists a record of cooperation and mutual borrowing that testifies to the similar psycho-socio-cultural effects of America-style racism on both groups.

In an effort to re-create some sense of this moment, this interdisciplinary project uses a range of cultural productions including visual media, newspaper articles, editorials, literary anthologies, and a selection of novels. I use this diverse array of materials as a backdrop to illuminate the workings of discourses of personal identity, representations of ethnic subjectivity, and literary forms and techniques present in both the Asian American and African American literary traditions during the Power period. To develop this interethnic cultural studies method of analysis, I draw on recent scholarly insights from a number of developing fields, including Asian American Studies, studies of the American sixties, and AfroAsian Studies as well as New Black Power and New Civil Rights Studies. Many scholars in these fields are revisiting the history of Black Power, the Black Arts Movement, and the Black Panther Party to critique reflexive dismissals of this period and open up investigations of local and grassroots resistance movements, while at the same time weaving together wide-ranging descriptive reassessments of this era and its cultural products.[14] In testing disciplinary boundaries, my methodology builds on the fields of history, cultural studies, and American literary studies in an effort to craft a mechanism relevant to the American experience of each group.

James Smethurst's impressive and comprehensive critical overview, *The Black Arts Movement: Literary Nationalism in the 1960s and 1970s*, models this type of scholarship. Smethurst traces the political, ideological, and literary influences that constitute the "matrix" of Black Arts, or more properly, literary nationalist cultural works by blacks during this period. Breathtaking in its scope, the ideologically, spatially, and chronologically messy nature of the Black Arts Movement seems to dictate the structure of Smethurst's wide-ranging study. Like much recent scholarship on Black Power, Smethurst begins with a critique of the at-times assumptive and reductive scholarly pronouncements about Black Power that are often associated with scholars and activists involved with the Black Feminism Movement of the 1970s and the New Black Aesthetic Movement of the early 1980s. Smethurst observes, "Even now, academic assessments of the Black Arts and Black Power movements are frequently made in passing and generally seem to assume that we already know all we need to know about these intertwined movements and their misogyny, homophobia, anti-Semitism, and eschewal of practical politics for the pathological symbolic."[15] Here, he responds to the longstanding trend in scholarship to critique the Black Power and Black Arts Movements for their homophobia and misogyny, dismissing these movements, and by extension many works from these movements, as narrow-mindedly ideological, strident, and exclusionary.[16] Academics, in particular those influenced by post-structuralist practices, also have summarily dismissed this moment for its often undeniably essentialist definitions of race and ethnicity.[17] For many years, these types of dismissals headed off much serious scholarship about the Black Power and Black Arts period. At the same time, Houston Baker has long recognized the Black Aesthetic moment as an exceptional period of literary production on par with the Harlem Renaissance.[18] Similarly, scholarship in Asian American Studies has recognized the Asian nationalist movement as precipitating campus activism and sparking an increased interest in the history of Asian peoples in America. Just as the concept of the "long Civil Rights Movement" encourages scholars to look beyond the "heroic narrative" of the movement to studies of grassroots-level resistance and organizing practices, as well as local institutional and personal histories, the New Black Power Studies looks beyond the "failure" of these national movements to the local and regional individuals and activities inspired by Power's principles.

In addition to thinking beyond the nationally significant figures and institutions that have long marked Civil Rights Studies, the New Civil Rights Studies also calls on scholars to rethink the chronology of the movement, to look backwards from the "Montgomery to Memphis" arc of the conventional narrative of the Civil Rights Movement to the advent of the Legal Defense Fund's legal strategy spearheaded by Charles Houston and Thurgood Marshall in the early 1930s, and to look forward to the "Reagan Revolution" of the 1980s when many of the legal and political gains secured using the LDF strategies were challenged and overturned in courts and municipalities across the U.S. [19]

Smethurst's work concedes, indeed embraces, the mélange of ideological and artistic influences that led to the multiple local iterations of what can collectively be thought of as Black Arts Movements; he goes on to point out that the "problem that makes both 'Black Power' and 'Black Arts' such elastic terms is that there was no real center to the interlocked movements. That is to say, that there was no predominant organization or ideology with which or against which various artists and activists defined themselves." [20] While on the one hand, his work lays the groundwork for more minutely focused critical studies of the networks of people, ideological movements, and artistic institutions that grew out of the interaction between Black Power activists and Black Arts practitioners during this period, his historiographic methodology leads him to preclude discursive investigations of the ideological structures that not only linked Black Power to Black Arts, but also linked Black Power and Black Arts to the affiliated Asian, Chicano, and Native American ethnic nationalist movements that receive significant treatment in his study. This work seeks to build on the work of Smethurst and others to develop a tool for literary analysis inspired by our continually evolving knowledge of the "long Civil Rights Movement" and the ideologies that linked artists, activists, and groups during this period.

Moreover, this project is indebted to an understanding of cultural studies that expands the range of texts acceptable for academic study and an understanding of Black Cultural Studies, which in the American context attempts to account for the political dimension of identity politics while rejecting essentialism. For Madhu Dubey, this commitment to antiessentialism is also "counternationalist" and suspicious of a "corporate" black identity.[21] Therefore, this project draws on the anti-essentialist insights of Black Cultural Studies to critique not only the prescriptive notions of "authentic" identity active during this period, but also the subsequent flattening and dismissive pronouncements about this period.

In addition to being interdisciplinary, this project is also comparative and cross-cultural. Throughout the project, I place African American and Asian American politics, literature, and study alongside each other. Much like Laura Pulido's regional study of the interconnections between Asian American, African American, and Hispanic American revolutionary groups in and around Los Angeles between 1968 and 1978, my comparative ethnic study focuses on the "distinct forms of activism that developed among the Third World Left," with a focus on how each group adapted and engaged international and domestic discourses of revolutionary and cultural nationalism as strategies for activism.[22] Indeed, Daryl Maeda argues that such studies "[demonstrate] the interdependence of racial formations strictly among people of color" and "refute the narrative" that Third World Left and New Left organizations devolved into "narrowly divisive identity politics."[23] Thus, comparative ethnic studies like this one reveal the pervasive effects of America's process of racialization and highlight shared strategies of resistance.

Thus, pairing the groups becomes less about figuring out which tradition had more influence than or borrowed more than the other; instead, I engage both traditions in an effort to elucidate the shifting meanings of "race" and "identity" in America from 1966 to 1981 and to better evaluate whether the promises of representational agency made by post-structuralist and postcolonial theory and practice are fulfilled or broken for African American and Asian American literary studies in the 1980s and '90s. "But," some may ask, "won't lumping together African American and Asian/Pacific Islander Studies undercut a concern with the particular and local, legacies of postcolonial critique that permeate African American and Asian American Studies?" I would answer that studying these traditions side by side allows a richer and more complex description of America's racialization process as captured in the literary and cultural objects of this process, the "African American" and the "Asian American." Studying Asian American and African American literature together also thwarts neocolonialist (and neoconservative) attempts to misappropriate the meaning of gains made by one group as evidence against another. The "model minority myth" is one example of the reductive trap that lurks within assimilationist narratives of immigrant success seeking to ensnare Asian and African Americans in a futile opposition that only serves America's oppressive binary racial system. Therefore, reading these traditions through each other frustrates the myth of the effeminate yellow and explodes the specter of the inarticulate brute black body, situating these cultural stereotypes as shades of the same racializing process.

A concern with the usefulness of the colonial paradigm and postcolonial theory also undergirds this interdisciplinary, comparative, and cross-cultural project. K. Anthony Appiah offers a definition of postcoloniality based primarily on its use value to the intelligentsia. He defines postcoloniality as

> the condition of what we might ungenerously call a comprador intelligentsia: of a relatively small, Western-trained, group of writers and thinkers who mediate the trade in cultural commodities of world capitalism at the periphery. In the West they are known through the Africa they offer; their compatriots know them through the West they present to Africa and through an Africa they have invented for the world, for each other, and for Africa.[24]

Appiah meditates on postmodernism and the postcolonial using examples of African art to discuss how the pressures of economic, cultural, and intellectual markets can shape a work's reception, evaluation, and valuation. In his discussion, Appiah distinguishes between postmodernity—the "aesthetics" of the postmodernist condition—and postmodernism—the political process whereby postmodernism is instituted. He goes on to make a similar distinction between the postcolonial and postcoloniality. Likewise, my project distinguishes between postcoloniality—the aesthetics of an imagined postrevolutionary society—and postcolonialism—the political process that brings about a postcolonial society. I believe this insight can also be extended to a discussion of the ideologies and aesthetics dedicated to the dissolution of the colonial: the anticolonial. Appiah, insisting on the distance between the postcolonial and the postmodern, questions the use of African art to emblematize the de facto postmodern condition, citing the danger of the traditions becoming, in Sara Suleri's phrase, an "Otherness-machine."[25] In his discussion, Appiah focuses on the *Man on Bicycle* sculpture, which James Baldwin had earlier singled out as an example of the cooptation of Western invention in African art. The sculpture, which depicts a Yoruba merchant in Western-inspired clothing riding a bicycle to the market, blends African adaptations of Western dress and technology. Baldwin praises the sculpture, not for its cultural authenticity, but for its perceived inauthenticity, its syncretism. The man on the bicycle transgresses the narrowly defined categories of "traditional," "contemporary," "Baule," and "Fanti," imposed by the curators and collectors putting together the exhibit. Baldwin observes that the *Man on Bicycle* "is challenging something—or something has challenged him."[26] Like the man on the bicycle, the guerilla represents a cooptation of Western form and technology. Also like the sculpture, the guerilla, as it appeared in the American context, embodies a spectacle of the other, a representation of difference that frustrates received racial and social categories. Both challenge the easy categories of colonized thought, thus embodying the anticolonial and representing a turn away from the overdetermined subjectivity of the colonized.

Unlike the sculpture, which Appiah praises for its unself-conscious ontology, the guerilla represents an uneasy cultural interface. This figure and subjectivity coalesced during the Power period as a symbol of militant resistance and political liberation, originating in Maoist socialist discourse and practice, then moving into the American consciousness through news reports of Vietnamese resistance to American neo-imperialist aggression. Quickly, the guerilla came to embody the effort to reconcile the at-times contradictory and contentious nature of revolution with the ideological, militant, and cultural struggles bound up in that heavily contested term. Revolutionary black nationalists, seizing on the Vietnam conflict as an example of America's hypocrisy, soon identified with this figure. In turn, Asian American nationalists reappropriated the Panthers' revolutionary guerilla imagery and rhetoric to represent their own brand of resistance and to provide a rallying point for Asian American racial solidarity. My project follows this trajectory of the guerilla from a symbol of radical resistance, to the embodiment of political ideology, to a representation of empowered ethnic subjectivity in texts from the Power period.

The guerilla exemplifies a "resistant" persona, embodying a revolutionary subjectivity that symbolizes resistance while advocating the overthrow of the American system. Understood discursively, which I believe is appropriate to Power's dialectical critique of the American racialist system, the guerilla operates within the system of American-style institutional racism that constructed black and yellow people as members of internal colonies of "Others." The process of becoming a guerilla, as outlined in the visual and print media, rhetoric, and novels included in this study, thus functions as an allegory for the development of a liberated consciousness and, eventually, a liberated society. Therefore, Black and Yellow Power are predicated upon the development of revolutionary consciousness as key to disrupting this Self/Other relationship between internal colony and the repressive American mainstream. However, disrupting this binary using culturalist practices without disrupting the discursive practices and transforming the knowledges that supported them has left the guerilla trapped within what Abdul JanMohamed calls "terminal alterity," stranded as an always already resistant subjectivity.[27] Thus, this project concludes by considering the downfalls of this revolutionary subjectivity and looking forward to its implications for representations of blackness and yellowness in the over forty years hence.

This project originated with the question "what connects political colonialism with academic postcolonialism?" Little did I know the critical, political, and textual terrain that simple question would require me to cover. Eventually, I settled on the narrower question: "How do the political critiques of American style colonialism as psychocultural pathology that were formulated by Black and Yellow Power revolutionaries relate to scholarly postcolonialism, in particular postcolonial theories of ethnic identity formation?"

The first chapter, "Translating Fanon: Black and Yellow Power as American Anticolonialisms," focuses on early academic and activist responses to the work of Martinique-born, French-trained psychiatrist Frantz Fanon, situating him as a node for African American and Asian American ideological cooperation. In this way, Frantz Fanon also operates as a bridge between Black and Yellow Power. Anticolonialism, as defined by Fanon, provided a rationale for active, sometimes armed, struggle against the system that was circumscribing the lives of and actively colonizing the minds of people of color. Thus, anticolonialism became a basis for ideologies that recognized the need to address the psychological wounds of oppression. I propose that this anticolonialism provided both a political and an academic framework for addressing the consequences of racism on what Hortense Spillers calls the "flesh"[28] of people of color in America. Thus, both Black and Yellow Power can be considered variants of an anticolonialist nationalism, anticolonialist in that proponents identified America as creating and sanctioning internal colonies that buttressed America's definition of itself and nationalist in that they believed the antidote to this oppression was greater representation and self-determination for members of these groups. Contrary to popular impression, however, this compelling call for self-determination contributed to the development of competing definitions of "blackness" and "yellowness" as defined by Huey Newton, Stokely Carmichael, Maulana Karenga, leader of the US Organization, Amiri Baraka, Ishmael Reed, Frank Chin, Maxine Hong Kingston, Larry Neal, and Jeffrey Paul Chan, among others.[29] Some felt self-determination would be best achieved by creating separate physical spaces for ethnic groups, others by creating separate cultural spaces, but all were seeking to articulate a revolutionary sense of their ethnic identity in the wake of the turmoil and tumult of the "heroic phase" of the American Civil Rights Movement and in the midst of increasing opposition to Vietnam.

By starting with the ideological origins of power, this chapter explores a given: Fanon's influence on the Black Power and Black Arts Movements. Fanon's theories of colonialism and anticolonial resistance facilitated identification with transnational discourses of revolution and between African American and Asian American revolutionary activists. Fanon's work subsequently informed transnational discourses of resistance during the waves of anticolonialist movements that raced across the twentieth century. This circuit of influence is embedded within the intersecting discourses of self-determined Asianness and blackness that are the focus of my analysis.

The second chapter, "From Gorilla to Guerilla: Defining Revolutionary Identity," charts the coming together of the guerilla trope and revolutionary aesthetic using images from *The Black Panther* and *Gidra* newspapers. The writings of Frank Chin, Huey Newton, and Ishmael Reed and the editorial cartoons and work of Emory Douglas, staff illustrator for the *Panther*, establish the figure of the guerilla as the agent for a *particular* form of revolution. The chapter begins with a definition of the guerilla as a disciplined, ideologically grounded, solitary agent who engages in political and cultural action designed to disrupt oppressive social practices. The chapter then considers the evolution of this guerilla posture or relationship to American colonialism into a location for launching political and social critiques of American culture.

As I define it, the guerilla is a usually solitary, radicalized individual, conscious of the inequities in his or her community and motivated by a counterhegemonic political sensibility to fight against those disparities. While this position was first thought of as a political one, the figure of the armed guerilla fighter later denoted a generalized antagonistic relationship towards American society signified by changes in dress, hair, naming, and other cultural practices. Within the poems, plays, and novels of the Black and Yellow Power Movements, the guerilla provided ideological and visual referents for a developing revolutionary consciousness and helped spread the gospel of revolutionary readiness on a weekly and monthly basis. However, while other global struggles against colonialism focused on the necessity of armed struggle, the focus of Black and Yellow Power activists in America quickly drifted from militant calls for political agitation and armed resistance to an emphasis on cultural nationalism and a preoccupation with cultural re-creation and re-formation.

During this period, *The Black Panther* had one of the highest circulation rates of any underground newspaper; Bobby Seale remembers a circulation of almost 125,000 in 1969–1970.[30] During its run from 1967 until 1980, the paper was a source of income for the Party and a vital space for debating theory, policy, and strategy. Likewise, *Gidra* was one of the most influential papers of the Asian American Movement. According to William Wei, *Gidra* was the "first radical Asian American newspaper."[31] In addition to being the longest-running Yellow Power paper, *Gidra* also had the highest circulation of any Asian American Movement paper.[32] While circulation, which centered around California and the West Coast with most of the nine hundred to thirteen hundred subscribers concentrated in the Los Angeles area, peaked at about four thousand, many more people likely saw the paper because underground publications tended to be passed along and read by multiple users.[33] In these papers, the guerilla was constructed as a disciplined, ideologically grounded, solitary agent engaged in political and cultural action to disrupt repression. Both newspapers helped to position the guerilla as an antidote to the nonviolent strategies of the Civil Rights Movement and an example to the "masses." Like the poems and plays of the Black and Yellow Power Movements, the rhetoric, images, and representations of the guerilla in newspapers and literature provided instructive illustrations of radical consciousness and revolutionary readiness for the development of revolutionary consciousness.

Since Vietnamese guerillas could be male or female, the guerilla subjectivity also allows for a critique of masculinist representations of resistance in the American context, as well as the problematic pan-ethnic Asian American identity.[34] For all these reasons, both the Black and Yellow Power nationalist movements have been particular sources of concern for scholars seeking to move beyond conceptions of race based on biology or genetics to understand race as a social and political construction with material consequences. Frank Chin's strident confrontations of Maxine Hong Kingston, Amiri Baraka's sexist pronouncements and Stokely Carmichael's sometimes irresponsible comments from exile are just a few of the misguided acts that have tarnished the reputation of Black and Yellow Power. This project seeks to complicate the Power moment in order to sift through the ideological influences that distinguish its promises from the personal excesses and misguided rhetoric that have led to popular simplifications and critical dismissals of the Power moment.

The third chapter, "Power in the Ivory Tower: Academics as Intellectual Guerillas," turns to anthologies of Asian American and African American literature as sites for negotiating the tensions between activism and academic standards that emerged as ethnic studies programs developed. This chapter uses the editorial comments and introductions from *Black Fire* (1968), *Black Arts* (1969), and *AIIIEEEEE!* (1974) to reconstruct the tensions between African American and Asian American scholars and mainstream academia and the tensions within African American and Asian American Studies. When writers "more on fire with political energy than inspired by literary insight" encountered the scholarly and intellectual traditions of the academy, they had to respond to both institutional and disciplinary pressures on the developing fields of ethnic studies.[35] Initially, some African American and Asian American scholars and critics positioned themselves as "intellectual guerillas" motivated by political ideology to collate, express, critique, and disseminate ethnic analysis and criticism from within academe. Rather than question the editors' choices or the perils of canonicity, I consider the introductions and epilogues of the anthologies as a space where these scholars negotiated the tensions between the demands of the academy and the demands of "the street." In these anthologies we can also see the move from literature as a political tool in the process of anticolonialism to the critical treatment of African American and Asian American literature as evidence of postcoloniality.

The chapter then turns to Ishmael Reed and Frank Chin as examples of "guerilla" scholars who used *Yardbird* journal and Publishing Company to subvert publishing and academic hegemony and the mounting ideological hegemony of cultural nationalism in Ethnic Studies.

The fourth chapter, "Reading Resistance: The Guerilla in Literature," traces the movement of the guerilla trope into a selection of novels by African Americans and Asian Americans published or republished during this period. As a literary trope, the guerilla challenges and complements the black-leather-clad "revolutionary" figure commonly associated with Power politics as it speaks to the ideological motivation and political purposes of revolutionary ethnic nationalism. After considering Sam Greenlee's novel *The Spook Who Sat by the Door* (1969) as an example of a stereotypical militant, revolutionary subjectivity, I then use Alice Walker's *Meridian* (1976) and John Okada's *No-No Boy* (1957; 1976) to examine how these literary representations of the guerilla synthesize politics and aesthetics in a textual subject that complicates representations of blackness and yellowness, as well as revolution and resistance. Following in the footsteps of *Invisible Man* and *Native Son*, novels of this period often feature an individual protagonist struggling with his place in larger society, with issues of identity and with his or her ability to exercise control in his situation. Thus, these novels illustrate the process of developing a radicalized consciousness. We see characters struggle to change; characters who, through their engagement with militant and military experience, engage pan-national discourses of resistance and revolution.

The conclusion revisits the ongoing debate about and competing definitions of cultural nationalism and revolutionary nationalism. While some scholars of this period continue to use the term "cultural nationalism" to denounce Black and Yellow Power as insufficiently revolutionary, this use of cultural nationalism rests on a flattened understanding of the dialectics of revolution in the American context. Ultimately, I would argue, the distinction is less important for understanding the effects of Power ideology on ensuing discourses of African American and Asian American identity, subjectivity, and representation. Instead, the continued "struggle" over this point hinders deeper, more incisive, nuanced and expansive investigations of this period. Ultimately, the conversation seems a continuation of the critique that the Black Panthers and Black and Yellow Power are not worthy of serious study because they failed to overthrow the American social and political system of their day. However, Power ideology and aesthetics undeniably informed radical revisions of identity symbolized by the militant, ethnic nationalist, guerilla figure, which was instated by power politics and continues to influence the contemporary representations of blackness and yellowness, as well as studies of American ethnic identity.

This study, at heart, surveys the wages of, as Abdul JanMohamed put it, "constituting one's self as a 'resistant' subject."[36] JanMohamed argues that the consequences of adopting a marginal subjectivity are more dire for African American and, I would argue, Asian American writers because the American process of constituting racial identity has become proficient at separating cultural meaning from political purchase. As with earlier "renaissance" moments, the Black and Yellow Power moments saw widespread political and social changes that were taken up in the literature and, like those earlier moments, continue to impact us. So while the guerilla may originate in libratory strategy, it has been received in our popular consciousness as a few painfully pitiful iterations of black and yellow caricatures that "keep it real" regardless of the consequences.[37] My project looks back to look forward to new representations of black and yellow identity that reflect the promises of a new millennium, rather than the scars of the last.

CHAPTER ONE

Translating Fanon

Black and Yellow Power as American Anticolonialisms

> Since I was born in the Antilles, my observations and my conclusions are valid only for the Antilles—at least concerning the black man *at home*. Another book could be dedicated to explaining the differences that separate the Negro of the Antilles from the Negro of Africa. Perhaps one day I will write it. Perhaps too it will no longer be necessary—a fact for which we could only congratulate ourselves.[1]

This sentiment, expressed in the closing lines of the introduction to Frantz Fanon's 1952 treatise on the psyche of the colonized, seems eerily prescient in light of Fanon's early death from complications of leukemia at the age of thirty-six, a mere nine years after the publication of his first book, *Peau noire, masques blancs* (*Black Skin, White Masks*). Intended as the doctoral thesis for his psychiatry degree, Fanon published the work, which grew out of his own eye-opening and gut-wrenching experiences as a black French colonial subject, elsewhere instead. Between the publication of *Black Skin, White Masks* and his death in 1961, Fanon married, became a father, served in the medical service in Algeria and Tunisia, joined the FLN (Algerian National Liberation Front), published articles on his innovative mental health management approaches, served as Algeria's diplomatic attaché to Ghana, and travelled extensively, giving speeches and presentations on his psychiatric work, the Algerian resistance, and the future of the Third World. During this frenzied period, he also published two more volumes–*L'An Cinq, de la Révolution Algérienne* (in English, *Studies in a Dying Colonialism*) (1959) and *Les Damnés de la terre* (in English, *The Wretched of the Earth*) (1961)—which, along with *Black Skin, White Masks*, had and continues to have a lasting impact on academic studies of the formation of postcolonialism, racial and ethnic identity and subjectivity, and revolutionary movements and forms of protest.

Though Fanon did refer to the Civil Rights Movement in America, he did not write at length about the condition of the "Negro" in America. Instead, he situated his work as a template that others could adapt in order to narrate their colonial experience and plan their own anticolonial struggles. His death meant that other theorists and activists would have to do the work of translating Fanon's insights into the American context themselves. In this chapter, I will read Black and Yellow Power as distinct though related efforts to "Americanize" Frantz Fanon's meditations on the psychosocial effects of colonialism, subsequently adapting his work into an ideology that supported an array of social, cultural, and even militant efforts against American-style colonialism.

This chapter considers how the early publication history of Fanon's works in America shaped his reception by American activists and academics. The order of publication, as well as the glosses provided by the introductory and prefatory materials included in each volume have contributed to later readings of Fanon as an insightful commentator on the psychic toll of racism, an incisive critic of colonialism, and an advocate of violent revolutionary resistance. This range of readings has contributed to a Fanon myth that obscures his specific influence on the evolution of Power ideology. Initially, Fanon's critique of colonialism and his advocacy of anticolonial resistance bolstered the argument for armed self-defense and he was read as endorsing militant struggle as an antidote to the damage inflicted by American-style colonialism. Later, his work drew fire from post-structuralist academics for the binaristic constructions of colonized identity and colonial society, which drove his political theory. Still it is important to understand Power as a uniquely ethnic American adaptation of Fanon's critique that attends to the particularities of American-style colonization and provides the basis for a plan to foster revolutionary social and political change in American society.

Key to translating colonialism into the American context (in addition to the examples of other anticolonialist and Marxist revolutions occurring contemporaneously around the world) was the growing awareness of the works of Fanon, a French-educated, Martinique-born, Freudian-trained psychiatrist who worked in French-occupied Algeria and ultimately championed the Algerian nationalist liberation movement. Fanon's analyses, which explored the "question of a socio-diagnostic," or the articulation and quantification of the effects of oppression and colonization beyond the individual psychiatric case and across a community of men, spoke to the political, social, and psychological symptoms of American institutional racism exhibited by people of color in America.[2] Understanding America as a repressive colonial system enabled Power advocates to distinguish themselves ideologically from the earlier nonviolent civil rights protest movement at a time when young African Americans were growing frustrated with the lack of enforcement of the legal gains made during the late 1950s and early 1960s. The concept of colonialism also proved useful to American Power activists seeking to hook up their struggle with anticolonial revolutionaries around the globe in hopes of importing the fire and dynamism of the anticolonial movements in Algeria, Zimbabwe, Nigeria, Vietnam, Cuba, Bolivia, Senegal, etc. Fanon's critique of the French colonial system also provided a theoretical matrix that set the stage for a radical revision of African American identity and the development of a uniquely pan-Asian American identity.

Indeed, Fanon's popularity and usefulness for the Black Power movement has been so oft cited as to be taken for granted. In *Waiting 'til the Midnight Hour: A Narrative History of Black Power in America*, Peniel Joseph, the scholar most responsible for the recent resurgence of Black Power studies, cites Fanon as part of a "self-fashioned radical intellectual canon" constructed by Huey Newton, cofounder of the Black Panther Party for Self-Defense.[3] In *The Black Power Movement: Rethinking the Civil Rights–Black Power Era*, the 2006 edited collection that preceded his monograph, at least four other contemporary scholars—Simon Wendt, Stephen Ward, Jeffrey Ogbar, and Komozi Woodard—also refer to Fanon's centrality and ubiquity in the evolution of the Black Panther Party's black revolutionary nationalist thought. That fully half of the scholars included in this seminal volume cite Fanon as an important ideological antecedent for activists and leaders during this moment seems to warrant a more sustained investigation of Fanon's reception and adaption during the period.

On the first page of the preface to his 1972 autobiography, *The Making of a Black Revolutionary*, James Forman, black activist and one time SNCC leader who became increasingly radicalized, quotes Fanon—"A society that drives its members to desperate solutions is a non-viable society, a society to be replaced"—identifying him as a great black thinker and African revolutionary.[4] Some, like Martin Luther King, questioned the Fanon fad, wondering whether and how deeply his works were read by the earnest young revolutionaries organizing on college campuses across the nation. Radical leftist groups like Students for a Democratic Society, the Student Nonviolent Coordinating Committee, the White Panthers, Red Guard (an Asian American radical group), and the Third World Liberation Front Coalition, which helped lead the student strikes at San Francisco State and the University of California at Berkeley in 1968 and '69, frequently listed *The Wretched of the Earth* (and to a lesser extent *Black Skin, White Masks*) as required reading for members. Likewise, the language of anticolonialism—"colony," "colonizer," "colonized," "decolonization"—began to appear in the rhetoric of leftist thinkers and student protestors during this period. But outside of appropriating Fanon's rhetoric, how did early reviews shape the way American readers interpreted his views and set the stage for this emphasis on *The Wretched of the Earth*?

At the time of his death in 1961, none of Fanon's works had been translated into English or offered through American publishing houses. In France, his earliest book, *Peau noire, masque blanc*, was initially published in 1952 by Editions du Seuil. All of his later texts—*L'An V de la Révolution algérienne* (1959), *Les Damnés de la terre* (1961), *Pour la révolution africaine* (1964)—were originally published by François Maspero, who worked with Fanon on the leftist, pro-Algerian nationalist magazine, *Partisan*.[5] Fanon's initial publication in French made his writings accessible to his primary audience, the French-speaking "natives" living in lands under French colonial occupation; however, translation delayed his introduction to most of American readers until much later.

Présence Africaine, the publisher that grew out of the Négritude movement journal headed by Alioune Diop, released the first English translation of *The Wretched of the Earth* (hereafter *TWE*), entitled *The Damned*, in 1963.[6] In 1965, a Grove Press edition of *TWE* and an edition of *Studies in a Dying Colonialism* (hereafter *SDC*) followed. Translations of *Toward the African Revolution* and *Black Skin, White Masks* (hereafter *BSWM*) were released in America in 1967.[7] Thus, Fanon's works were published in a very different order in America, with the two works devoted to more specific considerations of revolutionary movements in Africa and the Caribbean sandwiched between the more personal and psychologically inflected works. In addition, *BSWM* and *TWE* were translated and released in English in reverse order from their original publication in French. The American translations of these works were also released over a much shorter time period, occluding the evolution of the political and social conditions to which Fanon responded in both his activism and writing. During the nine years between 1952 and 1961, Fanon became increasingly involved in the Algerian movement on a local, then national, and, finally, international scale. As he became more exposed to the leadership of the Algerian resistance and to movements outside of North Africa, Fanon responded to the need for a political theory of revolution that would be relevant to francophone Africa and the African diaspora in his writing. Though he touched on the conditions of blacks in America in *BSWM* and *TWE*, it is only tangential to his primary concern, the revolutionary anticolonial movements in primarily francophone Africa and the Caribbean.[8]

Since Fanon's untimely death prevented him from an in-depth analysis of the condition of American blacks and the feasibility of revolution, young activists poised to push the movement for full liberation further had to accomplish that translation themselves. In the absence of his specific, extended treatment of America's racial dynamic, reviews in general interest, scholarly, and activist journals played a large part in setting the stage for the reception of and response to Fanon's ideas in America. As in France and the rest of Europe, the attention of most American reviewers and commentators was drawn to *BSWM* and *TWE*. In America, *BSWM* and *TWE* were the most widely reviewed of his four book-length publications and also exerted the greatest influence on Black and Yellow Power activists then and scholars and students today. *TWE*, published just before Fanon's untimely death, was released first in America and has been reviewed more often than *BSWM*.[9] At the time of its release, *TWE*'s American marketing capitalized on its revolutionary reputation. On the book jacket, *TWE* was heralded as a "classic work of modern revolutionary theory" and "a veritable handbook" for radical activists and therefore "necessary reading for anyone who wants to understand the psychology of the oppressed."[10] In it, Fanon presents a picture of colonialism as an inherently and irredeemably violent system and calls for colonial subjects to liberate themselves and their occupied territories through organized militant resistance. In the vein of philosophers Albert Memmi and Jean-Paul Sartre, Fanon unpacks the toll of the psychic and cultural violence that the colonial system unleashes on both native and settler. As in other philosophical treatments of subjectivity, this relationship revolves around a central tension—in this case, the dynamic of struggle between the processes of colonization and its inevitable resistance. Thus *TWE*, which includes an oft-cited preface by Jean-Paul Sartre, whose *Anti-Semite and Jew* (1948; *Réflexions sur la question juive* 1946) profoundly influenced Fanon's work, was received as an illustration of colonialism, as well as a proposal for its eradication.

Almost every review of *TWE* picks up on the theme of violent resistance articulated throughout the text, and while some contemporaneous reviews take Fanon to task for what they read as an endorsement of racist violence, most pick up on the dynamic he traces. A *Time* reviewer acknowledges that Fanon does not provide a wholesale endorsement of racial violence—"Fanon argues that hatred alone is not enough to sustain a war of liberation; only constant political work and propaganda can convince the peasant masses that freedom must be worth the ordeal; brutality must be used purposefully"; however, he concludes that liberation has to mean more than "harping on the guilt of the white man" for "if they cling to Fanon, they will only live as prisoners of their own hates."[11] Even though the reviewer understands Fanon's attempt to justify violent resistance within the Algerian context, he still reads it as a dead end for colonized subjects. Other reviews acknowledge that some critiques of Fanon's stance on violence may be self-serving: "The French established and maintained their rule in Algeria by violence, including violence against civilians; the conquered have the right to use equivalent violence to end that rule; they will rightly refuse to allow their conquerors to instruct them, on what forms of violence are to be considered legitimate."[12] In *Saturday Review*, Emile Capouya, leftist essayist and writer who went on to serve as literary editor for *The Nation* magazine, reads this treatment of violence even more generously: "Violence characterizes the colonial situation from first to last, and Fanon tells the colonial people, if you wish to be free you must fight, that is reverse the current of violence. You will find your manhood in so doing. And in this period of history, colonial rebellion makes good sense. . . ."[13] Significantly, these reviewers all note how Fanon links violence and subjectivity; just as it takes violent repression to create the colonized, it will take violent struggle to develop a liberated consciousness.

While reviews in general interest and public policy–oriented magazines inevitably drew comparisons between the Algerian revolution and race relations in America, reviews in academic outlets treated the text as more political theory than commentary and social observation. Significantly, most reviewers also read Fanon in relationship to Marxism, another political theory predicated on revolution as the engine for radical social change. Reviews of the work in more scholarly outlets like political science and African Studies journals also place *TWE* within the context of ongoing revolutionary struggles across Africa and around the globe. Rather than engage in sensationalism and cast Fanon as a "threat" to Western civilization, scholarly reviewers delve the ethical and political implications of Fanon's analysis and resulting strategies for liberation, focusing on issues like torture (*Modern Age: A Quarterly Review*) and the feasibility of a "process" of decolonization (*Journal of Modern African Studies*). In an extensive book review essay in *Middle Eastern Journal*, Irene Gendzier, who went on to publish a biography of Fanon, points out the danger of those initial reactionary readings in more general interest magazines that characterized Fanon as an apostle or advocate of violence: "Understandably, it was *Les damnés* that brought Fanon instant fame. In France, it evoked lyrical praise; in the United States, with less sentiment but more persistence, it was taken up by the advocates of anti-colonialism, the admirers of Castroism, the uncertain student leaders of the civil rights movements. But by translating Fanon's last book, the apostle of violence was misrepresented."[14] Gendzier goes on to argue that reading Fanon through *TWE* feeds a "myth of pure violence, of a justified catharsis of destruction."[15] Instead, she reminds readers, "[M]uch as it reflected Fanon's passion, *Les damnés* was only one of four books he had written and its birth had been scarred by the conditions of its emergence into the world."[16] Even in this early assessment, which comes after the publication of only *TWE* and *BSWM*, Gendzier accurately predicts the effects the scrambled publication order will have on readings of Fanon, particularly by more mainstream American audiences.

As in general interest magazines, reviews in radical magazines focused on the link between violence and consciousness; however, activists also read Fanon in relationship to global anticolonial movements and theorists, just like academic reviewers. A 1964 review of the first American edition of *TWE*, *The Damned*, appears in the summer issue of *Freedomways: A Quarterly Review of the Negro Freedom Movement*, a special issue devoted to the Caribbean portion of the African diaspora. While the reviewer, Calvin Sinnette, an M.D., acknowledges Fanon's warnings about the rise of the "black autocracy" and his commentary on the process of rebuilding a nation after the end of colonialism, he concentrates on Fanon's "case study of the anatomy of violence."[17] The reviewer reads Fanon as a challenge to the doctrine of "creative suffering" associated with Négritude in the francophone Caribbean and West Africa and the Civil Rights Movement in America. Sinnette concludes, "The dogma of supine resistance has been effectively challenged and it can enjoy no longer the sacrosanct privilege of an eternal verity."[18] Likewise, a review of *TWE* from the April 8, 1966 newsletter of the University of Chicago chapter of the Students for a Democratic Society praises Fanon's clear and incisive take on colonialism. The reviewer notes that Fanon "does not recklessly or thoughtlessly glorify violence. . . . The concept of struggle is not implanted on the situation from without. Violence is not an export of the Red Chinese, but a necessary consequence of the colonial setting."[19] In a somewhat more nuanced take, rather than criticize or valorize Fanon's take on violence, the reviewer focuses on the role that violence plays in creating the colonized consciousness and the subsequent role that political struggle plays in raising the consciousness of the "native" masses and creating the sense of shared purpose necessary for decolonization. Linking violence to China, and by extension Maoism, places violent resistance within transnational AfroAsian discourses of resistance. While both reviews emphasize Fanon's analysis of the social, cultural, and psychic structures of violent resistance, each also highlights Fanon's treatment of colonial systems as a political and cultural system, an insight central to the later development of both Black and Yellow Power.

In *Wretched of the Earth*, Fanon constructs the colonial condition as pervasive and all encompassing, forcing the "native" to wholly accept the culture of the "settler" and, indeed, to acknowledge and even espouse the superiority of the colonizing culture. As a hegemonic ideology, colonialism operates under the illusion of totality and cohesiveness:

> Cultural domination, because it is total and tends to oversimplify, very soon manages to disrupt, in spectacular fashion, the cultural life of a conquered people. This cultural obliteration is made possible by the negation of national reality, by new legal relations introduced by the occupying power, by the banishment of the natives and their customs to outlying districts by colonial society, by expropriation, and by the systemic enslaving of men and women.[20]

The remedy for colonialism, therefore, would have to be equally all encompassing: "The destruction of the colonial world is no more and no less than the abolition of one zone [the colonial], its burial in the depths of the earth or its expulsion from the country."[21] Fanon likens the psychological and sociocultural effects of colonialism to pulling "every string shamelessly" to ensure that the political, cultural, and social institutions of the occupied country replicate the "mother country" and bear no trace of the native.[22] Most tragically, colonialism remakes the mind and culture of the colonized, eventually convincing them that the colonial influence could indeed "lighten the darkness" of their native culture.[23] Thus, colonialism works on all levels of a society to control the colonized. Violence in the colonial system is also epistemological, creating a cultural "current" that relentlessly shapes representations and attitudes of both colonizer and colonized to reinforce the political and economic system of colonialism. Therefore, anticolonialism and "decolonization," the struggle to defeat colonialism, would have to involve routing the colonizer's institutions and value systems, then remaking native culture and identity. Significantly, Fanon goes on to caution that this insidious construction of colonialism continually complicates attempts to combat it, making the colonial subject's every interaction with the colonizing system fraught with the threat of complicity and continued cultural erosion.[24] For this reason, he warns against nationalism, ethnocentrism, the reification of the native bourgeoisie, and wanton violence, all of which could short circuit change and stall the movement towards liberation for the masses. While most early critics and reviewers responded to the clinical and philosophical implications of Fanon's work, black and Asian American activists launched "translations" of Fanon as a template for political and cultural action.

The first of these translations appeared two years after the first American edition of *TWE* with the publication of *Black Power: The Politics of Liberation in America*. The essays in *BSWM* provided a vivid illustration of the toll that colonialism takes on the consciousness of the oppressed. While originally taken as an indictment of colonialism and an exposé of the psychological toll taken on colonized subjects, American commentators took the work as an illustration of the process of colonization and decolonization, ultimately reading it as a guide to the development of black consciousness. For activists, *BSWM* provided a powerful, personal portrait of the toll that racialization takes on the oppressed. Described in a 1967 *Newsweek* review as a "strange, haunting mélange of existential analysis, revolutionary manifesto, metaphysics, prose poetry and literary criticism," this work was read as humanizing the specter of the mythic black man haunting oppressed and oppressor alike.[25]

The groundbreaking *Black Power*, published two years after the Grove Press edition of *TWE* and the same year as the American edition of *BSWM*, clearly responds to both works. As one of the most important American adaptations of Fanon, the book, by Stokely Carmichael and Charles Hamilton, incorporated several of Fanon's major themes: colonialism as a cultural system supported by violent repression, the need for militant resistance, and an analysis of the psychic effects of colonization on the colonized. In their manifesto, Carmichael and Hamilton assert that American-style institutional racism constitutes a form of colonialism: "black people in this country form a colony . . . they stand as colonial subjects in relation to the society."[26] Carmichael and Hamilton observe that as in colonial sites in the Caribbean, Africa, and India, colonization in America operates politically, economically, and socially. In other words, the *effects* of the American system of racialization—the process of establishing and imposing a racial identity through socialization, cultural representation, and political and legal decisions—mediates the racialized subjects' relationship to the state through their identity, rendering black, and by extension yellow, people in this country as "colonial subjects." Based on this observation, Carmichael and Hamilton assert that blacks, Asian Americans, and other people of color in America have a "colonial relationship" to the larger culture, though they acknowledge that the "analogy is not perfect" and does not fit the "classical" colonial paradigm.[27] Instead, Carmichael and Hamilton argue, colonialism in the American context takes the form of "institutional racism" that nonetheless circumscribes the lives and opportunities of blacks in America in several ways: through a black leadership system that is indebted to a white political party machine rather than "the people"; electoral manipulation; wage and labor exploitation; and the continual denial of equality and equity.

In its form, tone, and themes of revolution and identity reformation, *Black Power* displays the clear influence of *TWE*. Drawing on Fanon's elucidation of the psychology of the colonized, Carmichael and Hamilton establish "Power" as a strategy for black American anticolonialism and decolonialization. Feeling that the Civil Rights Movement's focus on legal strategy, nonviolent action, and assimilation into the mainstream did not address adequately the cultural losses that centuries of repressive laws and social practices had inflicted on blacks and other people of color, Carmichael and Hamilton propose a political ideology centered on self-determination and political strength, rather than assimilation or integration, as the proper response to American-style colonialism. This political agenda would be driven by "black consciousness" or "the revolutionary idea that black people are able to do things themselves."[28] This consciousness has to accompany any drive for political equality. Thus, "Power" represents an adaptation of Fanon's critique of colonialism that attends to the particularities of the American racial system and begins to construct a road map for revolutionary social change in America's colonial-style system. This desire for a more powerful social "position" also reflects a Fanonian-inflected understanding of the influence of institutional discourses on the oppressed subject.

Black Power activists felt that the treatment of blacks and other people of color in America rose to the level of colonialism precisely because inequalities were tolerated, and even inherent in, America's political, economic, and social systems. "There is no 'American dilemma,'" Carmichael and Hamilton thunder, "because black people in this country form a colony, and it is not in the interest of the colonial power to liberate them."[29] Assimilation, implicit goal of the Civil Rights Movement, would only mask these injustices. Using colonialism as a theoretical paradigm, Black Power constructs routes to political empowerment that would expose the "white" structures operating simultaneously to oppress blacks and other people of color, and shore up "white" power and hegemony. The ultimate aim of Power, then, is to create a Gramscian dialectic with "white" power wherein the uneven access to freedom and citizenship in America could be exposed and addressed.[30] Therefore, Power rests on an understanding that radical social change would also require a new understanding of what freedom entailed, a new understanding of the "struggle" required to secure "a bargaining position of strength in a pluralistic society."[31]

While *Black Power* is philosophically indebted to *TWE*, Eldridge Cleaver's equally influential collection of essays, *Soul on Ice* (1967), published the same year as *Black Power*, also owes much to the structure and tone of *BSWM*. In the introduction, Maxwell Geismar touts Cleaver as a "cultural critic" and calls our attention to the similarities between *Soul on Ice*, a collection of essays written during Cleaver's stint for rape, and *BSWM*. He draws our attention to Fanon's influence, asserting, "In a curious way Cleaver's book has definite parallels with Fanon's *Black Skin, White Masks*. In both books the central problem is of *identification* as a black soul which has been 'colonized'—more subtly perhaps in the United States for some three hundred years, but perhaps ever more pervasively—by an oppressive white society that projects its brief, narrow vision of life as eternal truth."[32]

Like *BSWM*, *Soul on Ice* chronicles the development of a racialized and revolutionary consciousness. In *Soul on Ice*, Cleaver cites his admiration for Malcolm X as key to his development; he "had a special meaning for black convicts. A former prisoner himself, he had risen from the lowest depths to great heights."[33] After joining and eventually becoming a leader among inmates loyal to the Nation of Islam, Cleaver becomes disillusioned with the organization following X's exile. Deeply influenced by X's travels to Africa and the Middle East, Cleaver even signs several outgoing prison letters "L. Eldridge Cleaver, Organization of Afro-American Unity," the OAU being the pan-African group Malcolm X founded following his ejection from the Nation of Islam.[34] Like X, Cleaver uses his time in prison to develop himself, keeping a prison journal, maintaining correspondence with leaders and writers whom he admires, and compiling extensive reading lists, including works on Négritude like Kwame Nkrumah's *The Last Stage of Imperialism*. Cleaver, who strongly identified as a writer, even taking classes on writing in prison, quickly picked up on the rhetoric of anticolonialism, substituting it for the racialist rhetoric of the Nation of Islam. Cleaver, who later served as Black Panther Party Minister of Information and the editor of the Black Panther newspaper, also incorporates the language of colonial critique in the later *Post-Prison Writings and Speeches* (1969): "black people are a stolen people held in a colonial status on a stolen land, and any analysis which does not acknowledge the colonial status of black people cannot hope to deal with the real problem."[35] The "real problem"—the system that facilitated the ascendance of America's racialist paradigm—has to be exposed in order to bring about lasting change, and the concepts of decolonization and anticolonialism offered in *TWE* were embraced as vital elements of any viable movement to address these problems.

In the first essay in *Soul on Ice*, "The White Race and Its Heroes," Cleaver rationalizes his rhetorical shift: "I have tried a tentative compromise by adopting a select vocabulary so that now when I see the whites of their eyes, instead of saying 'devil' or 'beast' I say 'imperialist' or 'colonialist,' and everyone seems to be happier."[36] Cleaver's language at once acknowledges the tension between integration or reform (civil rights) and self-determination or radicalism (Black Power), exposing the cultural and intellectual distance that the colonial paradigm imposes between the two. Cleaver appropriates Fanon's terms and turns them inside out so that "everyone" can be satisfied with the softening of his rhetoric. However, his dismissal of this substitution as an empty rhetorical move does not account fully for the change in register from ad hominem to anticolonialist, from barbaric to "civilized." "They" are still "devils" and "beasts," but "they" are also agents of a comprehensive system of oppression. Thus, Fanon's discourse of anticolonialism informs Cleaver's change, enabling a rhetorical switch to an attack on institutions and systems of oppression, not the individual agents of the system. Significantly, Cleaver's construction also picks up on the reification of language, a residue of Fanon's occupation and language as a medium for psychotherapy. Additionally, this anxiety about not being able to speak underscores the importance placed on having a voice and "speaking," or having agency in the social and political discourses shaping perceptions of racial identity and representation. Thus, Black Power advocates adapted Fanonian anticolonialism to include an emphasis on language and culture, understanding that the ability to revise representations and communicate protest are as important to securing freedom as the ability to engage in armed struggle against oppression. For Cleaver, Marxist-inflected Fanonian anticolonialism proved a valuable tool for describing the systemic nature of American oppression and establishing a connection with nationalist liberation movements around the world; however, he ultimately dismisses abstractions of language as distractions unable to radically change America's black/white racial system. Only a militant struggle would bring lasting significant change—true revolution.[37]

As in Fanon, Cleaver's essays also exhibit a transnational understanding of the struggle against colonialism, an awareness of the global nature of anticolonialism that links the fate of African Americans and Asian Americans with African, Asian, and Latin nations around the world. According to Cleaver's construction, the subjection of any people makes the subjection of any other people possible. Cleaver laments being unable to "utter a sound of protest" in any useful way against the treatment of the Vietnamese.[38] In "The Black Man's Stake in Vietnam," Cleaver asserts, "The Black people must have a guarantee, they must be *certain*, they must be sure beyond all doubt that the reign of terror is ended and not just suspended, and that the future of their people is secure. And the only way they can ensure this is to gain organizational unity and communication with their brothers and allies around the world, on an international basis."[39] Here Cleaver equates the fates of blacks at home with the Vietnamese abroad. Indeed, the treatment of each is abetted by the same racist structures; thus, the oppression of the Vietnamese makes possible the subjection of blacks and vice versa: "The American racial problem can no longer be spoken of or solved in isolation. The relationship between the genocide in Vietnam and the smiles of the white man toward black Americans is a direct relationship. Once the white man solves his problem in the East he will turn his fury again on the black people of America. . . ."[40] Using the trope of slavery to illustrate this "relationship," Cleaver urges American blacks towards a coalition of black, brown, and yellow people arrayed against the global threat of capitalism and neo-colonialist aggression. He concludes:

> The black man's interest lies in seeing a free and independent Vietnam, a strong Vietnam which is not the puppet of international white supremacy. If the nations of Asia, Latin America, and Africa are strong and free, the black man in America will be safe and secure and free to live in dignity and self-respect. It is a cold fact that while the nations of Africa, Asia and Latin America were shackled in colonial bondage, the black American was held tightly in the vise of oppression and not permitted to utter a sound of protest of any effect. . . . The only lasting salvation for the black American is to do all he can to see to it that the African, Asian and Latin American nations are free and independent.[41]

Cleaver takes the metaphor of colonialism and extends it to encompass America's enslavement of blacks. Once he establishes this similarity, Cleaver goes on to reverse the trope and responsibility, charging American blacks with the need to resist the "colonial bondage" of "Africa, Asia and Latin America." Rhetorically, this chiasmus further strengthens the equation between slavery and colonialism that animates Cleaver's argument. Ironically, the trope holds because of the brutal histories of oppression shared by people of color around the world.

Like Black Power activists, Yellow Power advocates recognized the value of translating Fanon's insights and applying them to their American experience. Yellow Power advocates like Amy Uyematsu, Franklin Odo, David Wand, and Larry Kubota were centered in the San Francisco Bay Area. Many of them contributed to or worked for the newspaper *Gidra*, which began publishing in 1969. The paper was started by and staffed largely with UCLA students. The founders, UCLA students Mike

Murase, Colin Watanabe, Laura Ho, Dinora Gil, and Tracy Okida and Cal State–Los Angeles student Ron Wakabayashi, were inspired by and involved in the student protests at San Francisco State, UCLA, and UC–Berkeley. While the Asian American Studies Center at UCLA provided the students with a meeting place and equipment, the university did not officially sanction the publication. Despite its perilous beginnings, *Gidra* published reports on conferences, trials, student activities, and local, national, and international politics, in addition to documenting the rapidly evolving radical community groups and organizations now considered part of the Asian American Movement: the Yellow Brotherhood and the Red Guard.

In "The Warren Report 1990," Warren Furutani reprises his man-on-the-street articles in a look back at *Gidra*'s impact. He refutes the idea that Asian Americans simply mimicked the Black Power or Civil Rights Movements: "Who was first [among revolutionary activist movements] is not important and any accusations that we were only copying the other movements are false. Our 'Movement' was the result of the racial, social, and economic oppression of Asian Pacific Americans and people of color in America."[42] Indeed, *Gidra* served as an incubator for Asian American radical thought and analysis that pertained to the various Asian communities. The paper published articles by budding activists and intellectuals like Ron Tanaka, Alan Nishiro, and Pat Sumi, as well as Amy Uyematsu and Larry Kubota, both of whom I will discuss at more length shortly. Significantly, the newspaper, like *The Black Panther,* also published poems, articles, and stories that advocated and illustrated a revolutionary pan-ethnic Asian American identity.[43] However, *Gidra* did not focus solely on issues and news related to the Asian American experience and movement. The paper also reprinted articles from *The Black Panther* and *Nommo,* the UCLA Black Student Union newspaper. On the international front, the paper published news from Vietnam and dispatches from Red Guard and Black Panther members in Cuba, China, and South America. Many of these articles echo Fanon's internationalist, Marxist-inflected, anticolonialist rhetoric and tone, while a significant number, like Uyematsu and Kubota, attempt to directly translate his ideas into the Asian American context.

In "The Emergence of Yellow Power in America," which appeared in the October 1969 issue of the paper, Amy Uyematsu, a Japanese American activist, heralds the beginning of "a yellow movement [. . .] set into motion by the black power movement."[44] She calls the "yellow power" movement a "direct outgrowth of the black power movement," enumerating similarities between the principles of Black Power and Yellow Power, including the need to develop political power to "improve the economic and social condition of [. . .] yellows."[45] Like Carmichael and Hamilton, Uyematsu also concedes that America's racial situation differs somewhat from the colonial model. She acknowledges, "Although the race situation in America is not strictly analogous to white colonialism and imperialism, the blacks and yellows have suffered similar consequences as Third World people at the hands of the American capitalist power."[46] Rather than try to justify the use of the term colonialism to describe the American racial system, Uyematsu instead points to the effects of American-style racism as reason enough for analyzing the condition of Asian Americans and African Americans using Fanon's anticolonial theory. Like Carmichael and Hamilton, Uyematsu justifies adapting anticolonialism as a paradigm for resistance because of the devastating effects of American racism on Asians in America.

In the introduction to *Asian American Heritage* (1974), David Hsin-Fu Wand also acknowledges the persuasive influence of the anticolonialist model formulated by Black Power advocates: "[T]he recent awakening of black consciousness in the United States further convinced some Asian-Americans to seek their ancestral roots."[47] Wand goes on to quote Daniel Okimoto's assertion in *American in Disguise*: "The new ethnic consciousness and defiance against racial prejudice [among Asian Americans] owes much to the Black Power movement which, by boldly challenging the status quo, brought vividly to light conditions of injustice that confront all minorities, leading the way for other races to join in the long delayed fight against discrimination."[48] Wand uses this excerpt from Okimoto's memoir to illustrate two imperatives for Yellow Power: to encourage the formation of group identity through knowledge of cultural history and to unify that group in the fight for political parity. As Yellow Power advocates read Fanon, the first strand was considered subordinate to the second, thus privileging struggle as the necessary prelude to the recuperation of culture.

Although Black Power provided an example for Asian Americans who were similarly frustrated by the continuing legal and economic challenges faced by segments of Asian America, Yellow Power had to reflect the Asian American communities' unique responses to American racism. Yellow Power did so by incorporating a unique call to recognize the reality of racism in the lives of all Asians in America (including "assimilated" third and fourth generation Chinese Americans and Japanese Americans on the West Coast), which would lead to group solidarity, political parity (rather than equality), and social agency to act on behalf of the community. Yellow Power also had to address the silencing produced by the "model minority" stereotype, which fostered an image of Asian Americans as "successful" immigrants largely assimilated into American society.

These Asian American activists limned out a definition of Yellow Power that required a recognition that the treatment of Asians in America had relied in part on oppressive racial and cultural systems and that true *group* autonomy was necessary so that Asian Americans could not be manipulated as foils to counter black and Hispanic American protests. One of the goals of Yellow Power, therefore, was to secure "greater control over the direction of [Asian American society]" in order to "be able to dictate some of the terms of entry into the American mainstream."[49] "Yellow Power" called for "all Asian Americans to end the silence that has condemned us to suffer in this racist society and to unite with our black, brown and red brothers of the Third World for survival, self-determination, and [in a nod to socialism] the creation of a more humanistic society."[50] Only by ending the cultural silence imposed by colonialism could Asian Americans unify, form a political pan-consciousness, and gain the social agency to "dictate" social policy and create a society that might foster these new expressions of self-determination. As an ideology, Yellow Power sounded the "call for ALL yellow people in America to unite as yellow *brothers*" creating a "group solidarity" that would meet the needs of the people by bringing about political awareness, greater political participation and group consciousness, all of which would be necessary for the complete expression of the community's "Power."[51]

In the preface to the 1971 anthology *Roots: An Asian American Reader*, Franklin Odo reifies group solidarity (both among Asians in America and between other American racial groups), configuring the struggle against American racism as a potential common ground for all Asians and their "black brothers," regardless of the relative prosperity evidenced by *some* groups of Asian Americans.[52] Odo echoes Fanon's cautions against nationalism and nationalist consciousness in *TWE*, arguing that group solidarity should precede group consciousness as a prelude to Asian American autonomy. His warning against class divisions also reflects Fanon's concern that an unreformed native bourgeoisie could be used to maintain the status quo and hamper the revolutionary will of the masses. Further, he endorses Fanon's assertion that group identity should be strengthened through struggle before engaging in larger political projects:

> Our questioning and thinking must relate directly to the issue of Asian ethnicity in a racist society but they must move from the particular to the universal, from personal identity to the identity of larger groups, to the nature of human experience and the human condition. And in all of this an essential identification with the people and a redistributing of power must be seen as both possible and necessary; that is, after all, what is meant by the demand for power to the people.[53]

Odo's remarks echo the socialist theories of revolution that influenced Fanon, figuring radicalized Asian Americans as a part of the proletarian vanguard. Odo also establishes a two-part process for this act of identification. First, one must recognize one's status as a subject of racism, then seek to identify with a community of other similarly oppressed individuals also agitating for change. Odo's articulation of the roots of Yellow Power gestures towards the original meaning of Carmichael and Hamilton's concept of power as an expropriation of the structures of society for the benefit of the powerless and oppressed. "Power" here denotes not violence, but social agency to dictate the construction of an Asian American identity and the political disposition of Asian American interests. The desire to "dictate" the "terms" of this relationship stems from Fanon's logocentric critique of the colonial system, and enables Odo's move away from Fanon's early advocacy of armed resistance and towards the cultural issues of identity, subjectivity, and representation as important battle fronts.

Creating a pan-Asian community and dismantling the "model minority" stereotype also inform two additional issues that contributed to the development of Yellow Power. The heterogeneity of the Asian American community and the long span of time and diverse conditions that motivated Asian American emigration made it difficult for early activists to define a unified identity and articulate a collective purpose and objectives sufficient to propel a political movement. The tenets of Yellow Power, therefore, had to negotiate the distinct histories of Asians in America to create a pan-Asian identity.

In his 1973 essay, "Yellow Power," Larry Kubota echoes Fanon's rhetoric about colonialism's psychic violence. Kubota denounces American racism, attributing the powerlessness and helplessness of the Asian American community to rootlessness and ignorance of history. According to Kubota, Yellow Power compels Asian Americans to "reject our past and present condition of powerlessness," signified in part by disidentification and factionalism.[54] In America's electoral system, numerical significance is vital to securing political power. Cultivating a pan-Asian "yellow" identity would shore up this effort, ensuring Asian American political significance.[55] Kubota understood the "model minority myth" as another expression of this powerlessness. The model minority myth placated *some* Asians in America who felt that there was no need for change because their own social and economic status was assured. However, this myth not only flattened the image of the community to a small group of successful second- and third-generation Chinese Americans and Japanese Americans, it also isolated Asian Americans from other ethnic minorities, hindering the coalitions which would be necessary for creating a revolutionary coalition in America.

Keith Osajima points to the model minority myth as it was articulated in 1966 by William Petersen and rearticulated in the mid-1980s in general interest publications like *Newsweek,* as a demonstration of the hardiness of essentialist cultural stereotypes.[56] Osajima observes that, despite the qualifications about earnings and opportunity included in most of the 1980s news stories, each articulation of this myth still attributes success in large part to the exoticizing catchall "traditional Asian cultural values."[57] Unlike previous immigrant success narratives that focused on successful assimilation, the model minority myth manages to laud "traditional" Japanese and Chinese values that *somehow* survived, while simultaneously reinforcing stereotypes of Asians as inscrutable and reinscribing the myth of American equality. The model minority stereotype functioned as a sop to a "bourgeoisie" class of Asian Americans and helped deflect charges of unfairness leveled by civil rights proponents.[58] The recognition of the damage done by this stereotype presented the first obstacle to group identity and agency for Asian Americans; repudiating it would be the next step in self-determination: "Precisely because Asian Americans have become economically secure do they face serious identity problems. Fully committed to a system that subordinates them on the basis of non-whiteness, Asian Americans still tried to gain complete acceptance by denying their yellowness. They have become white in every respect but color."[59] According to Uyematsu, Asian Americans face two identity problems. They are not white; they are not yellow enough. The resolution to this crisis would be the formation of a new identity predicated on resisting an outwardly imposed racial narrative that reinforced America's myth of itself. Helping the community retire this myth would also be part of realizing their unconscious implication in the racist American system: "Asian Americans are perpetuating white racism [. . .] as they allow white America to hold up the 'successful' Oriental image before other minority groups as the model to emulate."[60] According to Osajima, the model minority myth provides a "direct critique" of Black Power activists.[61] Rather than be treated as the "anti-Black," the "successful" minority, Asian American activists call for the recovery of the history of Asians in America as colonized people as part of the effort to reveal the oppression that earlier generations had to overcome in order to achieve the success for which the "group" was lately lauded. Uyematsu urges Asians in America to unite, arguing "the yellow power movement cannot begin to move forward until the yellow people in America have reached the primary stage of 'yellow consciousness.'"[62] By banding together under a "yellow" consciousness, a correct consciousness aware of the effects of racism on Asians in particular and people of color generally, Asian Americans could agitate for change and begin to heal the fractures within their community and claim more representation in America's racially charged political system.

Building on Fanon's critique of colonialism and his expositions on the pervasive cultural and psychic damage produced by colonialism, Asian American activists constructed Yellow Power as a cultural strategy to combat stereotypical representations of Asians in America and as a political strategy to raise awareness of and combat the effects of American institutional racism on Asian Americans and Asian communities. While Yellow Power also launched an anticolonialist critique of America's racial situation, it adapted Fanon to explain how this process operated uniquely in the Asian/Pacific Islander experience.

Just as Cleaver's *Soul on Ice* reflects the influence of *BSWM*, Daniel Okimoto's 1970 memoir, *American in Disguise*, also echoes Fanon to illustrate how the psychosocial dynamic of immigration, assimilation, and identity formation plays out in Okimoto's story of his life as a young Japanese immigrant to the U.S. Okimoto, who later distinguished himself as a professor and expert on Japanese and Asian political and security affairs, relates his upbringing in America. The memoir covers his arrival in America at the age of four, his internment with his family during World War II, his early experiences of racism in school and in his neighborhood, and his Ivy League education; it culminates with his marriage to a white American. Though a memoir and not a collection of essays, Okimoto spends a lot of time narrating the internal turmoil precipitated by his experiences and tracing the development of his identity as a Japanese and American. As in *BSWM* and *Soul on Ice*, he constructs a sense of personal identity that is initially dualistic and fractured, marked by splitting and fracturing produced by his encounters with racism and the hypocrisy of America's internment of the Japanese: "For much of my life, I had struggles with the conviction that I was an American in disguise, a creature a part of, yet somehow detached from, the mainstream of American society."[63] As the work progresses, he acknowledges the influence of the Civil Rights and Black Power Movements on Japanese Americans and urges his community to get involved in the larger struggle for civil rights: "Borrowing the insights and even some of the rhetoric of the blacks, the Asian-American movement represents a sharp divergence from the old pattern of silence and passivity. While Yellow Power may never become the rallying cry for Orientals in the same way that Black Power has for Negroes, the affirmation of racial ancestry is the kind of major shift in attitude that could have far-reaching implications for Asian subcultures in the United States."[64] In this passage, Okimoto adopts power's rhetoric of racial consciousness to advocate for a group consciousness that, he hopes, will lead to a drive for self-definition, self-determination, and self-representation for Asians in America. He also uses examples from his life to illustrate the danger of the "model minority" myth and the evolution of Japanese American identity and representation.

By the end, Okimoto expresses the same desire for an uncompromised subjectivity that Fanon longs for at the end of *BSWM*. Fanon writes, "At the conclusion of this study, I want the world to recognize, with me, the open door of every consciousness. My final prayer: O my body, make of me always a man who questions!"[65] Okimoto also ends expressing a desire for wholeness, which, in his vision, is a more personal project:

> Although my wife and I can do little to influence the basic treatment that awaits our children in American society, we can try to provide them with the option of learning about, and perhaps accepting, the rich Asian legacy that is theirs to inherit so that they need not feel apologetic, as I have for most of my life, for their dual identity. It will be somewhat different for them than it was for me. Physically, at least, half the disguise I have worn will be lost; emotionally, I hope the day will come when they and all my country's racial minorities are no longer made to feel any less American because of their ethnic heritage.[66]

This conclusion is more humanistic, like *Black Skin, White Masks*. Though he does feel the impulse to react against his treatment, in the end, he does not hold out for structural change that might ensure equal treatment for his children. In contrast, both *Black Power* and *Soul on Ice* argue that political remedies have to accompany changes in social conditions and popular representations in order to ensure parity for oppressed groups. In this way, Power attempts to bring together both the personal and psychosocial dimensions of Fanon's work and the political and economic critiques that motivated his activism. Thus, these early "translations" of Fanon struggle to reconcile somewhat divergent impulses in his work, tendencies that are exacerbated by the inverted publication order to the works in America. Later scholars would continue to struggle with these seeming contradictions with no less mixed results.

"One of the signal developments in contemporary criticism over the past several years has been the ascendancy of the colonial paradigm," begins "Critical Fanonism," Henry Louis Gates, Jr.'s survey of critical assessments of Fanon by Edward Said, Homi Bhabha, Stephen Greenblatt, Abdul JanMohamed, Benita Perry, and Gayatri Spivak. Gates addresses the Fanon "fad" of the late 1980s, citing the "current fascination" as having to do with "the convergence of the problematic of colonialism with that of subject-formation."[67] His reading of readings highlights the slipperiness of Fanon's theoretical and critical discussion of colonialism. Calling him a "Rorschach blot with legs," Gates maps out the multiple faces of Fanon revealed in his appropriation by a number of theorists using approaches ranging from postcolonial to Lacanian, post-structural to counterimperialist.[68] Gates concludes that, despite his eloquent work on the problem of identity, Fanon ultimately falls victim to the inability to "speak through" the frustrating aporia of identity that he so eloquently addressed. According to Gates, this inability lies in part in Fanon's own complicated history and psychology. On the one hand, he was a forceful theorist of revolution and spokesman for Algerian independence who never became fluent in the language of his many Afro-Algerian patients and had to make his diagnoses through translators who were largely Anglo-Algerian.[69] On the other, he was a provocative social critic whose views on violent resistance actually evolve throughout his body of work. So, who is Fanon? Whose Fanon offers a more productive understanding of colonialism as it informed political struggle and intellectual inquiry in America during the Power period? And how could the same figure prompt such an array of appropriations?

Gates's article, which focuses on academic appropriations by humanities scholars, concludes by gesturing toward a rehistoricizing that would place Fanon alongside Albert, Sartre, Memmi, and other European social theorists. While these philosophers and theorists exerted considerable influence on Fanon, such a prescription is born of Gates's milieu—the theoretically inflected, post-structuralist literary criticism of the 1990s. Embedding Fanon in the discourses of existential philosophy that inspired him help us understand his constructions of identity and his poignant conclusions about the personal effects of racism; however, recontextualization does not negate subsequent appropriations of his work that attend to the shared structure of oppression and colonialism experienced by various groups around the globe. Gates's Derridian reading of Fanonian discourse is insufficient to bridge the gap between the historical and theoretical Fanons, between Fanonian anticolonialism as cultural studies theory and as revolutionary political praxis. In his article, Gates ends by concluding that the multiple appropriations of Fanon point to a weakness in the colonial paradigm that the psychologist is most strongly associated with: "This may be the clearest way of representing Fanon's own self-divisions, that is, as an agon between psychology and a politics, between ontogeny and sociogeny, between—to recur to Memmi—Marx and Freud."[70] Though he draws attention to Fanon's doublevoicedness, Gates's solution, to cease using Fanonian anticolonialism as grounds for a "grand unified theory of oppression," highlights the true motivations of his suspicious reading of Fanon and his tendency to downplay Fanon's work as primarily responding to the material conditions of colonized people in Algeria, West Africa, the Antilles, and elsewhere.[71] Gates employs Memmi in his critique of Fanon's seemingly simple binaristic formulation for the transformation of consciousness brought about by decolonization, citing *The Colonizer and the Colonized*, published in 1957, four years before *The Wretched of the Earth*, where Fanon engages the cultural process of decolonization at greater length. Even as he gestures toward the "provisional, reactive and local nature" of Fanon's work, Gates's subject is not Fanon's reality as a historical figure whose work grew out of real social and political situations. As a post-structuralist critic, Gates interrogates instead the divisions and oppositions in Fanon's discourse as symptoms of Fanon's textual and metaphorical "slipperiness," slippages that motivate the multiple theoretical appropriations of his work.

In "The Appropriation of Frantz Fanon," Cedric Robinson critiques Gates's treatment of Fanon: ". . . the search for the *real* Fanon takes Gates from interpretive text to the next text, from one clever exposition to its more clever critique. Fanon is what occurs at whatever moment one intercepts the daisy-chain."[72] Even "reading" Fanon alongside other European scholars of identity and subjectivity like Memmi and Sartre still treats his work as mere theoretical exercise. Fanon can be "read" as a theorist of subjectivity, but he must also be read as a political theorist analyzing the ongoing anticolonial struggles in North Africa and the Caribbean. Hence these oppositions are not just examples of Hegelian or Manichean dialectics; they are evidence of Marxist dialectical materialism, the discursive model underlying Fanon's critique of colonialism and his discourse of revolutionary strategy as it is filtered through the lenses of race, class, and colonialism. That said, Fanon's work remains an important touchstone for theorists, activists, and political strategists who must necessarily build on and adapt his anticolonial critique to suit their particular struggles for independence and autonomy.

Other scholars also focus on Fanon's "slipperiness," but they foreground Fanon's political context in their assessments. In the 1974 article "Frantz Fanon: Portrait of a Revolutionary Intellectual," Emmanuel Hansen traces Fanon's biographical wanderings and his importance to the Algerian revolution. In his sympathetic mythologizing of Fanon, Hansen, attempting to read Fanon as both an advocate of Algerian revolution and as a theorist of anticolonial resistance, figures him as a "revolutionary intellectual" who saw his work as a part of the struggle against colonialism in Africa and other areas of the world. Unlike Gates, Hansen reads Fanon as a political theorist of revolution; thus, Fanonian anticolonialism becomes another method to achieve radical social change. For

Hansen, the "slipperiness" of Fanon and his concept of colonialism are due in part to the evolution of his ideas as he becomes more involved with the Algerian revolutionary movement.[73] Fanon's analysis informs his involvement, his involvement tested his analysis, and both were intended to aid the revolutionary cause. Thus, in Fanon, personal and political subjectivity is bound up with the struggle for liberation; who he and other colonized subjects are and who he and they become depends upon their participation in the struggle for radical social change.

Ross Posnock launches a reassessment of Fanon within the context of the black intellectual tradition. Posnock reads Fanon alongside Du Bois to establish the postmodern critique of Fanon as another iteration of the debate about authenticity and identity that rages through much of the African American intellectual tradition, linking Fanon to Du Bois through Négritude. Posnock addresses the issue of praxis, arguing that struggle is but one stage, though a vital one, in the process of radical social change. He argues that the colonized subject "deriv[es] identity from action" and situates action as a necessary stage on the way to universal freedom: "In Fanon, this shift is analogous to his plea that anti-colonial nationalism move rapidly from national consciousness (preoccupied with people who are) to political and social consciousness (focused on people acting in relation to others)."[74] Thought of in this way, decolonization renders everyone outside of the cultural and social centers produced by colonialism and, through the struggle to dismantle the structures of the colonial system, rebuilds relationships between radicalized members of a society.

Just as Black and Yellow Power advocates adapted Fanon's Marxist, anticolonialist mode of analysis to critique American-style colonialism, they also adapted his concept of decolonization through struggle as the mechanism for undoing the psychic and cultural damage inflicted by colonization. In African American literature, the struggle for freedom and equality are powerful, recurring themes. In Asian American literature and culture, the struggle to maintain cultural traditions and achieve citizenship emerge as similarly significant tropes. Fanon's concept of decolonization through struggle adds another dimension to this concept in both traditions and becomes a central tenet of Power ideology. In Fanon's analysis, revolutionary action has the ability both to overturn the colonial system and to repair the damage done to the colonized psyche and society. Struggle, or "the mobilisation of the masses," could produce a new shared consciousness "when it rises out of the war of liberation, introduces into each man's consciousness the ideas of a common cause, of a national destiny and of a collective history. [...] [T]he native's violence unifies the people."[75] Struggle, not wanton racialized violence, would produce a liberated consciousness and keep the masses and their allies focused on the need for continual radical social change.

In *Black Power*, Carmichael and Hamilton prescribe struggle as the remedy for the cultural violence inflicted on the oppressed society and psyche. Although Fanon initially held the pessimistic view that the native's culture is completely destroyed during occupation, he later modifies this view, arguing instead that although the native culture can't exist side-by-side with the colonial culture, it is sustained on the fringes of society.[76] It is this relationship between margin and center that should be redefined according to Carmichael and Hamilton.

> Our basic need is to reclaim our history and our identity from what must be called cultural terrorism from the depredation of self-justifying white guilt. *We shall have to struggle* for the right to create our own terms through which to define ourselves and our relationship to the society, and to have those terms recognized. This is the first necessity of a free people and the first right that any oppressor must suspend [emphasis added].[77]

Whatever the name—"true equality," "power," or "self-determination"—Carmichael and Hamilton agree that the antidote to colonialism differs from earlier goals of equality and access. "True equality," according to Carmichael and Hamilton, must include the ability of African Americans to "define ourselves." "Recognition" is integral to the process of "true equality." As Judith Butler later postulates, the ability to recognize and sustain a social identity rests in the initial and continuing recognition of that position by other agents in a discursive system.[78] Thus, the struggle for viable subjectivity results from the struggle against racist representations and sociopolitical marginalization.

Cleaver calls the struggle in America a "war for the national liberation of Afro-Americans from colonial bondage to the white mother country" and cites "guerilla warfare" as the "vehicle for national liberation," noting the enshrinement of *The Wretched of the Earth* "among the militants of the Black liberation movement in America as the 'Bible.'"[79] He calls the book a "classic," citing Fanon as one of his "ideological heroes." On Fanon's usefulness to the liberation struggle of blacks in America, he writes:

> Fanon provided a great service to revolutionaries by explaining and analyzing the consciousness of a colonized people and showing how they move from an awareness of being oppressed all the way to the ultimate, the height of consciousness: the point where they are willing to fight for their freedom. Part of the fight for freedom entails violence.[80]

Cleaver reads Fanon as arguing that violent struggle is a psychological response to repression, thus "legitimiz[ing] these feelings and strip[ping] away the feelings of guilt that one might have had over, for instance, wanting to kill his slave master."[81] Cleaver later reiterates the need for colonial struggle laid out by Fanon, linking revolutionary violence with "manhood." Cleaver glorifies "open" war, the armed phase of anticolonialist struggle, while Fanon comes to recognize this stage as transitory, one stop on the road to freedom. This time, Cleaver reads Fanon as "teach[ing] colonial subjects that it is perfectly normal for them to want to rise up and cut off the heads of the slavemasters, that it is a way to achieve their manhood, and that they must oppose the oppressor in order to experience themselves as men."[82] In Cleaver's conception of black anticolonialism, opposition to oppression not only fosters the development of group consciousness, but also encourages individual evolution. Since Black and Yellow Power advocates reinterpreted struggle as occurring between races rather than classes, Power calls for a reformation of American identity politics that would facilitate coalition building across racial lines and allow for a revolution in identity making and meaning that would lay the foundation for the revolution in America's racist political and economic structures.

Thus, Power provides a bridge for cooperation between blacks and Asians similarly subjected to oppression in America's racial system; however, Power, because of its international theoretical antecedents, also draws attention to the consequences of American struggle abroad. Vietnam, which represents both an ideological and a military struggle, is a particularly compelling example of the "direct,"[83] "structural relationship"[84] between American repression at home and American aggression abroad. Martin Luther King, Jr., acknowledges the link between the conditions of Vietnamese fighters and the oppressed in America: "[T]he security we prefer to seek in foreign adventures we will lose in our decaying cities. The bombs in Vietnam explode at home; they destroy the hopes and possibilities for a decent America."[85] However, King does not agree that Vietnam justifies increased black militancy. While King agrees that violence is a tool of American racism, he believes that advocating violence would be a trap. Therefore, he characterizes the violent strain of resistance arising out of the civil rights struggle as an expression of internalized racism. While King appreciates the appeal of violent resistance and the connection it provides to other struggles, he does not endorse it as a legitimate response to racism because, according to his philosophy, it would morally erode the oppressed just as it does the oppressor.

Many Power advocates read America's actions in Vietnam as a warning to leaders of emerging militant movements in America. While Eldridge Cleaver calls for a stronger response to American racism, Carmichael and Hamilton embrace Fanon's early assertion that political and social struggle against a "common cause" could foster a group consciousness. For Carmichael and Hamilton, the ongoing conflict in Vietnam provides a ready example of armed resistance to American neocolonial aggression. Perhaps most importantly for my purposes, the Vietnam conflict also provides a rallying point for Asian American and African American activists. Carmichael and Hamilton seem to see Vietnam as a wedge. As America's geopolitical resources are stretched thin in various imperialist ventures, blacks in America, along with a multicultural coalition of the similarly oppressed masses and their allies, should seize the opportunity to press for radical social change from a weakened central government. In *Soul on Ice*, Cleaver deals extensively with the similarities between the black and Asian struggles for freedom in America and anticolonialist struggles in Africa, the Caribbean, Latin America, and Southeast Asia.[86] Cleaver, who led the U.S. People's Anti-Imperialist Delegation to North Korea in 1970, understood the links between Asian Americans and African Americans as an extension of global relationships between anticolonial struggles abroad. Likewise, Yellow Power activists shared this view. In an interview with Deanna Lee published in the June/July 1970 edition of *Gidra*, Bobby Seale observes: "The people are oppressed in America; the United States Government is the most hypocritical in world history. Black people, Latin people [. . .]; Puerto Rican; Chinese people, and all Asian people; American Indians, poor whites, progressives and liberal White people; and Eskimo people are all oppressed and are being subjected to fascist oppression by the United

States Government."[87] He goes on to call for cooperation between the Black Panthers and Asian peoples in establishing community programs: "I think that the Asian peoples could also set up a community center and function with the Black Panther Party in alliance [. . .]. In the Asian communities, the Asian people must see that they are categorized as a second-class citizen and in some cases third-class."[88] In addition, America's deeply compromised image of itself was made even more precarious by the stark contradictions between the violent treatment of black civil rights protestors in America and the parallel aggression in Vietnam. Cleaver diagnosed America with a case of "schizophreni[a]," which allowed the nation to hold "two conflicting images of itself [land of the free, home of the multiply oppressed]." Cleaver goes on to say that this divide was "never reconciled, because never before has the survival of [America's] most cherished myths made a reconciliation mandatory."[89] However, this instability at the heart of America's national identity also allowed Asian American and African Americans discursive space to exploit this slipperiness in the social meaning system.[90]

In many ways, the adoption of the rhetoric and ideology of anticolonialism was meant to assuage fears of increasing militancy, which was off-putting for the previous generation of civil rights activists. No less than Martin Luther King, Jr., criticized the embrace of violent resistance inspired by Fanon:

> Over cups of coffee in my home in Atlanta and my apartment in Chicago, I have often talked late at night and over into the small hours of the morning with proponents of Black Power who argued passionately about the validity of violence and riots. They don't quote Gandhi or Tolstoy. Their Bible is Frantz Fanon's *The Wretched of the Earth*. This black psychiatrist from Martinique [. . .] argues in his book [. . .] that violence is a psychologically healthy and tactically sound method for the oppressed. And so, realizing that they are a part of that vast company of the "wretched of the earth," these young American Negroes, who are predominantly involved in the Black Power movement, often quote Fanon's belief that violence is the only thing that will bring about liberation.[91]

King points out a contradiction in Fanon, citing in full the same passage that Carmichael and Hamilton use to close their preface. Whereas Carmichael and Hamilton cite the passage as evidence of the need for

African Americans to join with other Third World groups in a revolutionary vanguard to lead a social revolution, King questions why Fanon would endorse violence, which had been used to repress, as the only means to freedom. King instead calls on Black Power advocates to set aside the "old concept of violence" and turn towards a "power infused with love and justice."[92] However, King's criticism seems directed more at Cleaver's militantism than Carmichael and Hamilton's "politics of liberation." For Carmichael and Hamilton, violence should be used as a defensive tactic. For Cleaver, militant violence is the only way to bring about change. While others interpret these disagreements as evidence of the untenablity of Fanon's theory, I read this discourse concerning the usefulness of violent resistance as an example of the sort of ongoing debate that Fanon hoped his work would foster among "revolutionists." Fanon understood that the "struggle" over strategy would positively inform the struggle against oppression and bind the various native classes together to work towards liberation.

Thus, Fanon's concept of anticolonialism and decolonization through struggle link Black and Yellow Power. Anticolonialism, as defined by Fanon, provided a rationale for active, sometimes armed, struggle against the system that circumscribed the lives and psyches of people of color. Both Black and Yellow Power ideology use Fanon's study of the colonial condition in *The Wretched of the Earth* and *Black Skin, White Masks* to diagnose American "institutional racism" as a form of colonialism. Drawing on Fanon, they argue that America, like other colonial powers, systematically institutes and reifies racial categories and racial difference to support the existing social structure. In Black and Yellow Power's translations of Fanon, American institutional racism functions as a type of colonial system, creating and sanctioning the internal racial divisions that buttress America's definition of itself. They "Americanize" colonialism, using the paradigm to argue that the systemic racism directed against black and yellow people constitutes the groups as de facto internal colonies. Although land or territory was not an issue, African American and Asian American activists found promise in struggle and resistance—Fanon's prescription for purging a colonized consciousness.[93] Anticolonialism thus became a basis for a Power ideology that theorizes the psychological wounds of oppression and provides a political and academic framework for addressing the consequences of racism on the "flesh" of people of color in America.[94] Linked by "institutional racism," a political and social system that conflated both Vietnamese guerilla fighters and radical black nationalists, Asian Americans and African Americans had an interest in overturning the American colonial system that ensnared them. Unless both sought Power, either group could be used as the menacing, threatening "Other" against which the American values of democracy, fairness, and freedom could be reinscribed and redefined. These activists use the language and rhetoric of Fanonian anticolonialism to more precisely delineate the structures of oppression for American blacks and others. Their adoption of this language underscores Fanon's assertion that all colonialism is global and related, linking the fate of African Americans and Asian Americans with African, Asian, and Latin nations around the world. Likewise, Fanon asserts that the oppressed would be compelled to overthrow colonialism once they became aware of its impact on their lives. Thus, Power advocates also recognize the "struggle" for self-determination as the best antidote to reversing the structural effects of American-style colonialism. Rather than read this "slipperiness" and doubleness as mere symptoms of essentialism or poor contextualization, I would argue that this element of Fanon reflects his embrace of dialecticalism, which Sylvia Wynder defines as the "relationship between the lived reality of choices and social options."[95]

How one interprets Fanon depends largely on how one "reads" Fanon. A flattening of Fanon is due in part to the idealistic philosophical origins of structuralist and post-structuralist literary criticism and the publication history that tilted attention to *TWE*. Postcolonial theorists' preoccupation with Fanon is motivated by *BSWM* and its compelling treatment of the problem of identity and subjectivity for the colonized. On the other hand, African and Asian American anticolonialist activists read Fanon alongside Che Guevara, Regis Debray, and Kwame Nkrumah as another revolutionary political theorist. These very different contexts for reading Fanon motivated their own analysis and theories of oppression and their strategies to resist American-style colonialism. The internal legacies of Robert Williams and the Deacons for Self-Defense and the Fruit of Islam, the highly trained security force of the Nation of Islam, also contributed to the preoccupation with militant resistance that became part of the ideologies of Black and Yellow Power. Though Fanonian inflected Black and Yellow Power are often criticized for their essentialist constructions of race relations and ethnic identity, perhaps a reading of Fanon that recovers his use of dialectical materialism—the tension between social forces, or struggle—offers another way to think about the messy, chaotic, contingent, asymmetrical, and fluid relationship between subjects in a colonial system.

Taken together, Fanon's works outline an ideology and politics of anticolonialism, a mode of militant resistance to the system of colonialism, as well as a way to recognize and redeem the psychological, cultural, and social damage inflicted on those oppressed by the system. According to this construction, African Americans and Asian Americans suffer as second-class "subjects," set apart from the rest of "white society" by a specific, indigenous American form of colonial oppression that stripped American blacks of their cultural identity and subjectivity as effectively as any colonial system: "Black and colored people are saying in a clear voice that they intend to determine for themselves the kinds of political, social and economic systems they will live under. Of necessity this means that the existing systems of the dominant, oppressive group—the entire spectrum of values, beliefs, traditions, and institutions—will have to be challenged and changed."[96] The focus on these "systems" is a crucial difference from other anticolonial struggles. Rather than retake territory, Carmichael and Hamilton call for challenging the material and political as well as the invisible discursive structures that support oppression. They acknowledge the dialectical relationship between self-definition and political agency and see the ultimate expression of self-determination as the ability to exercise power, or, as Newton called it, "the will of the community" to enact social change. Ultimately, the political aims of "Power" depended on the development of "cultural integrity"[97] and "redefinition" through the struggle to achieve liberation.[98]

CHAPTER TWO

From Gorilla to Guerilla

Defining Revolutionary Identity

The title of this chapter plays on gorilla/guerilla, but it also signifies on dehumanizing discourses of American-style racism that compared black and yellow people to gorillas, apes, and orangutans in order to justify the array of legal, political, social, and religious ideologies that upheld a longstanding and sometimes lethal system of racial discrimination and segregation. From Thomas Jefferson's *Notes on the State of Virginia* to the mocking Civil War and Reconstruction-era cartoons of Thomas Nast's *Harper's Bazaar*, from the nativist anti-Chinese rhetoric of the nineteen teens and twenties to the Yellow Peril propaganda of World War II, this racist trope lurks in the dark corners of racial representation even today. In light of this history, listeners have sometimes reacted with suspicion and, on occasion, anger when I outlined my assertion that African Americans and Asian Americans adopted a guerilla subjectivity to represent the ideology of ethnic nationalist revolutionary struggle against racist oppression in America. Time and again, I have had to explain that I meant "guerilla," not gorilla. Yet, the echo remains, adding another layer of meaning to my formulation. The guerilla subjectivity asserts a full and empowered humanity that defies the disempowering, dehumanizing racist tropes that for so long justified the oppression and repression of the descendents of Africans and Asians in America.

Ironically, this troping on guerilla and gorilla is not uncommon in contemporary African American and Asian American popular culture. Rappers like Gorilla Joe and Guerilla Black, rap groups like the Gorillaz, and even 50 Cent's G(uerilla)-Unit all play on the menacing associations linked to both terms. On the surface, both terms evoke aggressive, resistant, and hypersexual representations of black masculinity and the black male body.[1] While we could read these namings as acts of playful, revisionary appropriation, these seemingly unironic appropriations often highlight the issues of representation and self-definition explored in this chapter. Ultimately, I assert that though the guerilla coalesced as a representation of revolutionary ethnic nationalism and icon of resistance, the political and ideological import of this figure was eventually appropriated in blaxploitation film and Bruce Lee/kung fu flicks to signify the very types of brutish black and menacing yellow masculinities that sell videogames, mp3s, and action games today.

Using the writings of Mao Tse-tung, Che Guevara, Regis Debray, and Eldridge Cleaver, I will begin by defining the parameters of the guerilla as a disciplined, ideologically grounded, solitary agent who engages in political and cultural action designed to disrupt oppressive social practices. Then, I will trace the development and institution of this identity position through the pages of *The Black Panther* and *Gidra* between 1969 and 1974. This five-year period encompasses the entire initial run of *Gidra* and the ensuing period during which the social implications of the legal changes of the 1960s were highly contested. Ultimately, I hope to show that the rhetoric and images of the guerilla found in the pages of these newspapers provided ideological and visual referents for a developing revolutionary consciousness on a weekly and monthly basis.

> I still think today as yesterday, that the color line is a great problem of this century. But today I see more clearly than yesterday that back of the problem of race and color, lies a greater problem which both obscures and implements it, and that is the fact that many civilized persons are willing to live in comfort even if the price of this is poverty, ignorance and disease of the majority of their fellow men, that to maintain this privilege men have waged war until today war tends to become universal and continuous, and the excuse for this war continues largely to be color and race.[2]

W. E. B. Du Bois's words from 1953 appeared in a full-page article commemorating the life of the African American scholar, activist, and expatriate in the January 4, 1969 edition of *The Black Panther*. His words update his famous 1903 dictum and provide a new paradigm for late twentieth century activists who were becoming familiar with Fanon's Marxist-inflected, anticolonialist critique of colonialism and neo-imperialism. Du Bois's remarks condemn the "civilized persons" who tacitly condone war against and tolerate the misery of "Others" to maintain their privileges as they live within the social mechanisms that both "obscure and implement" color and race as problematic social categories. Reading Du Bois through Fanon, any counteroffensive against oppression must penetrate the "back of the problem," in order to disrupt the "systems" of privilege. Du Bois's remarks rearticulate the "problem of the color line" from a matter of "the relation of the darker to the lighter races" to a problem of social constructs.[3]

The solution? Revolutionary "struggle." Mao, Regis Debray, and Che Guevara stressed the need for armed ideologues that could operate underground to weaken and ultimately disrupt the "universal and continuous" matrix of political and economic inequality. But Du Bois's remarks also imply that the struggle to uproot racist social systems would have to include uprooting social mechanisms of power and oppression built on longstanding hierarchies of class, race, and identity. In each case, this new relationship would have to be revolutionary and radical; realizing this change would require a revolutionary subject position that I call "guerilla."

As the primary representation of radical struggle, the guerilla serves, in effect, as the arms and legs to the vanguard's mouth.[4] Initially, the "guerilla" subject was meant to function as a type of a "transitional" ethnic consciousness designed to usher people of color from "rhetorical change to substantive change."[5] For African American and Asian American revolutionary nationalists, the figure came to symbolize both a revolutionary ideology and a new social consciousness, one that heralds both self-determined black and yellow masculinities and the legitimacy of black and yellow community power. The adoption of the guerilla subjectivity by African American and Asian American activists who shared similarly anticolonialist nationalist politics descends from Fanon's assertion that the route to political, psychological, and social freedom runs through anticolonialist struggle. This revolution against "white definition" in Fanon is retained in revolutionary and cultural nationalism and black and yellow nationalism as the imperative for group determination and the purpose for group struggle. The unconscious, uneasy realization that white definition may not be entirely resisted, which emerged earlier as "double consciousness," accompanies the realization that one's representation may ultimately be out of one's control.[6] In the rhetoric of revolution, the figure of the guerilla seems to function as an answer to the problems of representation and powerlessness created by American-style neocolonialist oppression.[7]

Fanon struggles with the tension between the need for and the sting of white recognition. In the following passage, Fanon first narrates the process of an "I" becoming aware of his "objecthood," and then his attempts to re-create a "self":

> I came into the world imbued with the will to find a meaning in things, my spirit filled with the desire to attain to the source of the world, and then I found that I was an object in the midst of other objects.
>
> Sealed into the crushing objecthood, I turned beseechingly to others. Their attention was a liberation, running over my body suddenly abraded into nonbeing, endowing me once more with an agility that I had thought lost, and by taking me out of the world, restoring me to it. But just as I reached the other side, I stumbled, and the movements, the attitudes, the glances of the other fixed me there, in the sense in which a chemical solution is fixed by a dye. I was indignant; I demanded an explanation. Nothing happened. I burst apart. Now the fragments have been put back together again by another self.[8]

While this passage may at first seem to describe a moment of interpellation in which the self is called into being by another, the object-self that Fanon describes looks to the "others" initially for self-determination. Their attention satisfies the self's desire for being. For Althusser, ideology necessitates subjects and governs the terms by which individuals gain a relationship with both the governing ideology and an understanding of their relationship to ideology. Althusser argues, "As a first formulation I shall say: all ideology hails or interpellates concrete individuals as concrete subjects, by the functioning of the category of the subject."[9] Interpellation doesn't just awaken the individual to some preexistent subjectivity; the call "recruits" or "transforms" individuals into assuming already existent subjects necessary for the functioning of the governing ideology.[10] The self in this passage looks to the others because he recognizes his own absence from existing structures of meaning. Fanon advocates psychic decolonization, which would disrupt this call and lead to a refusal of the identity intended by colonial ideology. Within his anticolonialist framework, Fanon understands colonized subjectivity as subjection to a Subject whose seeming preeminence is supported by every material apparatus of the colony—military, religious, legal, educational, etc. Thus, psychic decolonization leads to a guerilla identity, which the people could readily occupy to subvert and dislodge colonized subjectivity. Hence, the development of this revolutionary aesthetic, which transcended racial and movement boundaries to offer both black and yellow revolutionary activists the promise of a decolonized identity through struggle.

The word "guerilla" descends from the Spanish *guerra* meaning "war," "warfare," or, in the familiar, "problems" or "trouble."[11] The word takes its form and spelling from the French "guerilla."[12] Since "-illa" designates the diminutive in Spanish, the term also carries dismissive connotations. Initially, the term referred to a type of "small war" during the eighteenth century. Originating as a pejorative for the Spanish participants in the conflict during the Spanish struggle against Napoleon, the usages listed by the OED show that the term has carried negative connotations almost from its inception. In addition to being characterized as "irregular," guerilla tactics were described as "baffling," "strange," and "improvisatory" and practitioners of this brand of conflict were called "degenerate," "dodges," and "doubtful, lazy and dirty."[13] Guerilla warfare, or *guerra de guerillas*, came to refer to tactics used by a weaker power against a more powerful and established foe. Ironically, guerilla tactics were, and are, routinely labeled unfair by those same stronger powers stymied by the guerillas' unexpected tactics and movements.[14] Today, guerilla has come to refer both to the combatant and the type of combat. Likewise in the Spanish, *guerrilla* now denotes a group of guerilla combatants or type of warfare.[15]

My use of the term is adapted from recent American usage denoting a participant engaged in "irregular" combat, the term referring both to the process of struggle and the person engaged in the conflict.[16] In this country, the term has been most closely associated with the nationalist resistance struggle of the Vietnamese National Liberation forces (more commonly known in America by the pejorative, Viet Cong) against first the French and then the United States from the 1950s to the 1970s. While the term may have initially referred to the relative weakness and disorganization of the nationalist Spanish forces, it specialized to denote a particular type of "revolutionary war, engaging a civilian population, or a significant part of such a population, against the military forces of established or usurpative governmental authority."[17] As such, guerilla warfare became, in Robert Taber's assessment, an effective "tool for political revolution."[18] Taking the Vietnamese as their example, black and Asian American political activists and artists identified with the label. A 1969 *Black Panther* article entitled "The Nature of Guerilla Warfare" expands this meaning of the guerilla to include "the political partisan, an armed civilian whose principal weapon is not his rifle or his machete, but his relationship to the community, the nation, in and for which he fights."[19] Likewise, the Black Panthers and related American revolutionaries also expanded the meaning of the word guerilla to refer not only to the strategies and practitioners, but also to the philosophies underlying the combat. Guerilla, therefore, came to refer to a counter-hegemonic revolutionary ideology. Taken together, a guerilla is a person who engages in political activism or combat based on a consciousness of the need for radical social change to end racial oppression and reform America's racist society. According to this definition, then, artists, writers, and academics, as well as their works, can be considered guerilla as long as revolutionary principles motivate and are reflected in their praxis and productions.

By the mid-twentieth century, guerilla forces were considered a vital element of anticolonialist and anti-imperialist nationalist movements. Indeed, an ideology of guerilla warfare arose out of a series of late nineteenth and twentieth century anti-imperialist struggles, and was brought together by Mao Tse-tung, whose *Ya Chi Chan (Guerilla Warfare)* was published in 1937.[20] Looking to movements in Central America, Asia, and Africa, young African American and Asian American activists read and studied Mao as an example of successful revolutionary action. Eldridge Cleaver acknowledges Mao's influence on the Panthers' belief in armed militarism: "Huey P. Newton took that step [towards armed revolution]. For the motto of the Black Panther Party he chose a quotation from Mao Tse-tung's *Little Red Book*: 'We are advocates of the abolition of war; we do not want war; and in order to get rid of the gun it is necessary to pick up the gun.'"[21] In his military strategy, Mao distinguished between conventional warfare and guerilla warfare, or "pick[ing] up the gun." While he considered conventional warfare the only means to emerge victorious over the standing forces of the government, Mao saw guerilla warfare as a necessary auxiliary to conventional forces.[22] For Mao, guerilla warfare was useful as an irritant to the conventional army of the opposition. He compared guerillas to "innumerable gnats, which by biting a giant both in front and in the rear, ultimately exhaust him."[23] In addition to this auxiliary martial role, Mao also understood the guerilla army as having an ideological function: to involve the people in support of the revolutionary struggle.

The unconventional nature of guerilla fighters and guerilla combat meant that special measures had to be taken to ensure the readiness of guerilla forces. Citing the corruption and lack of discipline in previous irregular armies, Mao established strict codes of behavior for the guerilla's conduct. This code—"The Three Rules and the Eight Remarks"—originally developed for the Russian Red Army was simple, but comprehensive:

1. All actions are subject to command.
2. Do not steal from the people.
3. Be neither selfish nor unjust.

1. Replace the door when you leave the house.
2. Roll up the bedding on which you have slept.
3. Be courteous.
4. Be honest in your transactions.
5. Return what you borrow.
6. Replace what you break.
7. Do not bathe in the presence of women.
8. Do not without authority search the pocketbooks of those you arrest.[24]

By adopting these rules, Mao acknowledged that though the guerilla warrior, recruited from the masses, may initially be less disciplined than a regular soldier, the guerilla must eventually be better trained than even a regular army member.[25] In addition to personal discipline, the guerilla soldier had to be more ideologically grounded than the regular soldier. The rules meant "both organization and discipline of guerilla troops must be at a high level so that [the guerillas] can carry out the political activities that are the life of both the guerilla armies and of revolutionary warfare."[26] Guerilla tactics also mandate that the forces operate by blending in with the populace. In this way, the guerillas serve as both paradigms and combatants. While the rules were intended to facilitate their peaceable coexistence with the peasants for whom they were ideologically mandated to fight, they also underscore the guerillas' role as representations of the change to come.

These rules also form the foundation for the code of ethics adopted by the Black Panther Party for Self-Defense. According to Bobby Seale's 1970 memoir *Seize the Time*, Seale and Huey Newton first framed the "Black Panther Party Program and Platform" in October 1966 at the time they founded the Oakland-based Black Panther Party for Self-Defense. Initially, the document was divided into two sections, "What We Want," the Party's demands, and "What We Believe," the philosophical and ideological underpinnings of those demands. Until March 29, 1972,[27] the ten points of the Panther "Program" were:

1. We want freedom. We want power to determine the destiny of our Black Community.
2. We want full employment for our people.
3. We want an end to the robbery by the white man of our Black Community.
4. We want decent housing, fit for shelter of human beings.
5. We want education for our people that exposes the true nature of this decadent American society. We want education that teaches us our true history and our role in the present-day society.
6. We want all black men to be exempt from military service.
7. We want an immediate end to POLICE BRUTALITY and MURDER of black people.
8. We want freedom for all black people held in federal, state, county, and city prisons and jails.
9. We want all black people when brought to trial to be tried in court by a jury of their peer group or people from their black communities, as defined by the Constitution of the United States.
10. We want land, bread, housing, education, clothing, justice, and peace. And as our major political objective, a United Nations supervised plebiscite to be held throughout the black colony in which only black colonial subjects will be allowed to participate, for the purpose of determining the will of black people as to their national destiny.[28]

The first point defines freedom as the power of self-determination and locates it within the ability to chart the "destiny" of the "Black Community," a unit that, the capital letters imply, shares common interests and goals due to a legacy of inequitable treatment at the hands of the American colonial system. Rather than calling for fairness or equality, the platform specifies the areas where the "privilege" of "civilized persons" has led to the repression of blacks and people of color and calls for the reversal of those inequities through radical political reorganization.

The "Platform" and "Program" were also usually accompanied by an almost verbatim repetition of the first two paragraphs of the Declaration of Independence, save for two sentences:

> . . . . That, to secure these rights, governments are instituted among men, deriving their just powers from the consent of the governed; that whenever any form of government becomes destructive of these ends, it is the right of the people to alter or to abolish it, and to institute a new government, laying its foundation on such principles, and organizing its powers in such form, as to them shall seem most likely to effect their safety and happiness. [. . .] But when a long train of abuses and usurpations, pursuing invariably the same object, evinces a design to reduce them under absolute despotism, it is their right, it is their duty, to throw off such government, and to provide new guards for their future security.[29]

A common move in the African American rhetorical tradition, this appropriation of the founding documents of the country is evidence of the Panthers' claim to represent America's "true" revolutionary values. The echoes of the Declaration of Independence also signify ironically on the persistant distance between the American myth of equality and its tortured reality. The "Platform" and "Program" embody, according to Seale's account, Newton's interpretation of "what all these revolutionary leaders [Malcolm X, Mao, Fanon] said we must do, what we must establish, what we must institutionalize. [. . .] Huey always had the people's desires and political needs in mind."[30]

In addition to the "Program" and "Platform," the Panther Party set up the "Eight Points of Attention" and "Three Main Rules of Discipline" as rules of conduct for their members in 1968.

Eight Points of Attention
1. Speak politely.
2. Pay fairly for what you buy.
3. Return everything you borrow.
4. Pay for anything you damage.
5. Do not hit or swear at people.
6. Do not damage property or crops of the poor, oppressed masses.

7. Do not take liberties with women.

8. If we ever have to take captives, do not ill-treat them.

Three Main Rules of Discipline

1. Obey orders in all your actions.
2. Do not take a single needle or a piece of thread from the poor and oppressed masses.
3. Turn in everything captured from the attacking enemy.[31]

Like Mao's code of behavior, the Panther Party's rules were intended to establish a standard of behavior for the "lumpen proletariat" who made up the rank and file. The strict code was meant to instill a sense of discipline and cohesiveness while also mediating the potentially intimidating martial power of the guerilla forces and heightening the ideological persuasiveness of their presence in the community. The rules were to remind the guerillas of their role in a war for the souls of the people, with the ultimate goal being to gain community support for a generalized uprising. These rules, distilled from a much longer work—"The Rules of the Black Panther Party"—also governed the relationship between local chapters and the national organization and enumerated prohibitions on Panther behavior. The Panthers' urban setting and the danger of its forces falling prey to a variety of social pathologies seem to propel many of the Panthers' rules. These proscriptions on Panther behavior presage the turmoil caused by later efforts to police the membership on the grounds of ideological consistency and community credibility.

In addition to Mao, Che Guevara, an important icon of anticolonialist nationalist struggle, became an ideological and a symbolic influence for the Black Panthers. Guevara's *Guerilla Warfare*, a handbook for armed revolutionary action, served as a blueprint for nascent revolutionary activists. Che Guevara, one of the architects of the Cuban revolution, also argues that the guerilla should embody revolution, acting as a "standard bearer" who works with the people and leads them towards social reform. In a famous photo reminiscent of Guevara, Huey Newton, the Black Panther Minister of Defense, appears heavily armed while seated in a fan-backed wicker chair. Newton and the Black Panther Party drew on the images of Guevara to build Newton's image as a forceful and effective leader of an organized cadre of military revolutionaries. *The Black*

Panther regularly included pictures of Huey Newton in profile, holding a gun, while seated upon a figurative throne evoking Che Guevara. Newton was always depicted in the black leather jacket, black pants, and blue or black shirt or turtleneck that became emblematic of the Panthers. The success of the Cuban revolution made other revolutionaries hopeful that Guevara's strategies would work for them as well. Appropriating Guevara's image was a way to symbolically align Newton, and the Black Panther by extension, to his brand of revolution. For Guevara, guerilla warfare was not just a supplemental military strategy; it was a foundation for revolutionary military action, and he posited a set of rules both for behavior and strategy that reflect that belief.

Among the specific characteristics that the guerilla should possess, Guevara lists vigilance, discretion, physical hardiness to tolerate the conditions of life in the field, and loyalty to his fellow combatants.[32] In addition, he advises guerilla combatants to maintain good relations with the inhabitants of the countryside in order to ensure aid when necessary and help recruit additional combatants. He also places as much importance on ideological readiness as combat readiness, because the guerilla serves as the representative of revolution. Going further than Mao, Guevara calls the guerilla a "social reformer" fighting for an ideological cause on behalf of the people.[33] This idea of the guerilla as a social activist became a significant aspect of the persona. In his classic 1965 study of guerilla warfare, *The War of the Flea*, Robert Taber cites the "first task" of the guerilla as drawing attention to a "great cause," then relating all action to it in order to give the movement meaning and cohesion and to "arouse great expectations and appear crucial at every stage, so that no one can stand outside of it."[34] Guevara likewise characterizes the guerilla as part of a revolutionary vanguard initially taking up the cause of revolution on behalf of the people and then, by example, bringing them in line until a small band "snowball[s] into a nationwide rebellion."[35] While Guevara's emphasis on the rural countryside as the staging ground for revolution made it difficult to translate his principles to an urban American setting, his reification of the guerilla's ideological function informed the guerilla subjectivity that grew out of the ideology of Power adopted by Asian American and African American activists.

Casting the guerilla as an ideological agent also underscores the ideologically motivated nature of guerilla warfare or "struggle." Guevara characterizes guerilla warfare as "the miracle by which a small nucleus of men [. . .] becomes the vanguard of a mass movement [. . .] establishing a new society, ending the ways of the old, and winning social justice. Considered in this light, guerilla warfare takes on a true greatness, a sense of destiny, without the need for further rhetoric."[36] Guevara, stressing action over continual organization and ideological refinement, deemphasizes the need to expend resources on creating a parallel bureaucratic infrastructure to replace the overthrown government. Instead, Guevara believes that the struggle itself would produce the ultimate goal of overthrowing repressive government, creating new structures for governance in the process. As a result, he reifies combat, placing it at the "climax of guerilla life."[37] Each battle offers an opportunity for guerilla forces to extract, through defeat or attrition, from the power and reserves of the hegemonic regime. For Guervara, combat, not rhetoric, functions as the ultimate expression of ideological conviction, because it is the only way to bring about social overthrow and institute a socialist system. Guevara's philosophy also heightens the tension between the guerilla vanguard committed to military action and the masses in need of radical change.

One more theorist would add to the development of the guerilla as an ideological agent. Using the language of missionaries, Regis Debray, the French theorist of the Latin American socialist revolutions, exhorts potential revolutionaries to spread the word of revolution like evangelicals, converting the masses, stirring up their "faith" in the legitimacy of struggle, and reiterating the message "again and again."[38] According to Debray, socialist revolution requires a vanguard to articulate its principles, but revolution could not be accomplished without a guerilla force to engage in the struggle. In *Revolution in the Revolution?*, Debray condemns the Soviet party for perpetuating a Communist bureaucracy, advocating for truly revolutionary movements that focus on engaging in the struggle rather than building an infrastructure that may or may not be responsive to the people and relevant to the overthrow of the government. In a review of *Revolution in the Revolution?*, Weusi (which seems to be the nom de guerre of a *Soulbook* contributor) reiterates this principle. In "For Black Guerillas," Weusi stresses the necessity for constant "guerilla conflict," citing it as "one of the most basic principles of popular revolutionary warfare, in fact the one which makes guerillas guerillas [. . .]. [P]opular forces must stay mobile to stay alive."[39] Weusi criticizes H. Rap Brown and Stokely Carmichael for philosophizing revolution rather than engaging in combat, saying that "there is a need in Black America for a unified together guerilla front which is based on taking care of business, not on talking about it."[40] Weusi, Debray, Guevara, and others believed that bureaucracy and "philosophizing" delayed the ultimate goal of complete overthrow of an oppressive or colonialist regime by taking the focus from armed resistance and focusing instead on bureaucracy and talk, which were associated with the bourgeois class demonized by most revolutionaries. Without constant struggle, conflict, and agitation, the oppressed and colonized masses stood to lose the context of conflict within which new societies and resistant identities like the guerilla could be constituted.

While Debray limns out a process for revolution, his blueprint or "program" is not an exact fit for America's struggle. Debray bases his theories on the relative success of Marxist revolutions in South and Central America, but he was criticized for advocating a plan that would be ineffective in an urban society like the United States. However, Debray's theory of armed struggle, like Fanon's theory of colonial consciousness, values the ability of individual combatants to "think outside the box" to accomplish their revolutionary aims. This willingness to improvise revolutionary strategy is largely based on Guevara's example. Some theorists of revolution criticized the romantic notion of an armed band of guerillas gaining strength, territory, and support in rural areas before advancing to overthrow the government. But for African American and Asian American revolutionaries, the guerilla strategy remained powerfully influential, primarily because the decentralized structure offered hope that even a small band of badly outnumbered believers could bring about widespread social change.

As constructed by Debray and Guevara, the guerilla functions as the main agent for revolutionary change. As such, he must be disciplined, prepared for action, empowered to act singly or in small groups, and ideologically grounded for his "primary effort, [. . .] militat[ing] the population."[41] In this way, the guerilla represents a threat to the existing order in that the guerilla disseminates revolutionary ideas, his actions lending force to his doctrine and demonstrating the route to radical change. Yet, it would be an error to consider the guerilla a mere strategic tool. The political dialogue between revolutionaries and the hegemonic regime establishes the guerilla as an expression of the revolutionary impulse, as well as a catalyst for the popular will toward such change.[42] The guerilla thus represents both the need for change and the means for accomplishing it.

So, how did advocates of Black and Yellow Power distill these principles into their own discussions of revolution? In an anecdote from *Soul on Ice*, Eldridge Cleaver recounts the denunciation of a fellow inmate who does not grasp the revolutionary program:

> "Do you know the difference between a gorilla and a guerilla?" the Eunuch on my right asked the Accused.
>
> The Accused appeared to be contemplating an answer.
>
> "I'll make it easier for you," the Eunuch said. "You're a gorilla, and a guerilla is everything you are not."
>
> The Accused opened his mouth to reply, but the Eunuch on my left [. . .] cut him off. "A guerilla is a man," he snapped, his eyes flashing, "but you're some kind of freak."[43]

This exchange occurs near the beginning of "The Allegory of the Black Eunuch," a fictionalized, dreamlike essay that occurs in the fourth and final section of Cleaver's *Soul on Ice*, "White Woman, Black Man." Most commentators note two things about this chapter: the denunciation of the "cowardly" older black male inmate, who is alternately called "Lazarus," "the Accused" or "the Infidel," and the extended discussion of the complicated psychosexual dynamic between black and white men and women in this society, a seeming takeoff on chapter three, "The Man of Color and the White Woman" in Fanon's *Black Skin, White Masks*. In this chapter, "Lazarus" explains his profound love for white women and antipathy for black women in relationship to the Supermasculine Menial-Omnipotent Administrator schema more fully developed in "The Primeval Mitosis." In addition to these issues of sexual and racial politics, it is also important to note Cleaver's use of genre and form to structure his discussion of race and sexuality. In other words, if this is an allegory, what idealized principles or values does Cleaver intend to associate with the guerilla?

Initially, Cleaver and the fellow inmates of his generation attack Lazarus/the Accused/the Infidel for not being revolutionary, for "cling[ing]" to life rather than rising up against America's oppressive system.[44] After the exchange replicated above, the Accused goes into a "self-searching, inward-looking" reverie, remembering the "blood and guns and knives, whips, ropes and chains and trees, screams, night riders, fear, nightsticks, police dogs and firehoses, fire, wounds and bombs," mechanisms of terror and control that had alternately "frozen," "destudded," or "burnt out" black men. The memories of white racial terrorism and black impotence stymie both Lazarus/the Accused and the paragraph, which ends in an ellipsis ". . .". In order to restart the conversation, the narrator changes the subject, asking, "Have you ever hit a black woman?" The enthusiastic response of Lazarus/the Accused constitutes most of the remaining essay. Again, while most readers comment on the problematic sexual politics of this passage, how can Cleaver's use of allegory help us recuperate any rehearsal of revolutionary politics in this loaded passage?

Drawing on Cleaver's allusion to Plato's "Allegory of the Cave," the essay seems to be most concerned with how racial consciousness changes one's perception of reality or truth. Since the essay begins and ends with denunciations of the "Lazarus generation" for their cowardice and lack of militancy, this dilemma seems to drive the deeper conflict between the prisoners. While the passage could be read as a generational conflict born of a pervasive anxiety about black masculinity, it is perhaps more productive to consider this as an instance of anxiety about the fundamental lack of agency of all of the inmates. Cleaver signifies on Plato's "prisonhouse" of reality to illustrate the ontological dilemma faced by both Lazarus and his tormentors. Like Plato's allegory, the essay is hypothetical, the imagined exchange seeming to take place in a dream. The narrator speaks rarely, preferring to "remain silent" (149) and later not knowing what to say, indicating difficulty or reluctance speaking. Even in an essay written from his perspective, the narrator struggles to voice his own experience of resistance within the competing discourses of masculinity, sexuality, gender, and resistance being rehearsed by his prisonmates. Like the subject of Plato's story, the narrator is aware of a world beyond his projections; however, he struggles to articulate his awakening consciousness to his compatriots.

Though Cleaver's example is problematic—the Eunuch who "cuts off" the Accused is himself, according to his moniker, not entirely a man—it does allow him to contrast the guerilla with Lazarus's mindset. A guerilla, possessed with a revolutionary consciousness as defined by Yellow or Black Power rhetoric, now becomes the norm; anything else is freakish.[45] By using Lazarus as a negative example and punning on the near rhyme of the two terms, Cleaver positions the guerilla as a man, not woman, and as a man, not animal. The gorilla, an animal, acts on instinct, unaware of the need for struggle to free himself from the dehumanizing effects of colonization. A guerilla, on the other hand, achieves manhood because he has become aware of the need for revolutionary change. In this way, Cleaver's anecdote also represents an attempt to rewrite earlier racialist narratives and racist tropes that equated blacks and Asians with primates like chimpanzees and orangutans. By becoming a guerilla, an unthinking "Lazarus" can evolve into a "man." Unfortunately, by endorsing this denunciation without critiquing the validity of the original gorilla reference, Cleaver fails to escape the dialectic established by the racist discourse to which the anecdote alludes, even as he offers the guerilla as a way beyond previously dehumanizing racial narratives. Thus, this humanity and manhood only extend to the narrator who has become aware of the light beyond the shadows, not his fellow inmates.

In a *Gidra* editorial, Alan Nishiro also voices an anxiety about Asian American humanity and manhood and the ability to assert a radicalized consciousness. Nishiro asserts, "Orientals in America have become [. . .] White Americans," having given up their greatest asset, a self-defined identity, in the rush to assimilate and gain acceptance in American society.[46] The solution to this "powerlessness" is to "act as Asian Americans," to reject the "stereotypes" of the mainstream and pursue "self-determination and self-defense" in concert with other oppressed peoples.[47] Nishiro's argument implies that the "Oriental," like the "gorilla," is unaware of the psychosocial damage that cultural assimilation does to the individual subject and is thus powerless to confront this psychic change. According to Nishiro, the most dangerous effect of this mental colonization is the loss of individual ethnic identity, leading to cultural impotence. His call to reject internal stereotypes also recognizes that self-hate motivates the Oriental, as it does the "gorilla."

In *Asian American Literature*, one of the first comprehensive studies of the field of Asian American literary studies, Elaine H. Kim, Jeffrey Paul Chan, and Frank Chin also address the problem of constructing an identity that is conscious, autonomous, and revolutionary. While Kim acknowledges that this period saw increased attention to the issues of "racial and cultural identity," she centers this dialectic around the tension between Asian American writers and activists who actively sought to reconnect with an "authentic" past, real or imagined, and those who actively resisted identification with romanticized images of the past to the point of demonizing early and midcentury "portraits" and relics of Chinese, Filipino, and Japanese American life.[48] Kim argues that the destructive stereotypes of Asian Americans as the "model minority," of Asian American women as emasculating, and of the men as effeminate and nonthreatening, were central to the reshaping of Asian American identity during this period. She references Jeffrey Paul Chan and Frank Chin, who attribute these seemingly salutary stereotypes to "racist love" as opposed to "racist hate."[49] While "racist hate" produces hypermasculine threatening stereotypes like those that haunt African American males, "racist love" paints Asian American males as "docile and compliant" and unthreatening. For Chan and Chin, the revolutionary message was not only transformative, but was also evolutionary, enabling the guerilla, Oriental, and kissass a route to full manhood in the face of these distorted and repressive representations. Daniel Maeda similarly asserts that, for Chin, "emulating blackness provided a way to recuperate Asian American masculinity."[50]

Thus, the acceptance of Power ideology leads to transformation in several important ways. Power ideology facilitates resolution of the oppressed subject's "identity crisis," enabling the initiation of ethnic consciousness. In addition, power's revolutionary ideology/rhetoric establishes a culture of cooperation, between the community and the vanguard and between ethnic groups seeking similar societal change. This ideology also creates individuals, not in the bourgeois sense, but in the sense that each revolutionary consciousness results from a personal "salvation" experience. In these ways, the revolutionary message of Black and Yellow Power leads to guerillas, people awakened.

A cartoon by Mantilaba in the May 4, 1968, edition of *The Black Panther* illustrates this transformation. Part of an ever-evolving series of cartoons depicting the Black Panther Party Platform and Program, the cartoon depicts Point 6, "We want all black men to be exempt from military service. [. . .] We will not fight and kill other people of color in the world who, like black people, are being victimized by the white racist government of America."[51] The cartoon shows six black men, four of them garbed in the Black Panther uniform—"blue shirt, with black leather jacket, black pants, and black beret"[52]—standing upright behind a kneeling figure, similarly clad, staring piercingly ahead. Emerging from the right of the frame is another male figure, in the midst of donning his Panther uniform while stepping out of (and stepping onto) a U. S. military uniform. Stooped, his slightly bowed head implies that

Figure 1. Mantilaba. "Cartoon." *The Black Panther* [Berkeley], 4 May 1968: 9.

WE WANT ALL BLACK MEN TO BE EXEMPT from military service

his service with the repressive American military has diminished him somehow, making him less than the other black men in the picture. The viewer can infer that this man will soon progress from the right of the image to the left, joining his "brothers" on the other side of the frame, standing upright and armed in service to "the Black Community."[53] This cartoon also approximates the process of transformation from "gorilla" to guerilla.

While the revolutionary function of poetry and drama is well documented, less has been said about the role of visual arts in articulating revolutionary ideology and the revolutionary character. In this instance, ideology dictates the aesthetics of this image. Mantilaba vividly portrays the process of a young man preparing to answer the call of Bobby Seale, chairman of the Black Panther Party, to "come home, [. . .] relate to the struggle here, [. . .] get mobilized and to amass together" to free the community and overthrow oppression.[54] Returning vets were seen as valuable potential Panther Party members because their military training could be useful in training other recruits and defenders of the black community in America. Thus, this image, as much as the articles and commentaries in the paper, reinforces the ultimate goal of the party: to revolutionize the black community and develop it into a vanguard.

Both *Gidra* and *The Black Panther* function as spaces where the formerly subjected could institute a discourse with mainstream American culture and, in so doing, develop a revolutionary consciousness. To that end, both *Gidra* and *The Black Panther* serve as "instruments of political education [. . .] published with the intent of countering the misinformation that often appears in the mass communication media" for the ultimate purpose of "educating the oppressed."[55] The newspapers characterized themselves as guides for evolving revolutionaries, battling mental colonialism and offering visual representations of the revolutionary aesthetic. Both papers were key to illustrating and disseminating revolutionary identity and principles.

Christian A. Davenport contributed a content analysis of *The Black Panther* paper to *The Black Panther Party Reconsidered* (1998), treating it as an example of the "dissident" press. According to Davenport, dissident media must:

1. Attempt to create an alternative evaluation of political, social, and economic reality that might provide new insights or different solutions from those that are already current in the mainstream;
2. Advocate political positions not expressed within the more established media;
3. Attempt to decrease the legitimacy of existing political and economic relations;
4. Increase the visibility of the dissident individuals/groups they represent by prompting the group's ideas in order to garner support and/or increase membership;
5. Help provide an identity for the dissident individuals/groups they represent as well as their constituency; and
6. Generate revenue for other activities.[56]

In addition, each paper should be thought of as an outlet for protest, highlighting inequality and injustice, while building a community of like-minded reformers. In this way, the papers provide a cultural and ideological commons wherein writers, artists, and activists can rehearse identities and strategies both useful for dissidents and attractive to "the people." I treat *The Black Panther*, published in Berkeley as the official news organ of the Black Panther Party, and *Gidra*, published by an ever-changing roster of young Asian American activists in Los Angeles, as archives of the rhetoric and visual images of revolution. In their photos, illustrations, and editorial cartoons, *Gidra* and *The Black Panther* perform the fifth function of the dissident press. For young activists, *Gidra* and *The Black Panther* were among the "alternative media" that "became crucial in establishing a new method for analyzing society and establishing models for 'revolutionary' changes and 'self-determination.'"[57] In addition to establishing a visual identity for the Black Panther Party and Yellow Power activists, both papers communicated the ideology and rhetoric of these movements, and illustrated those principles for public consumption.

The Black Panther, cornerstone of first the Black Community News Service and later the Liberation News Service, was the organ of "the People's Party" and as such was designed to broadcast the demands and Party platform. Emory Douglas, Black Panther Party Minister of Culture, produced and oversaw the illustrations in *The Black Panther*. It fell to Douglas to "bring to life" the principles outlined by Newton, Seale, and others.

On the other hand, *Gidra* was not the communication organ for any particular organization, but within its pages we find rhetoric and imagery clearly identified with the Power principles of self-determination, political parity, and self-definition. Nelson Nagai reflected on the importance of *Gidra* to young Asian Americans seeking self-awareness: "*Gidra* taught us that we were no longer to be called 'orientals,' and should call ourselves Asian Americans. *Gidra* told us about the struggle for Asian American Studies at San Francisco State, University of California at Berkeley, and UCLA, the anti-war movement, and the I-Hotel, and how Asian activists should band together to make a national political movement."[58] In their pages, both papers overturned old notions of identity, circulating new possibilities and encouraging newly self-determined subjectivities. Containing a mix of news, rhetoric, advertisements, cartoons, drawings, poems, dramatic pieces, and short fiction, both papers first articulate and then illustrate the revolutionary ideologies of Black Power and of Yellow Power. These newspapers did much more than dispense information; they were essential tools in the revolutionary project, disseminating rhetoric and ideology, news about community service projects, national political news affecting black and Asian American communities, and global news of the world-

Figure 2. "Cartoon." *Gidra* [Los Angeles], May 1971: front cover.

Figure 3. Emory Douglas, "In Revolution One Wins, or One Dies." *The Black Panther* [Berkeley], 27 April 1969: back cover.

wide struggles against imperialism. Ethnic publications, according to Espiritu, "promote ethnic ideology and keep alive ethnic symbols and values, heroes, and historical achievement. It is the very business of the ethnic media to be concerned with the events and progress of the ethnic group."[59] Along with the writings and speeches of those involved in black and Asian anticolonialist nationalist politics, these papers acted as avenues for the development of revolutionary ideology and guerilla subjectivity.

I will now turn to some of the images of the guerilla found in the pages of *Gidra* and *The Black Panther* to discuss how each illustrates the principles of Power ideology and revolutionary ethnic subjectivity.

In figures 2 and 3, the lone, armed men crouch stealthily, tracking their designated targets. The beret in figure 2 and the scarf in figure 3 outwardly signal their membership in the revolutionary cadre. Both figures are anonymous, indeterminate, ready to be called into being by the struggle. The black face of the figure from the back cover of *The Black Panther* is even more indeterminate. Their crouching stances suggest a readiness to engage the enemy. The National Liberation Front soldier appears on the 1971 *Gidra* cover peering into the distance at an opponent who is presumably unaware of his presence. The Black Panther guerilla in figure 3 faces the viewer, seeming to move towards us. We could be his target. His steadily approaching body challenges us to identify ourselves as either enemy—an agent in the American imperialist system or an unradicalized black person—or friend and fellow guerilla. The slogan reinforces this ambiguity—"In Revolution One Wins, or One Dies"—implying death to either the member of mainstream culture or to the unconscious black person.[60] His figure forces us to choose. Do we identify with him or will we be attacked? The indeterminate locations of the pictures, the vague background of the Black Panther, and the slight vegetation of a rural locale imagined by the Socialist revolutionary theorists, all imply that the revolution could be anywhere and everywhere. The pages of both newspapers reify this type of lone, almost exclusively male figure over and over during the years from 1969 to 1974.

These figures embody and model the type of person needed to achieve the evolutionary revolution articulated by activists in the pages of both newspapers. It was not enough simply to agree with the rhetoric of anticolonialism; the struggle demanded that hearers become doers, ready to participate in any action necessary to overthrow the American system.

In addition to modeling the figure of the guerilla, these images also illustrate principles of revolutionary organization. Figures 4 and 5 exemplify the cooperative struggle envisioned by Fanon, Debray, and Newton. The illustrations suggest a ready alliance between Asian Americans and African Americans against American oppression as facilitated by anticolonial ideology. Although they could be seen as facing each other in opposition, the black American GI and South Vietnamese National Liberation fighter instead express solidarity. In figure 4, they shake hands with weapons pointed down, indicating a lack of aggression. The absence of other figures hints at the furtive, subversive character of this alliance. Just as the NLF was the guerilla companion of the regular North Vietnamese Army, the alliance suggested by this illustration positions African Americans in the armed forces as an extension of this guerilla force. The illustration suggests that instead of fighting in America's military interests, African Americans have more in common with the ideological, political, and military struggle of the North Vietnamese. The next illustration depicts this alliance more forthrightly.

Figure 4. (right) "Cartoon."
The Black Panther [Berkeley],
20 September 1969: 2.

Figure 5. (Below) "Cartoon."
The Black Panther [Berkeley],
4 January 1969: 8.

WHAT WE WANT

6. We want all black men exempt from military service.

In figure 5, the racial differences of the soldiers are clearer, as are the symbols of cooperation. The soldiers stand in close physical proximity while the body of a U.S. soldier depicted as a "pig" and representing their common enemy, lies dead at their feet. This cartoon often illustrated point six of the 1969 version of the "Ten Point Program for the Black Panther Party"; it demanded that all black Americans be exempt from military service. Like the previous illustration, this drawing figures African American soldiers as an internal threat because of the ideological affinities created by similar struggles against American aggression and oppression. These illustrations indicate the repeated and

Figure 6. Boris. "Cartoon." *The Black Panther* [Berkeley], 7 June 1969: 18.

emphatic identification made between the Black Power Movement and the struggle of the Vietnamese Nationalist Army, which, by extension, provided an avenue for cooperation between blacks and Asians in America.

In addition to targeting blacks in the armed forces, considered prime recruits due to their military experience, the cartoons also targeted audiences beyond the "lumpen" or "peasantry." As a June 7, 1969, cartoon from *The Black Panther* illustrates, the revolutionary message is aimed also at narratives of black middle-class respectability that played out in the Civil Rights Movement. The idealized integrationist couple on the left in figure 6 conforms to tropes of middle-class American respectability; indeed, they win approval from the white bystander who tearily whispers, "Beautiful, beautiful." The dress and hairstyles of the 1965 couple mimic the dress of the bystander, while the Bible and flag that they hold affirm the values of the so-called American dream, signaling a desire for acceptance through exemplifying white American standards and waiting quietly for recognition and acceptance. Lastly, the lyrics unfurling above their heads ironically echo the well-known Civil Rights Movement anthem. Here the words imply an

Figure 7. "Cartoon." *Gidra*
[Los Angeles], April 1970: 9.

otherworldy confidence in a moral law that they believe will prevail: "We shall overcome . . ."[61] By 1969, the couple, after exposure to the revolutionary message, manifests a new consciousness that is reflected in their dress and demeanor. The man peers out at the reader while his wife's eyes are hidden behind dark, defiant shades, rather than demure glasses. Their "natural" hairstyles defy the beauty norms of mainstream society. The man wears ammo, a beret, and work boots, indicating both an identification with the working class and a readiness for paramilitary action, while the wife wears a jumpsuit with a plunging neckline, reclaiming rather than hiding her black female sexuality as she holds a "Free Huey" placard revealing her political sympathies. This time, the white bystander, visibly shaken, exclaims, "My God! Anarchy!," a fear justified by the new slogan unfurling above the heads of the couple and alongside the husband's upraised fist: "We shall overthrow. . . "

A similar tale of transformation holds for the *Gidra* mascot (figure 7). The humble caterpillar has been transformed by the anticolonialist Yellow Power revolutionary message, having "search[ed his soul] for the flame of the Asian warriors who fought for their people and their pride without fear of death."[62] The hat, the *non la*, reminiscent of those often shown on Vietnamese Nationalist Army fighters, his upraised fist, and

Defining Revolutionary Identity   77

the sword slung across his chest identify him as a guerilla, prepared and willing to participate in armed struggle. The upraised fist clearly mirrors the Black Power salute in figure 6, signaling his identification with a specifically American form of revolutionary ideology. Ironically, this humble caterpillar, tired of waiting, has evolved into a warrior worm.

As these newspaper images and Black and Yellow Power organizational rhetoric demonstrate, guerilla identity goes beyond the iconic black beret and black leather jacket dress code that distinguished members of the Black Panther Party.[63] The goal of raising the consciousness of African Americans and Asian Americans was to transform them into guerillas, suitable for the fight against the oppressive American system. Robert Taber summarizes the material, physical, and mental supplies that the guerilla should need. While the guerilla would need little—"his rifle, a blanket, a square . . . to shelter him from the rain, a knife, a compass, stout boots"—to withstand the deprivations of a long uncertain struggle, he had to be mentally prepared: "cheerful, stoic and ascetic; he must like the hard life he leads."[64] However, the guerilla's ideological temerity was the one trait that would sustain him through this "hard life": "what is indispensable is ideological armor. Above all, the revolutionary activist must stand on solid, moral ground, if he is to be more than a political bandit."[65] As a soldier, the guerilla was expected to be disciplined, proficient, comfortable, and knowledgeable about the care and operation of guns. Because the success of insurrectionary actions depended on secrecy, the guerilla had to be able to operate singly or in small groups in order to retain the element of surprise and increase the chance of the mission's success. Also important, the guerilla had to be fit to fight. Emboldened, enraged, or embittered, depending on the polemicist, by the imprint of American oppression on his life, the guerilla needed to be prepared to participate actively in the struggle for change when called. Most importantly, as a member of the vanguard, the guerilla had to be ideologically stable, having already had his "salvation" moment when he developed a radical consciousness after becoming acutely aware of his position within the American racial hierarchy.

The figure of the guerilla gave both Asian American and African American nationalists a new identity and subjectivity, one opposed to the political status quo and representing ideological readiness and militancy. The guerilla figure also represents the intersection of multiple national and international discourses of anti-imperialist and ethnic nationalist struggles against oppression and repression. In *A Dying Colonialism*, Fanon sums up the ultimate import of the guerilla.

> [T]he power of each guerilla fighter does not rest simply in himself, his weapon, and his army unit. He is the reincarnation of the will of the people to struggle, of the resistance, of the anonymous and innumerable ways in which the people seek to harass and liquidate the oppressor and refuse to collaborate with him. This is the only "magic" the guerillas have—that they are the representatives of the social force immensely superior to their own numbers and firepower, a social force that constantly encircles, attacks, and intimidates the enemy.[66]

The guerilla represents the spirit or will of the native community, a force that Fanon felt was inherently in opposition to the colonial status quo. Just as the guerilla military agent disrupts the "us vs. them" dichotomy of military engagement, the guerilla's commitment to radical social change offers a way to disrupt social dichotomies and secure access to discourses of representation for the formerly colonized.

Therefore, the guerilla significantly represents novel avenues for black and Asian activists to represent and express a revolutionary, anticolonialist relationship to the American state apparatus. As the representation of ideology, which Althusser defines as the "imaginary relation to real relations," or the discourses that motivate mechanisms of material and social meaning.[67] This "imaginary" mediates the "system of the real relations which govern the existence of individuals" and the "imaginary relation of these individuals to the real relations in which they live."[68] To gain intelligibility, the individual has to take up the subject position within discourse in order to "tell the story" of its existence.[69] For Carmichael and Hamilton, any ideology that opposes institutional racism has to provide people with the hope that it would also enable the expression of the "will to power" of the community. As ideologies, Black Power and Yellow Power virtually predicated a guerilla subject capable of acting on behalf of the community. According to Althusser, "the subject is the linguistic occasion for the individual to achieve and reproduce intelligibly, the linguistic condition of its existence and agency."[70] The subject is "always-already" constituted by ideology: "there is no ideology except for concrete subjects and this destination for ideology is only made possible by the subject: meaning by the category of the subject and its functioning."[71] Contemporary studies of the subject and subjectivity have stressed the necessity of repetition and reiteration to create the illusion of an independent self outside of ideology and discourse. This self is illusory precisely because subjecthood and subjectivity are contingent upon discourse and ideology for agency. According to Judith Butler, the subject can be formed only through subjection, that "fundamental dependency on a discourse we never chose but that paradoxically initiates and sustains our agency."[72]

Just as struggle provides the occasion for the reiteration and reproduction of subjectivity for Fanon, Black and Yellow Power ideology conceive of struggle as providing the "occasion" for the individual to exercise a guerilla subjectivity. Struggle and resistance represent moments where oppressed subjects could frustrate the "rules of recognition" and create "hybridity" in America's racial caste system.[73] Struggle becomes the mechanism by which the iterability of identity can be disrupted in order to achieve power or self-determination, or the agency (cultural authority) to posit new sites for identity. The road maps to these new sites are the cultural programs Fanon dictated as a part of the decolonizing process: poems, stories, plays, as well as newspapers could be the units of the utopian psychic economy he theorized.

While the guerilla identity arose to fulfill a need in a particular moment, its adoption as a continuing position within American society has proven problematic. The guerilla may have been well suited as a representative of militant resistance, but the figure has proven to be deleterious when taken up in contemporary representations of black defiance.[74]

As a result, it is difficult to conclude that Fanon, Black Power, and Yellow Power ultimately imagine a way outside of colonized subjectivity. Instead, they offer at best a way for American colonial subjects, who have gained access to the "inadvertently enabling power" of subjectivity through their subjection, to divest their identities of their colonial significance and reinvest them with self-significant significance. By definition, the guerilla's ideological motivations limit the range of representations available to her/him. Since the guerilla has some degree of agency only when she or he acts within the program articulated by his movement, these identities leave little room for what yellowness and blackness could be after the struggle ended. The guerilla identity is also deeply implicated in the continuation of the American racial hierarchy, because it functions as a "definitive" subject position, inherently in opposition to the mainstream against which "critical questions about the efficacy of nationalist rhetoric can center and thus themselves still be recognizable as nationalist discourse."[75] In seeking to rewrite stereotypical depictions of themselves, Asian American and African American activists reinscribed an identity in opposition to the "model minority" and "inferior" identities placed on them by the mainstream. However, the guerilla figure, while libratory for its time, became confining and confusing as the struggle for liberation moved (some would say was co-opted) from the streets into the classrooms and boardrooms of America.

Susan Koshy argues that the constantly changing composition of local and global communities and politics continually destabilizes monolithic ethnic identities. Seen through this lens, the problem with retaining the guerilla as a representation of an as yet unfulfilled revolution is that it cannot adapt to a transformed social context. Thus, the identity remains frozen within the ideological visual limits framed in the pages of *The Black Panther* and *Gidra*. While this visual referent achieved iconic status, social discourses continued to change. By the hip-hop era, "Power to the People," "Revolution," and the guerilla became symbols of protest evacuated of meaning. This move from political symbol to iconic totem was facilitated, in part, by the adoption of an anticolonialist critique into the academic construct of postcolonialism. Though the armed offensive envisioned by some may not have been fully realized, Power ideology continues to be a whetstone against which we sharpen our thinking about race, repression, struggle, and identity.

CHAPTER THREE

Power and the Ivory Tower

Academics as Intellectual Guerillas

Gidra and *The Black Panther* facilitated the guerilla's move from image to identity position. This transition from subject to subjectivity established the guerilla as a participant in American political discourse. With the broadening of this identity, those who believed in the anticolonialist ends embodied by the guerilla could take up the markers of this subject position even without engaging in combat. As militant activism fell out of favor, the guerilla figure drifted from its original military significance to become synonymous with militant resistance. In turn, some early activists-turned-academics adopted this subjectivity, envisioning the early Ethnic Studies, African American Studies, and Asian American Studies programs that they populated as vehicles to infiltrate and subvert academia. In this chapter, I consider how some academics took up the guerilla subjectivity, positioning Ethnic Studies as a critique of the mid-twentieth-century canon and positioning themselves as what Abdul JanMohamed termed "border intellectuals."[1]

Most of the writers and activists involved with *Gidra* and *The Black Panther* were in college or college-aged. As Fabio Rojas notes in his chronicle of the development of Black Studies, *From Black Power to Black Studies: How a Radical Social Movement Became an Academic Discipline*, the university became an important site of interaction for radical activists and young people seeking to liberalize their educational experience. Expanding the curriculum to formalize Black and Ethnic Studies programs provided an opportunity for students and community activists to use their previous experiences with RAM, SNCC, SDS, and the Black Panther Party in campus protest movements. Of course, education had long been seen as a route for African American empowerment and community development; however, the 1968–1969 Third World Strike at San Francisco State College represents the moment when Black and Ethnic Studies programs, not just courses, were instituted as part of the established curriculum in mainstream institutions of higher education. Significantly, this move required a sustained effort; Rojas notes that "universities did not formalize this knowledge in courses, curricula, or degree programs. This would happen only when nationalist politics prompted black students to demand new academic units and to stage strikes pushing for their creation."[2] Under pressure, San Francisco State and many other colleges and universities made space for Ethnic Studies courses; however, this concession was by no means the end of the struggle.

The advent of Ethnic Studies went far beyond the addition of a few courses and majors. Just as this new field drew on the methodologies of history, sociology, political science, and literary studies, these fields adapted and changed as a result of the information and insights uncovered by Ethnic Studies scholars. Likewise, Ethnic Studies changed from a confrontational critique of American higher education to a field of study supported by the mechanisms of institutional authority and control endemic to academia: graduate programs, departmental status, dedicated hires, journals, conferences, textbooks, and course materials. Rather than rehearse the events that led to the development of Ethnic Studies, this chapter will focus on one of the most ubiquitous tools of higher education: the anthology. Anthologies have been an important tool in the effort to establish the autonomy of literary traditions. Thus, looking at the evolution of African American and Asian American literary anthologies during the late 1960s and early 1970s through the 1980s and 1990s provides insight into the struggle for primacy between the political and scholarly functions of literary studies. Though much has been written about matters of representativeness, the nexus of aesthetics and cultural politics, and, of course, canonization, I draw on a selection of Asian American and African American literature anthologies to analyze how scholars use the prefaces of these volumes to negotiate the tensions between activism and academics and establish themselves as subjects within discourses of academia.

Among the chief concerns of activists in the Black and Yellow Power movements were losing the vestiges of mental occupation and rebuilding "authentic" identities. According to Fanon, colonization wreaks both social and psychological havoc on the colonized. Fanon's *Black Skin, White Masks* (1952; 1967) and *Wretched of the Earth* (1961; 1963) revolutionized identity politics in America by assigning a name to the system of social, economic, political, and psychoanalytic oppression—colonialism—and outlining a remedy for the effects of that oppression—anticolonialism. Preeminent among these injuries is the mental colonization that associated the colonized with inferiority. These academic guerillas used the university as a site for developing and deploying revised representations of Blackness and Yellowness to newly conscious young people.

This chapter examines the editorial comments and introductions from *Black Fire* (1968), *Black Arts* (1969), and *AIIIEEEEE!* (1974). During the Power period, anthologies of Asian American literature provided early Ethnic Studies scholars a space to negotiate the issues of ideology, disciplinarity, canonicity, and aesthetics that shaped the fields during these early years. Within these pages, some African American and Asian American scholars and critics positioned themselves as "intellectual guerillas," assimilating, expressing, critiquing, and disseminating ethnic analysis and criticism. After surveying a sample of anthologies, the chapter turns to Ishmael Reed and Frank Chin as examples of "guerilla" scholars who used *Yardbird* journal and Publishing Company to subvert publishing and academic hegemony, as well as the mounting ideological hegemony of cultural nationalism in Ethnic Studies. In these ways, academia was figured as another type of battlefield where scholars engaged in struggle in order to legitimate the preservation and study of African American and Asian American culture and letters and recast colonized representations of African American and Asian American life and culture.

Early advocates of Ethnic Studies saw the field as functioning in three ways to open up the academy and provide spaces to decolonize black and yellow minds. First, Ethnic Studies could function as a staging ground for activist teachers interested in reforming the academy and aiding in the mental decolonization of students and communities by producing scholarship and curricula that reflected the true history, priorities, and perspectives of "the people." Secondly, Ethnic Studies programs challenged the university system, calling into question methods of study and criteria by which "knowledges" were judged worthy of "knowing." Finally, Ethnic Studies departments marked a point of convergence where politically active students and teachers could advance the radical decolonizing objectives of African American and Asian American revolutionary ethnic nationalist politics. Anthologies of the period between 1967 and 1985 often contained highly incendiary works or works critical of the government, works that mainstream publishers were reluctant to publish. Many Black Arts Movement works espoused the nationalist ideology of Black Power and were committed to overthrowing the "New Negro" for an "Afro-American" prepared to take his place in American society. These works not only continued the protest tradition by decrying the social conditions of African Americans; they also asserted new, powerful, aggressive social identities, "stable and coherent" black identities.[3] Anthologies, therefore, provided handy forums for the shorter fiction and poetry favored by Black Arts Movement and Yellow and Black Power artists.[4] These early functions figured the "ethnic" as outside of and counter to an American educational hegemony. In fact, early Black Studies and Ethnic Studies programs classes were often configured as critiques of "mainstream" knowledge communicated in the average college classroom. Thus, early on it could be said that Ethnic Studies functioned as a guerilla camp at the base of the ivory tower.

Many early Ethnic Studies programs came about as a result of prolonged activism and demonstrations by students and community activists; therefore, Ethnic Studies departments were, and in some cases continue to be, politically charged environments. Early student proponents of Ethnic Studies programs demanded that they be "relevant," reflective, and authentic.[5] Often students saw Ethnic Studies programs as extensions of the political project started by Black Power and the Asian American Movement. According to longtime activist Yuri Kochiyama, the movement for Ethnic Studies provided a foundation for the eventual development of an Asian American community: "Without ethnic studies, we Asians wouldn't know about our histories. [. . .] We came to understand ourselves better. [. . .] And we saw how much we had in common with other people of color who were also afflicted with a colonized mentality."[6] As Gary Okihiro put it, "[T]he drive for Ethnic Studies in the university was a conjoining of the domestic struggle for civil rights with the international struggle for Third World liberation."[7] Ethnic Studies, then, extended the larger social project of self-determination and self-definition as articulated by Power politics. The inclusion of African American, Asian American, and Ethnic Studies programs symbolized an engagement with the organizations, bureaucracies, and institutions of the university. But perhaps more significantly, the presence of these courses, students, scholars, and programs also represent a symbolic challenge to the "knowledges" replicated by the university.

The rhetoric of a 1969 manifesto from the Asian American Political Alliance also reflects this belief in education's power to overturn the effects of oppression:

> The Third World feels at the gut level that Western imperialism and colonialism has been the number one factor in the continuing state of deprivation seen all over Asia, Africa, and Latin America; in the colonies of Algiers, Hong Kong, Singapore, Calcutta, and the internal colonies of the black, brown, and yellow ghettoes of America.
>
> A Third World College can begin to investigate and teach us what the nature of the predator is, and how we as non-white people in America can work to end the workings of the generals, corporate elites, and political hacks which keep our people enslaved in poverty and psychological deprivation. An Asian Studies Department is essential in order to complete the Third World picture; it is up to us to do it. Nobody else can.[8]

Education in this instance has both, in the words of Gates, a "backward-glancing" and an inward-gazing function. The Third World College, according to this manifesto, would investigate the creation of whiteness to expose its complicity in the hegemonic system of "institutional racism," also known as American-style colonialism. This preoccupation with the "gaze" of the colonizer locks the ethnic American "Other" in a deadly embrace with the Subject that is the mechanism of perpetuation and repression. But the manifesto also implies an inward-gazing function that situates the ethnic American as a subject that may be capable of "complete[ing]" the "picture," or the circuit, of social discourse. Indeed, the manifesto claims, no one else can initiate this discourse. Therefore, by bringing Asian American and African American Studies into the academy, scholar activists hoped to shape political discourses by redirecting the critical and scholarly discourses of black and yellow representation.

However, not everyone's concept of ethnic studies was the same. Richard Gambino authored a 1975 report, commissioned by the Rockefeller Center on Ethnic Studies programs and curricula, that captures the competing approaches—assimilationism versus ethnic nationalism—that existed in early Ethnic Studies programs, particularly those devoted to the study of non-European groups. Although Gambino claims that his study was done in part to encourage the development of programs that would preserve America's heterogeneous heritage, it contains course rubrics for only European ethnic programs; the bibliography of "Black" sources runs for only about a page (and doesn't include any bibliographic information for the books that are listed), and there is a total of only six entries for "Oriental." Meanwhile Slavic, Eastern European, and Russian Studies texts occupy six pages.[9] The study goes on to laud those programs that follow an "area studies" or multicultural model versus those that use "racial" categories as the basis of identity, lest it inspire nationalism.

Literary anthologies from this period interestingly illustrate the mix of professional, pedagogical, popular, and political functions that mirror the tensions experienced by the activists turned academics who often populated early Ethnic Studies programs. Rather than crunch numbers and consider inclusions and exclusions in "mainstream" anthologies, or, in the case of African American literature, earlier anthologies of the milieu, this chapter focuses on the rhetoric of the prefaces, introductions, and afterwords from a selection of Asian American and African American fiction anthologies, to discern how scholars navigated the social, political, historical, literary, and professional pressures during this period. In particular, I also consider how the anthologies engage the rhetoric, ideology, and principles of revolution and cultural decolonization articulated by Fanon.

For this study, I chose texts published between 1967 and 1985, slightly shifting the time frame of my larger study to accommodate the longer horizon for developing and publishing anthologies due to their often collaborative nature. I will then consider where the anthology falls in one of three phases of development for anthologies of ethnic literature: legitimation, self-determination, and critical appreciation. During the legitimation phase, anthologies provide evidence for the existence of a literary tradition, chronicling the earliest examples of writing by members of the group and highlighting "exceptional" and "representative" authors and texts. Anthologies of the self-determination phase assert the development of a cultural aesthetic, offering texts that present "authentic" or "righteous" representations of group members. Anthologies of this period tend to resist mainstream criteria for worth, instead establishing their own aesthetic. The final phase, critical appreciation, consists of anthologies that combine literature with critical glosses and commentaries that provide a scholarly context for reading the texts. Some anthologies, particularly during the legitimation and self-determination phases, can be considered guerilla because they envision themselves as overturning canons, infiltrating the mainstream with a variety of "worthy" texts by people of color, past and present.

The Asian American anthologies of this period also performed the legitimating function of ethnic anthologies, collecting texts that proved the existence and depth of an Asian American tradition. However, the need to identify "literature" worthy of consumption by the academic community often seems in tension with the need to be "authentic" to in-group readers, accessible to out-group readers, and valued by both in-group and out-group critics. Ultimately, anthologies of African American and Asian American literatures evolved to function as repositories not just for literature, but also for the social struggles, political demands, and histories of these cultures in America.

While canonization in Asian American and African American literary studies was influenced and informed by the processes of formation and legitimation that shaped the American literary canon during the latter nineteenth century, the process had to also respond to the sociohistorical and political conditions of African American and Asian American life in the United States. Looking at the somewhat longer history of African American literary studies reveals a sense of the effects of racialization on canonization. African American literary canon formation has undergone historical revision and renovations as new works are uncovered, previous works by known artists are resurrected, and trends in literary and political fashion lead to new works by writers who often radically resisted and rewrote their predecessors. As a result, strategies of canon formation in the African American literary tradition have changed in response to literary trends, political climate, and academic conditions across three eras: the Harlem Renaissance to the early 1940s, the civil rights era and Black Arts Movement, and most recently, the "Black Intellectual Renaissance" of the 1990s to the present. Over the course of the past century, anthologies in the African American tradition have had to attend to a number of concerns, including historical representation (making available the unknown or ignored history of a group), political representation (making known the social condition and concerns of a group), and aesthetic representation (appealing to literary worthiness), a formalist appeal. Additionally, professional concerns motivated canonization in the African American tradition. Since anthologies also include a payoff in the form of professional legitimacy for the scholars who produce them, these concerns produce a unique dialectic that influences the selection of texts for African American literary anthologies.

Many of the "canon" debates in African American literature have taken anthologies as a well-established tool for canon formation and professional legitimation. In "The Master's Pieces," Gates expounds on the development of the African American literary tradition, using anthologies as evidence of this process. Gates defines canons alternately as the "commonplace book of our shared culture" containing "the texts and titles that we want to remember, that [have] some special meaning for us," and as an "'essence' of the tradition [...] that reveals the tradition [...], its internal rationale."[10] He also points out that canon formation has always been caught up in ideology and nationalism. Gates's essay decries a "dark essentialism" lurking in African American studies of the 1960s and 1970s that situates the "blackness" of literature in terms of ideological fealty. Gates goes on to tie the future of black literary studies to the vernacular, an oral tradition that is not just "part of a larger discourse on the nature of the black, and of his or her role in the order of things," but that constructs critical tools for evaluating the enduring themes of the tradition.[11] Before we look at how anthologies of the Power period participate in discourses of representation, it may help to outline the principles of canon formation that emerged during the "canon debates" of the late 1990s.

Arguably, representativeness lies at the core of all of the purposes of an anthology—social, historical, political, literary, and academic. Michael Bérubé asserts that "'representation'" operates in "canon making" along three avenues: texts and authors represented, representations of a particular culture, and academic use by critics and in classrooms.[12] In the case of ethnic literary anthologies, these modes of representation are used to paint a picture for a reader or educator of the literary tradition of a particular nation, ethnic group, or gender using the *best selections* from that larger body of texts. While these avenues are similar for Asian American and African American literature, the political and culture-making functions of the canon seemed to overwhelm the other categories of representation during the Power period. During that period, the question seems to have become not how well do the anthologies expose the mechanisms of cultural reproduction, but how well do the collections represent the political will or advance the political aims of the community? For many editors, the political imperative overrode aesthetic or academic concerns entirely. When evaluating Asian

American and African American anthologies, therefore, yet another set of questions concerning the role of scholars as the agents of cultural reproduction must be considered: How do editors of anthologies position the texts in relationship to their audience, whether academic or popular? And what ideology or ideologies do scholars advance through their selections? These early African American scholars were attempting to establish a new mechanism for cultural reproduction, using anthologies that included selections based on political imperatives, social advancement, preservation, and cultural history to justify the existence of these literary traditions and legitimize the study of these cultures in the newly expanding academy.

However, efforts to make the canon "representative" of class, gender, or ethnic groups are necessarily limited, since cultural equity cannot be achieved by merely "correcting" the literary choices of the academy. Paul Lauter investigates canon revision in American literature in the 1920s in order to limn out the institutional pressures that shape canonization. Lauter defines the "'American literary canon' [as] that set of authors and works generally included in basic American literature college courses and textbooks, and those ordinarily discussed in standard volumes of literary history, bibliography or criticism."[13] To illustrate this connection, Lauter specifically examines the mechanisms by which women and African Americans were excluded from academe and the American literary canon. The process by which access to academe and, consequently, the ability to influence critical and literary work was curtailed, Lauter argues, closely tracks the status and power allowed to these groups in larger American society. Lauter identifies three factors that shaped the academic profession at this moment and facilitated the gradual "disappearing" of African American and women writers from the American literary canon: "the professionalization of the teaching of literature, the development of an aesthetic theory that privileged certain texts and the historiographic organization of the body of literature into conventional 'periods' and 'themes.'"[14] According to Lauter, the professionalization of the professoriate led to a commensurate rise in "social capital" ascribed to academics and increased pressure to secure the privileges of this status for white men, resulting in the exclusion of white women and the "ghettoization" of black scholars.[15] As a result, these scholars and the works by women and people of color that they often studied were marginalized. As the strictures on women, African Americans, Asian Americans, and other "Others" loosened, their access to the critical apparatuses—university education and the professoriate—increased along with their ability to shape the canon. If, as Lauter argues, the canonization process depends upon the workings of the university system and, therefore, reflects the values of that system, then the way that system operates has to adapt as large numbers of "Others" are incorporated into it. While this system would react reflexively to preserve itself, the increased demand for writings by women and people of color can not be met by "mainstream" anthologies that incorporate too few entries to sustain a focused, semester-long study of the literary traditions of these groups. Thus, this inequity exposes the existing canon to attacks based on gender and racial representativeness.

The absence of commensurate numbers of female and African American scholars and the devaluation of works by these groups as legitimate topics of academic discourse and study provide evidence for Lauter's claim that "the literary canon is, in short, a means by which culture validates social power."[16] At its worst, the canon can reflect the politics of exclusion practiced by the larger American society during the early part of the twentieth century. However, some canon revisionists also see a revised canon as a mechanism for representing the complexity of American society that it previously ignored. Lauter identifies two "aesthetic systems" that developed during the 1920s and 1930s to reinforce the exclusion of texts by women and African Americans.[17] The first is the concept of a "usable past" that legitimates the United States as a "world power."[18] This aesthetic led to a narrative of American history that privileges the American pioneer character, chronicling the development of American literary works in a way that could be likened to European literary traditions. The second is a formalist aesthetic that focuses on literature as isolated works of genius with little regard for the social and historical contexts within which a text is embedded.

For critics and scholars concerned with "alternative" canons, Lauter argues that there must likewise be an alternative strategy that "asks whether the work acts effectively in the world of which it and we constitute parts, by touching human feeling and shaping consciousness."[19] For anthologies of African American and Asian American literature, the question of who occupies this "world" is important. Many anthologies of the Asian American and African American literary traditions conceived of themselves as directed towards an ethnic cultural audience rather than an academic one. This perceived need to educate people about their own history and offer "black" and "yellow" knowledges translates into anthologies that often include a mixture of historical, archival, and rhetorical texts chronicling the struggle for political freedom, as well as literary works depicting the "experience" of this struggle, particularly during the period of my concern, 1967 to 1985.

Historically, anthologies of ethnic American literature often appealed to general cultural audiences, and the textual choices were as influenced by social and political issues as by aesthetic or academic use value. In the early twentieth century, the study of African American life and culture was undertaken almost exclusively by the system of historically black colleges and universities and journals and magazines like *Negro Digest*, *Crisis*, and *Opportunity*. This critical establishment worked during the 1920s through the 1960s to study, preserve, analyze, and theorize the African American literary tradition. For Asian Americans, there was no similar independent system of universities and critics. The historical conditions of citizenship for many early Asian Americans also severely limited access to education and delayed the development of Asian American studies until the last third of the twentieth century. At that point, the early Ethnic Studies departments and programs that developed at schools along the East and West Coasts during the 1970s came to function as a network for scholars and critics of Asian American literature. Consequently, the late 1960s and 1970s brought the publication of anthologies geared towards the educational and entertainment needs of an Asian American audience. Because the process coalesced at almost the same time as Asian American and Ethnic American Studies, it became open to the pressures of professionalization, authority, and aesthetic merit, as well as questions of canonization and transmission almost as soon as it was established. Anthologies of various ethnic literary traditions, therefore, labor under slightly different sets of imperatives from those articulated by Bérubé. Anthologies of both Asian American and African American literary traditions must represent their cultural tradition "accurately," recover and preserve literary artifacts, select works of literary value for classroom use by a largely out-group audience, and include works that may be enjoyed by a largely in-group audience located outside of the university.

In addition to what is read and where, canonization also affects who reads and why. John Guillory undertakes an investigation of canonicity that goes beyond a critique of academe to explore the relations of power that result in a privileging of the professoriate: "The deligitimation of the canon is premised upon a structural homology between, on the one hand, the distinction of the canonical from the non-canonical, and on the other, the process of inclusion or exclusion by which social groups are represented or not represented in the exercise of power."[20] In Guillory's analysis, alternative canons that actively include and actively exclude texts replicate the professional dynamics of the mainstream canon, reifying social distinctions between authorized readers and nonreaders rather than accomplishing a substantive revision of the real problem, which is, according to Guillory, access to literacy. Thus, "canonicity is not a property of the work itself, but of its transmission."[21] Alternative canons, therefore, cannot escape scrutiny of their means of institutionalization and transmission raised in previous debates about the literary canon. In other words, canon revisionists who neglect to investigate access to literacy fail to reveal the social systems that are masked by discussions of representation and value: "Hence the question of the effects of social struggle upon certain protocols of the educational institution bypasses the articulation of canonical selection upon the social foundation of regulated reading and writing, and degenerates into quarrels about the value of individual works."[22] Guillory implies that attempts to revise the canon will be unsuccessful because they do not address the social pressures that shape who is authorized to "read" and assign "value" to texts. Only by empowering a broader and more diverse set of readers can the canon truly be opened. Early activists saw Third World colleges and Ethnic Studies departments as the mechanisms to accomplish this empowerment. However, inclusion in the academy opened these new departments to the same discourses of legitimacy. As soon as scholars and students in Third World, Ethnic Studies, Asian American, and African American Studies departments became constituents of the discourses operating within the academy, they also became implicated in the mechanisms of power governing these discourses. As these disciplines developed, the discourses of "dark essentialism" asserted themselves, establishing competing professional, political, and cultural aesthetic criteria that determined both authorized texts and "readers."

Anthologies of African American and, later, Asian American literature developed canons that had to attend to shifting standards of artistic merit, political usefulness, and cultural identity. Neither the African American nor the Asian American literary canon developed as a simple adoption of the criteria of the mainstream canon in an act of unreflective "cooptation."[23] Thus, the tension between legitimation and authenticity represent an adaptation of the canonization process for ethnic literary anthologies. Later, anthologies concentrated on elaborating critical and aesthetic standards that grew out of these adaptations. In addition, the tricky question of identity was salient for initial anthologies seeking to counter negative stereotypes and images of African and Asian Americans. To do so, early critics often collapsed the whole of Asian and African America into categories—the "New Negro" or the "Asian American"—to bolster their authority to speak on behalf of their respective communities. It could be said that identity and the related issue of representation are always primary concerns of the ethnic literature anthology.

In an effort to address this preoccupation with representation, Asian American critics and theorists adapted postcolonial discussions of identity and identification to articulate how the process of identity-making both depends on and creates cultural meaning. Using the works of Bhabha, Said, and Fanon, these theorists have focused on confronting and overturning stereotypes imported from European colonialist rhetoric and homegrown stereotypes springing from American nativist fervor and military policy. These postcolonial scholars have enabled theorists and critics to go beyond an understanding of how difference is constructed, to an understanding of how it operates to reinforce social hierarchies and maintain social power. The recognition of difference, which leads to the "problem of identification," illuminates the process by which identity is made meaningful in particular cultural contexts.[24] The process of creating difference first delineates characteristics that denote difference and then naturalizes them. As a result, the identities sanctioned by society acquire social power, reinforcing their naturalness and increasing the difficulty of exposing and escaping their strictures. Stuart Hall applied this understanding of a cultural economy to a delineation of the formation and use of racial and ethnic images throughout a culture. The assignation of power *to representation* illuminates the process by which stereotypes are created and uncovers the values that they are deployed to protect.[25]

While the process of canonization helped both traditions gain cultural and academic "power," the politics of representation also extend to the tools of criticism and analysis. David Palumbo-Liu argues that as ethnic literatures become emblematic of the postmodern condition, the specificity of those works gets diluted. Acknowledging the contributions of ethnic literatures to the American tradition, Palumbo-Liu argues that it is also necessary to have an awareness of the "limitations of critical and theoretical categories unable to address ethnicity and race and their relationships to cultural production."[26] He chastises critics who would transform ethnic literature into an "aesthetic" that values difference without attending to the multiple valences that constitute it. Lisa Lowe also attempts to get beyond the bagginess of "ethnicity" as a critical category by offering immigration as a more culturally specific tool for analysis. An immigrant subjectivity, according to Lowe, is desirable because it recognizes that "subjectivity is multiply determined ... [and] that each determination is uneven and historically differentiated."[27] By focusing on the act of migration, of moving from there to here, it is possible to more sensitively define how the American process of racialization molds identity and its representations.

Lowe argues that understanding Asian American identity formation through the experience of immigration can also undercut the homogenizing effects of racialization in ethnic cultures. By acknowledging the heterogeneity of experience embodied by the process of immigration, it is possible, Lowe argues, to free up the "material, racial, and sexual aspects that contradict and are in excess of [. . .] generic state formation."[28] Acknowledging and attending to the many dimensions of nationality, class, gender, and language that govern one's introduction to the American acculturation process makes it more difficult to transform Asian Americans into a "racialized group" that can be readily assimilated into American social, cultural, and political life. It is first necessary to attend to the various conditions of immigration in order to consider the impact of the process of Americanization on Asian Americans. The trope of immigration, therefore, becomes a "Gold Mountain" for critics and theorists interested in delineating the process of identity making and the accompanying concerns of reconstructed and recovered history, community, and language.

Thus, the anthologies of each tradition can be thought of as spaces for developing culturally sensitive scholarly hermeneutics. With all of these concerns in mind, this chapter will now turn to a closer analysis of selected anthologies of the Power period.

While many anthologies, particularly those created by professional academics rather than activist academics, deal consciously with aesthetic and pedagogical concerns, identity and its representations remain major preoccupations of Asian American and African American anthologies of the Power period. Many Power anthologies are invested in rethinking and reformulating these identities in order to "authentically" render the Asian American and African American "experience." Thus anthologies of the Power period, by either embracing or criticizing a black or yellow aesthetic, respond to discourses of political representation, cultural authenticity, and aesthetic ideology in ways that go beyond protest, appreciation, or legitimation.

Black Fire: An Anthology of Afro-American Writing (1968) was edited by Amiri Baraka (formerly LeRoi Jones) and Larry Neal and published by William Morrow. Three times longer than the later *Black Arts* anthology, *Black Fire* contains a mix of essays, poems, drama, and fiction that provides a comprehensive collection of the works of the "founding Fathers and Mothers, of our nation."[29] It contains works by writers identified with the Black Arts Movement and the politics of the Black Nationalist Movement and is designed, first, to articulate the revolutionary ideology of Black Nationalism, and then, to present poems, stories, and dramatic pieces that express the struggle for liberation. According to Neal, *Black Fire* participates in a critique of "Western," particularly American, thought: "Most of the book can be read as if it were a critical re-examination of Western political, social, and artistic values. It can be read also as a rejection of anything that we feel is detrimental to our people."[30] Neal labels this anthology as a work of "art of liberation" prioritizing the political function of the text. In the foreword, Baraka hails this collection as valuable to those seeking "The black artist. The black man. The holy holy black man."[31] He encourages readers to find themselves (of course, this might be difficult for "holy, holy" black women) in the poems, short stories, essays, and dramatic pieces in the volume. Although the foreword also exhibits the sexism that infected the Black Nationalist Movement—"tho the wimmens sell they men, then cry up hell to get them back out here agin"—it demonstrates a primary concern that the works be accessible to politically conscious black readers who are interested in art that is also politically conscious.[32]

In the afterword, "And Shine Swam On," Neal argues that previous literature by writers "like Charles Chesnutt and William Braithwaite" failed, because it looked to white America for "justice" and recognition rather than addressing itself "to black people, to their needs, suffering, and aspirations."[33] He argues instead that *Black Fire* contains "literature primarily directed at the consciousness of black people. And, in that sense, it is a literature that is somewhat more mature than that which preceded it."[34] Thus, the editors of *Black Fire* judge works primarily according to the social and political will of the black community. Literature can be "righteous" only if the artist can "move people to a deeper understanding of what this thing is all about, be a kind of priest, a black magician, working juju with the word on the world."[35] The editors self-consciously target a popular black audience rather than a professional academic one, making almost no argument for the "aesthetic" value of the texts they include, instead urging black people to apply their own judgments as to the "righteousness" of their choices. Thus, this anthology also engages discourses of protest and professionalization as critiques of mainstream canons of African American literature, in addition to discourses of representation, authenticity, and the principles of Power: self-definition, self-determination, and anticolonial resistance.

Black Arts: An Anthology of Black Creations (1969) was edited by Ahmed Alhamisi and Harun Kofi Wangara and dedicated to "third world peoples the spiritual warriors."[36] In the introduction, Keorapetse Kgositsile describes this anthology as part of the process of "self-examination" and "self-assertion" necessary to free the oppressed mind and prepare for racial liberation: "These creations attempt to capture the mood, the spirit of a people engaged in liberatory struggle."[37] In this anthology, critical, pedagogical, and aesthetic motives are not only subordinate but are declared anathema to the political and social struggle for black liberation. Kgositsile has "no respect" for any "'artist' who will not put his creative talent and ability to work in the street along with the people."[38] Art, according to the editors of this anthology, must measure up to a libratory standard and a revolutionary aesthetic. No judgment of value can be made apart from the social and historical condition of the cultural community. Indeed, these editors figure formalist aesthetics as separating art from social and political contexts. For Kgositsile, art for art's sake is a potentially dangerous affectation that prevents black writers, or indeed any writers of color, from being "effectively instrumental in freeing people."[39] According to this standard, art must be of value in the larger struggle for liberation. Kgositsile encourages black writers to "free themselves from mannerisms and get directly involved in very concrete community action."[40] *Black Arts*, which features on its cover a black Christlike face crowned by thorns, eschews every other function except those that service the political and the social. According to these writers and editors, the struggle for freedom that Brawley saw limiting the artistic development of black authors has not yet been won. The anthology also seems intent on trumping the "righteousness" of the earlier *Black Fire* anthology. Its title, *Black Fire: An Anthology of Afro-American Writing*, splits the difference in the naming debates, labeling its individual works "Black," but labeling the artists "Afro-American." *Black Arts*, subtitled *An Anthology of Black Creations*, displays no such ambivalence. Its title endorses a black identity and espouses a black aesthetic. Unlike *Black Fire*, the work is published by a black publisher, features the works of black artists—many of whom have adopted African names—and contains an interview with Amiri Baraka about the influence of Islam on the Black Nationalist Movement. The entire anthology, not just its individual selections, consciously and conspicuously conforms to a revolutionary, libratory aesthetic dictated by Power ideology.

Two years later came the publication of *Dark Symphony: Negro Literature in America* (1971). Edited by James Emanuel and Theodore Gross, it represents the fullest manifestation of the formalist approach to canon construction during this period:

> The criterion for inclusion in this volume is the intrinsic artistic merit of the story, the poem, or the essay. Most previous collections of American Negro literature have necessarily brought together works of historical and social as well as of literary importance; scholars have occupied themselves with the primary task of gathering the written materials of Negro culture without making those aesthetic distinctions that help to create a literary tradition. But we have reached the moment in our history when it becomes possible, and indeed necessary, to designate which works by Negroes deserve to be part of the heritage of American literature.[41]

In the introduction to this volume, the editors posit a history of the development of African American literature from its "early instances of lasting achievement, with works that skillfully initiate or characterize dominant trends" to later works that represent the emergence of an independent black aesthetic.[42] As in earlier anthologies from the Harlem Renaissance, the editors of *Dark Symphony* set out to confront stereotypes by presenting a comprehensive picture of the black literary tradition. The anthology contains a range of texts from Douglass to Locke, Ellison to LeRoi Jones. There are, however, relatively few authors from eighteenth- and early nineteenth-century literature (no

Phillis Wheatley or Olaudah Equiano, a.k.a. Gustavas Vassa). Nor are there many selections from the Harlem Renaissance (120 of 600 pages from 8 authors—Johnson, Locke, McKay, Toomer, Fischer, Walrond, Brown, and Cullen), largely because the editors seem to have found many early works by early African American authors derivative and wanting. Instead, it contains texts selected for their "quality and significance" in order to "convey historical development in the way that elevations mark out the contour of terrain for the traveler."[43] The four essays that close the volume—"Trends in Negro American Literature," "Emerson and the South," "Society and the Self in Recent American Literature," and "Into the Mainstream and Oblivion"—indicate the editors' strong academic and integrationist motives, themselves a black and white pair. In response to the politicized "rhetoric as literature" of the Black Arts Movement, the editors of this anthology of "Negro Literature in America" retreat into aesthetic considerations of the literary tradition and almost totally divorce it from the political construct and cultural conditions of the texts, distinguishing it from most other anthologies of African American literature from the time. Indeed, the editors don't even claim to be critiquing the process of canonization by creating a separate canon of African American literature; instead, they hold their choices as candidates for inclusion in the mainstream American literary canon.

In *Black Writers of America* (1972), editors Richard Barksdale, who served many years as a professor of African American literature in the English department of the University of Illinois, and Keneth Kinnamon, also a former professor of English at the University of Illinois, reject a strictly formalist construction of the African American canon and acknowledge the literary and social concerns motivating their textual selections:

> Recognizing the limitation of a narrowly esthetic approach to a body of writing of great social import, we have provided generous selections of autobiographies, essays, speeches, letters, political pamphlets, histories, journals, and folk literature as well as poems, plays, and stories. Our criteria for inclusion were both artistic and social; indeed, facile or rigid separation of the two seems to us misguided. For this reason, our anthology serves as an introduction not only to the literature of Black people in America, but to their intellectual and social history as well.[44]

Barksdale and Kinnamon's preface displays a mix of the motives that also shaped later collections. Barksdale and Kinnamon, according to Barksdale, were "driven by political furies" and "more on fire with political energy than inspired by literary insight" when editing *Black Writers of America*.[45] The anthology attempts to be comprehensive in its historical scope and breadth while also remaining "suitable to a variety of [classroom] activities."[46]

The editors of this "comprehensive anthology" strive not only to collect literary works based on artistic merit, but to also collect sociological and historical writings chronicling the development of an African American literary tradition in order to provide an apparatus to "examine the literature and relate it closely to the life and circumstances out of which it grew."[47] Their aim was to restore a sense of the social conditions and concerns motivating their creation in order to dissolve the "facile" separation between the artistic and social functions of literature. Thus, the anthology moves beyond a formalist consideration of the merits of various works in order to paint a fuller picture of the "usable past" that shapes the African American literary tradition. Barksdale and Kinnamon argue that this picture of the past cannot be complete without the voices of all groups active in the formation of an American identity. This anthology, then, tries to reconstruct the discourse between the cultural mainstream and the descendants of Africans over the course of America's changing historical, political, and cultural contexts.

William Adams, editor of *Afro-American Authors*, which includes Amiri Baraka and Eldridge Cleaver along with Langston Hughes, Countee Cullen, and Arna Bontemps, also attends to the political function of the anthology, but in a way somewhat different from the editors of *Black Fire* or *Black Arts*. Instead of merely identifying and collecting works with a nationalist agenda, Adams links protest literature from the time with a tradition of protest within the African American literary tradition. The thematic structure situates the "Afro-American" writer within a polemic and rhetorical tradition tied to political imperatives: "Historically, for the Black writer, literature was a calling not unlike the ministry, a cause within a larger cause, with freedom as the hoped for effect."[48] In the introduction to this 1972 volume, Adams goes on to map out a trajectory for the development of African American literature that originates in "protest" and moves to "awakening," then "assertion," the moment when the black writer "sees the world as essentially varied and multi-faceted, organically knit together by a common historical experience and its concomitant heritage. He neither apologizes for his blackness, nor celebrates it. By projecting an individual identity, however, he often reflects a collective one."[49] Adams includes a range of writers to illustrate this powerful thread within the African American literary tradition. He brings together works like "We Wear the Mask" by Paul Laurence Dunbar, "In Bondage" by Claude McKay, "Ballad of the Landlord" by Langston Hughes, "Kitchenette Building" by Gwendolyn Brooks, "I Have a Dream" by M. L. King, Jr., and "The White Race and Its Heroes" by Eldridge Cleaver as evidence of a progressive tradition of protest in African American literature. By compiling examples of the protest oeuvre from throughout African American literary history, Adams links contemporary writers and activists to earlier canonized writers and thinkers in order to legitimate the contemporaneous examples of protest literature. By making the political thematic, Adams, like Barksdale and Kinnamon, attempts to balance the academic and formalist discourses with the political and ideological functions of ethnic American literary anthologies.

Paralleling the pattern of development discerned in the African American anthology tradition, Asian American scholars and critics also struggled to balance the tensions between the aesthetic, political, and academic functions of anthologies. Like African American anthologies, early Asian American anthologies also take up the issue of naming, participating in the effort to define the meaning and scope of the term "Asian American." Additionally, these anthologies play a role in identity formation, offering up representations of Asian American life and culture. But Asian American anthologies of this period, like African American anthologies of the early twentieth century, are also concerned with identifying and legitimating an Asian American cultural and literary tradition. Many anthologies, therefore, function as historical repositories, collecting artistic pieces for academic study, providing exposure for little-known artists and often overlooked cultural voices, and preserving the rapidly fading firsthand accounts of Asian immigrants to America.

Early anthologies of Asian American literature, intent on casting off the stereotypes created by popular American culture during the nativist and Yellow Peril scares of the late nineteenth and early twentieth centuries, herald the maturation of a literary tradition. However, these anthologies also deal with issues of political representation and naming that also characterize African American anthologies of the

Power period. In many ways, the heterogeneous nature of the Asian American community in America made the issue of identity even more fraught. Initially, the term "Asian American" was used to encourage political solidarity and suggest a common experience of America. The homogeneity of experience implied by the term, however, became problematic as later critics and theorists considered its implications. Just as racial identities separate "them" from "us," the term Asian American could be thought of as working to institute a racial category that strengthens notions of whiteness while codifying a small number of available social and cultural representations of Asianness. Drawing on post-structuralist, postcolonialist, and cultural studies discussions of the functioning of social discourse, later scholars began to explore and attend to the cultural and historical specifics of each of the peoples grouped within the term "Asian American." Respecting the heterogeneous experiences and national differences became an ongoing concern for "Asian" American writers and theorists. Anthologies of Asian American literature, therefore, developed as a way to represent the many voices that make up Asian America, while also providing a forum for the community's shared cultural experiences, and doing so in their own words.

In the introduction to *AIIIEEEEE!* (1974), the editors proudly label their anthology "exclusively Asian American" and announce their intent to give voice to this previously silenced group: "Asian America, so long ignored and forcibly excluded from creative participation in American culture, is wounded, sad, angry, swearing, and wondering, and this is his *AIIIEEEEE!* It is more than a whine, shout, or scream. It is fifty years of our whole voice."[50] Although *AIIIEEEEE!* was not the first anthology of Asian American writers, it was the first to state a desire to collect Asian American texts in an anthology that would provide a "corrective" to the mainstream canon.

The editors of *AIIIEEEEE!* bring together works that they consider authentic representations of the life and experience of Asians in America. Although the editors take great pains to trace the history of Chinese, Japanese, and Filipino American literature in America, the academic and literary merit of the works contained in the collection is clearly subordinate to issues of social and cultural representation. The subtitle of the anthology, *An Anthology of Asian-American Writers*, signals this preoccupation. By adopting the pan-ethnic terminology, the anthology can be seen as a response to Power's call for self-definition and self-determination. In this way, the framing of the anthology supports efforts to outline a distinct identity position for Asians in America. These negotiations also indicate that political use value eclipses the academic and literary functions of the anthology.

In addition to this concern with self-definition and naming, the anthology also claims to represent the "voice" of Asian America, the Asian American experience. In "Introduction to Chinese and Japanese American Literature," Frank Chin, Jeffrey Chan, Lawson Inada, and Shawn Wong chastise critics who "have forgotten that the vitality of literature stems from its ability to codify and legitimize common experience in the terms of that experience and to celebrate life as it is lived. ... [T]he literary establishment has never considered the fact that a new folk in a strange land would experience the land and develop new language out of old words."[51] Like these immigrant speakers of the "new language," the editors figuratively adapt the anthology form to reflect life as it is lived in the Asian American community. The editors of *AIIIEEEEE!* figure the anthology as a protest of the active exclusion of the Asian American voice from American political and cultural discourse, as well as a space for literature of the Asian American experience: "American culture, protecting the sanctity of its whiteness, still patronizes us as foreigners and refuses to recognize Asian American literature as 'American' literature."[52] Like Alain Locke, the editors of *AIIIEEEEE!* believe that the recognition of Asian Americans as a vital part of American cultural, social, and literary history is long overdue. They conclude by asserting, "We're not new here."[53] *AIIIEEEEE!* is a collection of texts, but more importantly it is a forum for social protest, an impulse that ties the Asian American literary tradition to the traditions of African, Native, and Hispanic Americans. In addition, the anthology provides a space for negotiating a recognizable cultural subjectivity; through the naming, introduction, and textual choices, the editors mobilize representations of this identity in ways that could be politically useful for the community.

Of course, as editors of *AIIIEEEEE!*, Chin and Wong were accused of essentialism and oversights in their own process of inclusion and exclusion. Compelled by the challenging tone of the anthology, Asian American literary critics and theorists took up the discourse about how definition, group identity, and social difference are determined within the Asian American community. Operating from a Bakhtinian understanding that just as every language and mode of language operates differently, some critics argued that each representation is "grounded in a completely different principle for marking differences and for establishing units" within Asian American literature.[54] Integral to this understanding is the recognition that "languages [and identities] do not *exclude* each other, but rather intersect with each other in many different ways."[55] Efforts to excavate the constructedness of the category Asian American and the heterogeneity badly contained by the term led critics, writers, artists, theorists, and activists to develop artistic, cultural, and political strategies to combat the homogenizing impulse of even politically useful racial categories. The issue of naming has been integral to this discussion. For example, Shirley Geok-lin Lim considers the "difficult[ies]" of "representative[ness]" for those who seek connections to their historic ethnic and American cultures and read the Asian American literary tradition as a chronicle of the negotiations that Asians in America had to accomplish on the way to realizing America as a truly multiplied culture.[56] She concludes that the heterogeneity of Asian America may serve as a template for understanding America's multiethnic future, a future where groups come together based on their historical engagement with the discourses of American identity and citizenship.

Though a little outside of the 1966–1981 framework of this study, Elaine Kim's *Asian American Literature: An Introduction to the Writings and Their Social Context* (1982) represents a more formalist approach to the literary anthology. Significantly, Kim focuses on providing a historical and literary critical context for reading Asian American literature. Kim's work then intervenes in an attempt to move the critical debates about Asian American literature beyond questions of cultural authenticity and representation. In the preface, Kim addresses the social, political, and cultural imperatives that inform canonization:

> Traditionally, one of the problems facing Asian American and other racial minority writers in America has been that many readers insist on viewing their writing as sociological or anthropological statements about the group.... For the purposes of this study, however, I have deliberately chosen to emphasize how the literature elucidates the social history of Asians in the United States. The problem of understanding Asian American literature within its sociohistorical and cultural contexts is important to me because, when these contexts are unfamiliar, the literature is likely to be misunderstood and unappreciated.[57]

Kim recognizes that the term "Asian American" encompasses many groups and many experiences of life in America. Her work also confronts the at times willful misunderstandings of Asian American literature and experience resulting from a distorted understanding of the history of Asians in America. However, Kim also argues that judging literature primarily according to political criteria will ultimately inhibit the development of the tradition.

In the foreword to Shirley Lim and Amy Ling's *Reading the Literature of Asian America*, Kim takes up this issue again. She recognizes that "cultural nationalism" as a strategy was crucial in early critical work because it was "crucial [to] Asian Americans' struggles for self-determination: insisting on a unitary identity seemed the only effective means of opposing and defending . . . against marginalization."[58] But Kim senses the potential danger in the reductive nature of this new strategy. Asian American anthologies display a mix of functions that reflect the efforts to create a literary history around the idea of a coherent ethnic identity.

The negotiation of social space and nomenclature, nationalist ideologies, and revolutionary aesthetics characterize the anthologies of the Power period. While Guillory argues that the ideological content of literary works is less significant, in terms of cultural use value, than the linguistic or symbolic capital, the anthologies produced during the Black Arts and Asian American Movements usually assign political ideology the highest possible cultural capital in light of the political climate of the time. Most of the anthologies display a revolutionary, libratory aesthetic designed to support the political goals of activists in both communities. For most of these anthologies, the value of each text resides in its ability to embody the struggle for freedom, or to portray black and Asian American life "like it is." Since *Black Fire*, *Black Arts*, and *AIIIEEEEE!* presume a radical politicized audience, they can afford to be polemical. But not all anthologies from the Power period prioritize political use value. *Afro-American Writers*, *Black Writers in America*, and *Asian American Literature* are less radical in their rhetoric because they are intended for academic audiences. However, they do recognize the importance of reclaiming representation as an act of self-determination, but to a lesser extent. *Dark Symphony*, alone in its narrow focus on aesthetics and academic value, presages the literary, theoretical, and critical purposes of the *Norton Anthology of African*

American Literature (1997) and *Call and Response: The Riverside Anthology of the African American Literary Tradition* (1998).

Most discussions of anthologies focus on the range of voices and approaches reflected in the included texts; however, the collections themselves reflect a range of aesthetic, political, and cultural positions adopted by the academics and artists who created them. The rest of this chapter will focus on a pair of scholar-artists, Frank Chin and Ishmael Reed, and their collaboration, which led to the publication of *AIIIEEEEE!*, the first significant anthology of Asian American literature.

Ishmael Reed and Frank Chin, a frequent early collaborator, were tagged "Two Angry Writers" by Myron Simon in a special MELUS forum on the stir Reed, Chin, Thomas Sanchez, and Karl Shapiro caused at a previous MLA panel. The panel was just one moment in Chin and Reed's substantial and productive professional relationship that developed during the early 1970s. Chin, a Berkeley native, and Reed, a transplant, both taught at the University of California at Berkeley, Reed beginning in 1970 and Chin starting in 1972. While Chin left within a few years, Reed was affiliated with the university for over two decades.

In negotiating their multipled status as artists, activists, academics, and publishers within the culturally and politically diverse Bay Area which gave rise to the Black Panthers, Asian American Movement, and widespread campus protests, Chin and Reed drew on what I call a guerilla subjectivity to construct and position themselves as agents of change, engaged in revolutionary struggle against the literary establishment. From the earliest a provocateur, Reed reacted against the ideological and creative orthodoxy of the Black Arts Movement to follow the avant-garde tradition within African American and ethnic American literature. He also rejected strains of ethnic revolutionary nationalism and cultural nationalism that espoused literature as an extension of ideology, choosing instead to pioneer another brand of cultural nationalism that sought to recover the goal of controlling the means of production. Chin, meanwhile, constantly negotiated his revolutionary posture, while remaining consistently convinced of the need for change. His highly polemical early writings were designed to call attention to the nascent Asian American literary tradition and challenge scholars to recognize the contributions of Asian American writers.

Ishmael Reed, early on, felt locked out of the Ethnic Studies "complex," because his work was not politically aligned with the agenda of reigning African American scholars née activists who dominated early

African American Studies programs. Reed, avant-gardist, ardent multiculturalist, publisher, editor, educator, novelist, and poet, championed a "transethnic" understanding of the development of not just individual ethnic literary traditions, but of the American literary tradition as a whole. However, Reed also defended the legitimacy of individual traditions. In an infamous exchange chronicled in the summer 1976 volume of *MELUS*, Reed attacked an article by critic Robert Moss that traced the origins of the black avant garde, erroneously Reed believes, to the beat poets. Reed vehemently criticized Moss's dismissal of black experimental poetry as derivative and unforgivably uninformed.[59] Creating an anthology that places the works of blacks, Asians, Hispanics, and Native Americans alongside the works of white writers would, Reed believed, counter these dismissals of ethnic American literary works, providing evidence of the interconnected development of the American literary tradition and the benefits of transethnic cooperation.

As a former popular radio personality, editor of the avant-garde *19 Necromancers from Now* (1970), author of the innovative novels *Freelance Pallbearers*, *Yellow Back Radio Broke Down*, and *Mumbo Jumbo*, and founder of the *Yardbird* journal and Yardbird Publishing Company, by the early 1970s Reed was well on his way to developing a reputation as a pioneer. Reed founded Yardbird Publishing in 1971 as a showcase for multicultural literature and a means to accomplish his aims. In an introduction to the 1972 inaugural edition of *Yardbird*, Reed promises that the "Yardbird Publishing Company, Incorporated, will publish the finest working Afro-American artists without regard to ideological or aesthetic affiliation."[60] In his remarks, Reed strongly denies that *Yardbird* is either assimilationist ("How anybody can read *Yardbird* and come away with the impression that we believe that the culture of one people is superior to those of all others, and that everybody ought to be like them is a mystery to us") or isolationist ("We feel that there are enough Black Worlds, Yellow Worlds, Red Worlds, Brown Worlds, and White Worlds for people who crave that"). Instead he proclaims that the journal "reflects cultural exchange!," capturing life in an increasingly diverse society.[61] Indeed, Reed establishes *Yardbird* as a mediator, "the messenger at the crossroads through which different cultures [communicate]."[62]

In the introduction, Reed constructs his journal as a craft to navigate the changing academy as well as the treacherous and deceiving waters of race and cultural identity in America. He locates the journal as an island in the "ocean" of American literature, a place to showcase works by writers who don't fit "European American" standards or cultural nationalist aesthetic orthodoxies: "*Yardbird* believes that a political revolution means nothing if hearts and minds are unchanged. Join in a real revolution by supporting *Yardbird*, the Reader of the New America!"[63] While Reed sympathizes with the impulses of revolutionary writers and activists, he criticizes the excesses of a particularly unreflective brand of ethnic nationalist revolutionary aesthetics, which he argues only recodify the systems and stereotypes it claims to destroy. Reed assigns blame for this breakdown alternately to publishers, academics, and ideological orthodoxy.

Reed also champions cooperation between ethnicities to achieve his vision of a multiethnic society. The range of artists in *Yardbird* journal, the makeup of the editorial board, and the publication of the Asian American volume in 1974 are proof of this commitment. Frank Chin cooperated with Reed to produce this special edition of the reader devoted mainly, but not exclusively, to Asian American literature. This third edition of *Yardbird* journal appeared the same year as *AIIIEEEEE!*, the notable anthology of Asian American literature and thought, and it previews the tone in some of the works found in the anthology. Edited by Frank Chin and Shawn Wong and dedicated to John Okada, Louis Chu, Duke Ellington, and William Gardner Smith, this special edition of the journal contains fiction, photography, drawings, and poetry by contemporary Chinese American and Japanese American authors including Nathan Lee, Shawn Wong, Jeffrey Chan, and Wing Tek Lum, as well as several works by African, Hispanic, and Native Americans, including Leslie Marmon Silko's "Lullaby."

The introduction of the journal maps out the challenges that Chin and Wong faced in finding publishers for their other collaboration. The introduction touches on many of the same themes and uses many of the same examples as *AIIIEEEEE!* (the discussion of Mori's *Yokohoma, CA*, the mention of the publisher's condescending letter, a dissing of Bill Hosokawa). Chin and Reed castigate the publishing industry for failing to publish *AIIIEEEEE!*, quoting a rejection letter from a publisher that stated that the "least ethnic" pieces were the best and warned Chin and Wong against a collection that celebrates writers "merely" for their Asian Americanness.[64] Chin and Wong express a desire to use the journal to claim an Asian American tradition of literary practice and to prove, to both white and yellow critics, that writing is not an "exclusively white practice."⁶⁵ They argue that the very existence of the texts in the collection counters the cultural "pathology" that labels certain writers "bananas" and illustrates the existence of an Asian American collective consciousness.⁶⁶ Chin and Wong speak to two main purposes for the collection, one historical and the other cultural. By collecting contemporary poems and stories by writers like Wing Tek Lum and Lawson Inada and republishing earlier works by authors like Ben Fee, they ally the journal with the preservation function of anthologies, creating within the issue a place to collect and catalog literary artifacts by Asian Americans. The journal also aims to be representative, providing proof of the existence of an Asian American identity in order to refute integrationist Asian American critics and myopic white critics who dismiss the very concept of a distinct Asian American culture. Chin and Wong thus align themselves with Reed's desire to collect contemporary works that do not conform to mainstream critical and aesthetic judgments.

Like Reed, Chin positioned himself outside of the "English business."⁶⁷ Writer, railroad man, lecturer, scholar, and dramatist, Chin consistently identifies himself as disenfranchised, silenced, underappreciated, and misunderstood. Chin characterizes himself as an outsider, rejecting what he sees as the prevailing assimilationist sentiment in establishment Asian American society. Like Reed, Chin uses the preface and introduction as an opportunity to call out several critics by name. Chin saw the special edition of *Yardbird* as an opportunity to "print up a little proof from the past" attesting to the existence of "Asian American writing" (v), thus validating his own identity as a writer and furthering his efforts to bring attention to the Asian American literary tradition.

At heart, *Yardbird* journal and Yardbird Publishing were reactions not just to the lack of publishing opportunities for writers of color generally, but also to the narrow ideological prescriptions of cultural and revolutionary nationalists. In a 2004 interview, Shawn Wong reflects on the difficulty getting *AIIIEEEEE!* published:

> Scholars now say what *AIIIEEEEE!* did was to define the literary canon in Asian American Literature. Our intent was to get people to take notice. We were going to be Asian American writers, and we felt the best way for people to know something about our writing would be to educate the audience about something called Asian American literature, the tradition. Our point was really in some ways selfish, as we were writers ourselves. At first nobody would publish it. They were pub-

lishing African American anthologies with riveting titles like *Black Fire, Black Rage*. There was only one voice that was being published—you had to be angry or in jail or from the ghetto. They weren't publishing Latinos or Chicanos, Asians or anybody, just African Americans.[68]

Contrary to Wong's assertion, the fashion for militant works also affected African American writers who did not conform to the revolutionary nationalist aesthetic. Thus, Yardbird Publishing and the *Yardbird* journal, which Wong does not mention in his interview, provided a space for writers of many backgrounds who found themselves bucking ideological trends of the time.

In this way, the journal, a part of Reed's pan-cultural literary project, functions as a locus of cooperation for these artists. In their praise of Reed and Yardbird Publishing, Chin and Wong intimate that Yardbird, "a black company," understands their efforts to chronicle "an Asian American cultural tradition that is not mere mimicry or exotic artifact."[69] While acknowledging the occasionally contentious history of social relations between blacks and yellows, Chin asserts that the journal is "no inter-racial treaty, vision of Utopia or crazy avant garde stunt.... We just don't believe yellows hate blacks and blacks hate yellows. Those that do hate, hate themselves and must hate hating by now."[70] Instead, Chin properly situates this tension in the legacy of repression experienced by each group in America and in the brutal process of racial identification which required blacks and Asians to suppress racial uniqueness in exchange for integration and American success. In resisting these assimilationist impulses, the journal represents a new type of success, claiming writing, reading, and the means of publication for all people of color.

As revolutionary characters, Chin and Reed develop a counterhegemonic subjectivity that borrows heavily from transcultural and transnational ideologies of revolution and resistance. Chin and Reed understood their efforts as writers, scholars, and critics as part of a larger revolutionary project informed by the dynamic, progressive atmosphere of the Bay Area. Understood within this context, their cooperation becomes an act of resistance and struggle intended to secure the rights to self-determination, self-definition, and self-naming for Asians and Africans in America. Chin and Reed can thus be understood as part of a vanguard, attempting to manipulate the mechanisms of publication in order to create works that reflected the multicultural, polyglot community to which they both belonged.

The rhetoric of the preface echoes this discourse of cross-cultural identification. In the preface to the *Yardbird* third edition Chin writes, "Blacks hated us for being a race of Toms bucking for honorary Whiteman. Whites love us for not being black" (iv). In this construction, Asian Americans again disappear in the middle of the black/white binary. Blacks hate yellows for what they are perceived as being. Whites seek to assimilate yellows because they are the "not black." The introduction also echoes the "racist love/racist hate" binary established by Chin and Jeffrey Paul Chan in the vitriolic 1972 essay "Racist Love." In "Racist Love," Chan and Chin equate blackness with effective cultural, political, or social critique. Blacks are "badass," while Chinese Americans are assimilationist, or "kissass."[71] Blacks are cast as "cultural villains" resisting white domination and thereby commanding "respect."[72] However, Chin and Chan fail to offer a positive iteration of what yellow is in either piece. Like Eldridge Cleaver, Chan and Chin equate masculinity with resistance and resistance with power. The "badass" garners attention; it is too "shocking" to ignore or easily dismiss.

However, the badass pays a price.

Chin and Reed both employ a confrontational masculinist vernacular that borrows from the rhetoric of the Power Movement. In *Writing Manhood in Black and Yellow*, Daniel Kim identifies a contradiction in Chin's rhetoric. Kim understands Chin as arguing that Asian American writers must articulate a "distinct Asian American vernacular" on the one hand, while simultaneously denying the possibility of the existence of this vernacular, a silencing that is one of the conditions of powerlessness and a legacy of the fraught relationship with the English language and American identity.[73] Kim concludes that this tension is a result of Chin trying to fit a "set of black nationalist arguments into a cultural context that is inappropriate to them."[74] I would argue that the cross-cultural origins of the principles of Power, derived from the anticolonialist ideologies of Fanon, Guevara, and Mao, and the masculine revolutionary agent, the guerilla, patterned in large part after the Vietnamese National Liberation Front, make this mode of revolutionary resistance not only attractive, but available and recognizable. The tension Kim notes may more properly be located in what he correctly recognizes as cultural nationalism, the dislocation produced when the rhetoric and principles of revolution are separated from the political struggle for systemic change.

However, the generative nature of Chin's cooperation with Reed contrasts with his often pessimistic and strident tone, making it possible to read their cooperation as a space for resolving this tension. Hence, their so-called guerilla subjectivity facilitates a revolutionary culture of cooperation, between the community and the vanguard, between individuals and groups seeking similar societal change, and between Frank Chin and Ishmael Reed. While Reed opposed the ethnic nationalist agenda of the Power Movement and Chin toyed with a variety of political ideologies, both identified with the need for change in the publishing industry, the "English business," and American society, and, while both taught at Berkeley, their primary identification as artistic creators meant that they were not totally within the authorizing institution of the academy. By positioning themselves as establishment outsiders, both were available to be part of the "leading edge," able to use their knowledge of the system in order to appropriate it for their own purposes.

For us as scholars this relationship is significant for several reasons. I hope that by offering another instance of black and Asian cooperation we may move from a model of exceptionalism, seeing transethnic cooperation as isolated incidents, and begin to recognize a history of engagement and constructive interaction between these groups. Their cooperation also points to the possibility for coalitions based on a shared understanding of the need for social change, not just shared history or shared identification. Lastly, Chin and Reed's articulations of revolution and struggle complicate our understanding of Power and revolution, providing a genealogy for multiple strains of cultural nationalism that continue to shape Asian American and African American studies and literature.

In black and yellow anthologies, we see a range of responses to the various political, social, cultural, academic, and aesthetic discourses pressuring the development of African American and Asian American studies during the Power period. The heterogeneity of these responses provides evidence of how the demands of the academy mediated the cultural and political functions of Ethnic Studies programs and the ethnic literary anthology. Within the academy, power and its critique of American colonialism had to compete with intellectual discourses that reified the aesthetic and critical functions of the literature. However, the question remains, did these anthologies intervene to change the mainstream canon, creating a "guerilla" process of canonization that addressed issues of inclusion and exclusion, representation and "authenticity," aesthetics and politics?

As Werner Sollers observes in "A Critique of Pure Pluralism," it is not right to lump "ethnic" writers together in one group or even one racial group. Although Sollers argues vigorously against approaches that do not acknowledge the relationships between cultural and literary traditions, his dismissal of "ethnic traditions" in favor of an understanding of the "transethnic" workings of American society is insufficient to account for the political and social discourses that have long shaped the relationship of Asian and African Americans to the mainstream. The discussions of historicity, cultural identity, and nomenclature *are* attempts to negotiate and record the American experience. Anthologies that make the literatures of Asian America and African America available have developed into far more than a mere "reflection of ethnically diverse 'experience.'"[75] By preserving the specific political, historical, and cultural contexts of people who share a cultural identity, these anthologies *make it possible* to study Stein and Wright, Chu and Roth, or Tan and Walker side by side. Harold Kolb argues that a canon "is a cultural mirror, imaging our notions of who we are. It is a national repository of historical and social values, of pedagogical notions, of ideas about the purpose of literature."[76] By recording the cycles of protest, assertion, and appreciation that also gave rise to America's literary tradition, anthologies of Asian American and African American literature act not as mirrors, but prisms that betray the multiplicity within the seemingly white light.

CHAPTER FOUR

Reading Resistance

The Guerilla in Literature

Since the beginning of this project during my graduate school days, the fields of Black Power Studies, Asian American Studies, and AfroAsian Studies have exploded. The increased attention to the areas directly related to my research has resulted in not only a rapid proliferation of scholarship, but also the recovery and republishing of numerous works from the Power period, which I date roughly from 1966 until 1981. Under the Black Arts Movement Series, the nonprofit Coffee House Press has republished a number of titles from the era, including William Kelley's *Dem* (1967; 2000); Rosa Guy's *Bird at My Window* (1966; 2001); John Oliver Killens's *The Cotillion* (1971; 2002); the posthumous collection *Echo Tree* from Henry Dumas, who was killed in 1968; and Kristin Lattany's *The Lakestown Rebellion* (1978; 2003). In addition to republishing the works of Frank Chin, Coffee House Press has also reissued works by Lawson Inada, Karen Yamashita, and Wang Ping. Thunder's Mouth Press has also released novels from the era by writers as diverse as John A. Williams, John O. Killens, Chester Himes, and Langston Hughes. This increased attention has also led to reassessments of other works from the period, like John A. Williams's *Sons of Darkness, Sons of Light*, republished in 1999 with a critical introduction by leading African American literary scholar Richard Yarborough, as part of the Northeastern Library of Black Literature Series, and *The Man Who Cried I Am*, republished in 2004 with an introduction by the prolific fiction writer Walter Mosley. The increased scholarly activity and available materials in these areas and during this period has inevitably reshaped our thinking about works and writers who do not fit the conventional periodizations in African American and Asian American literature, about lesser-known works that appeared early or late in an author's career, and about works overlooked due to previous critical dismissals of Black and Yellow Power and the Power period. The rapidly changing contours of these fields means that there are many avenues for continued archival research and critical evaluation. For the moment, however, I have chosen to focus on several essentially canonical works from the Power period, works that I feel provide a range of representations of the guerilla subjectivity that I have endeavored to outline so far.

This chapter applies the multiple facets of guerilla subjectivity outlined in the previous chapters—resistant, anticolonial, self-defined, self-determined, ideologically grounded, revolutionary agent—to a discussion of Sam Greenlee's *The Spook Who Sat by the Door* (1969; 1990), Alice Walker's *Meridian* (1976), and John Okada's *No-No Boy* (1957; 1976). These novels represent literary responses to the contingent, contentious social and political atmosphere of the Power period. For example, Greenlee's *Spook* responds to the black aesthetic imperative to illustrate revolutionary culture.[1] Greenlee's explicitly revolutionary paramilitary fiction takes up the Black Arts call to meaningfully depict the meaning, motivation, and mechanisms of revolutionary activity for "the masses." Okada's *No-No Boy*, originally published in 1957, anticipates the demands for self-determination and issues of representation and racial consciousness that characterized the Power moment. Republished in 1976, Okada's story of Ichiro's struggle to forge a Japanese American identity against the backdrop of World War II and the unjust internment and imprisonment of Japanese American citizens resonated with young Asian Americans struggling to secure their place in America even as the war in Vietnam raged on. Finally, Walker's *Meridian*, often called a "Civil Rights Movement" novel, illustrates the protagonist's journey towards an "authentic" revolutionary subjectivity. Meridian's struggle to formulate an enlightened and enduring revolutionary praxis reopens discourses of resistance to revise sexist and superficial cultural materialist posturing. As the characters in each novel struggle to negotiate racist, sexist, and nativist social discourses, they become guerilla subjects capable of intervening in these repressive discourses to create narratives of resistance and portraits of revolutionary identity. As guerilla subjects, Dan Freeman, Kenji Kaano, Ichiro Yamada, and Meridian Hill can exercise agency within the revolutionary context. However, once the violent, martial Power period that supports guerilla subjectivity passes, what are the consequences of continuing to employ such a subjectivity? While each novel enacts a revolution in self-definition, each also points towards the violent nihilism and empty spectacle that lurks within the guerilla identity, especially when detached from its particular political milieu.

At heart, all of these novels critique dehumanizing and diminishing American narratives of blackness and yellowness. Asian American and African American ethnic nationalists also employ this tactic, basing Power ideology on an anticolonialist critique of American racialist sociopolitical syntax. Huey Newton, one-time head of the Black Panther Party and a proponent of dialectical materialism (how rigorously and consistently he applied it notwithstanding), understood power as working through a competitive interplay between the community interests of blacks and other minorities, as well as mainstream American political interests. "So the people do not want assimilation, integration or separation," he argued, "[t]hey want some freedom. We will not be free until we negate the power of the aggressor."[2] In a later article, he goes on to discuss the origins of the term:

> When we coined the expression "All Power to the People," we had in mind emphasizing the word "Power," for we recognize that the will to power is the basic drive of man. But it is incorrect to seek power over people. We have been subjected to the dehumanizing power of exploitation and racism for hundreds of years; and the Black community has its own will to power also. What we seek, however, is not power over people, but the power to control our own destiny. For us the true definition of power is not in terms of how many people you can control, to us power is the ability to first of all define phenomena, and secondly the ability to make these phenomena act in a desired manner.[3]

Although his rhetoric in this quotation, from a 1971 *Black Panther* article "Black Capitalism Re-Analyzed," offers a theoretical reading of the real obstacles to black economic development, the "phenomena" to which he refers were not imagined. They were the real social and political emblems of racism—"power" distributed inequitably. Newton's comments also display an ambivalence about the purposes of "power" and the most effective means to use it. The first quotation, a "Statement" from the April 1971 *Black Panther*, comes from a polemical attack on civil rights solutions to the problem of racial oppression. According to Newton's statement, the only solution involves not just assimilation—being incorporated into the existing system—but an end to the systems of power that maintain oppression. Since the "aggressor" exerts a self-serving control over the "people," that influence must be countered or nullified, not accommodated. To do so, Newton argues, the people must organize and mobilize to undermine the aggressor's control and disrupt the aggressor's hold over the community. His dismissal of previous solutions, like "assimilation, integration or separation" as inadequate, underlines his belief that solutions for the problem of racism should originate with "the people" of the affected communities.

Likewise, the second comment condemns the distorting, oppressive exertion of power "over people" for "control." Newton rails against those who replicate repressive capitalist systems of power within the black community. Again, the "power of the aggressor" cannot be neutralized through equal opportunity; it has to be overturned to bring about equity. Otherwise, equality will only lead to elite blacks and yellows oppressing the black and yellow masses just as whites did. In his rhetoric, Newton claims for "the people" or "the Black community" power through access to and agency within economic and political systems. Freedom would lie in the ability of the community to participate in these systems on their own terms.

Black and Yellow Power critiques of American institutional racism thus constructed inequality as a crisis in representation. Power's advocates, both revolutionary nationalists and cultural nationalists, sought to address the problem of self-determination by rewriting discourses of resistance, revising legal discourses shaping American citizenship, and creating new modes of blackness and yellowness. The guerilla subjectivity arose to address this crisis in representation. Militant but not military, the guerilla functions as a mediating figure, ideologically constituted, but able to blend into in- and out-group communities without losing his ideological readiness. Unlike the protagonist of mid-century African American literature, the guerilla protagonist constitutes a "resistant subject," subverting and penetrating to overturn, not to integrate. This chapter examines three novels, two published and one republished during the Power period. Each features narrators who function as guerillas or develop guerilla subjectivity during the course of a personal journey to self-definition and self-determination. Their struggle to realize revolutionary practice either posits or revises revolutionary methodology, providing an example to the masses.

The guerilla subjectivity arose in response to Power's demand for self-defined and self-determined representations of African American and Asian American sociopolitical identity. Drawing on the Black Power call to "define the world in their own terms," African American and Asian American artists and writers began to create "art that [spoke] directly to the needs and aspirations of Black America" and Yellow America.[4] According to Larry Neal, this art had to be based on "separate" systems of "symbolism, mythology, critique, and iconology" that did not originate in racist American culture.[5] Neal and others saw the espousal of an African American or Asian American "cultural tradition" as part of "the destruction of the white thing, the destruction of white ideas, and ways of looking at the world."[6] By extension, the uncovering of black and yellow contributions to this "white thing" would uncover the falsity of an American mythic past marked by hardy pilgrims, infallible Founding Fathers, and the inevitability of Manifest Destiny. While much has been made of poets like Sonia Sanchez, Nikki Giovanni, and Haki Madhubiti, who urged blacks and yellows to "resist—/as a 'manchild' should,"[7] and playwrights like Amiri Baraka and Frank Chin, who exposed the self-annihilating violence at the heart of the American colonial system, less attention has been paid to how novels were also used to act out this textual revolution in self-definition during the Power period. Novels, because they took longer to go from conception to execution and publication, were considered less immediate, less topical, and, therefore, a less effective medium for illustrating revolutionary thought and action than poetry and drama. The characterization of novels as an artifact of the expansion of the bourgeois and leisure time enabled by advances in home economics and consumer capitalism made the form politically suspect for most Marxist-based movements. Indeed, according to this line of thinking, the length and relative expense of novels was thought to make them less appealing and less accessible to the working- and lower-class masses looking for affordable and dynamic representations of their everyday struggles in artistic form. Novels of this period are invaluable, however, in part because they depict extended treatments of the issues and ideologies propelling the political and social dynamics of this period. The length of the novel also allows for extended character development; thus, novelists can show characters evolving into revolutionary subjects as they struggle with the effort to enact radical social and political change. Ultimately, these novels show the "process" of revolution, in addition to imagining its consequences for communities and individuals.

As a vehicle for change, the guerilla provides a pathway to a revolutionary subjectivity for African Americans and Asian Americans ready for radical social and political change. As we have seen, several factors make the guerilla a fitting signifier of revolutionary difference. First, the guerilla functions as a strategic figure, facilitating the distillation of radical and revolutionary theories to prepare the masses for the liberation struggle. Secondly, the guerilla is a mediating figure, existing at the hub of a cross-cultural web of revolutionary ideological antecedents. The figure of the guerilla provides a handy vehicle that embodies the theories of Fanon and references the African, Asian, and Central American struggles for justice. As a revolutionary subjectivity, the guerilla figure acts as a comment on the outrages in Vietnam, while illuminating the irony and tragedy of violent oppression here at home. As a descriptive trope, the guerilla provides another bridge for comparativist explorations of American identity formation. Its cross-cultural origins allow scholars and critics insight into how the American process of racialization functions across and within groups to instate difference. Finally, the guerilla bridges ideological purpose and practice. The guerilla allows us to see how revolutionary cultural productions imagined sympathetic communities. Thus, the guerilla subjectivity challenges its reader to consciousness, even as these novels illustrate the perils and promise of revolutionary resistance.

So, how does this subjectivity function as a "trope" in African American and Asian American novels during and after the Black and Yellow Power Movements?[8]

The Spook Who Sat by the Door, a paramilitary fantasy, features Dan Freeman, the novel's protagonist, as a guerilla modeled on Guevara, Mao, and Debray. Freeman studies martial arts, is well trained in gun use and maintenance, and lives a self-contained life that allows him anonymity and mobility. But most importantly, he is willing to give up his life for his revolutionary cause. Freeman is a Chicago social worker who, despite the obvious pun of his name, submits himself to a CIA training program with the hidden purpose of polishing his combat and leadership skills. Unbeknownst to the class-conscious bourgeois blacks and the rabidly racist whites who populate the text, Freeman participates in this callow gesture towards integration as part of a larger insurgent plan. He patiently waits out the sabotage of a bigoted martial arts instructor and the backstabbing by his fellow recruits to emerge at the end of the eight-week training program as the only recruit to "stick it."[9] After "painstakingly" transforming himself into "squaredom" as "CIA Freeman," he rises to the glorified post of "special assistant to the

Director" of the CIA, i.e., the "spook" of the title, consigned to a desk job with high visibility and low responsibility. Freeman then quits the CIA and goes undercover a second time as the executive director of a Chicago social service agency, a move the black elite consider the next logical step for a well-positioned black person leaving public service. This new position provides Freeman an opportunity to "make a greater contribution to his people" while giving him a cover to recruit and develop a cadre of budding guerilla revolutionaries from youth gangs in urban Chicago and beyond. When the "inevitable" Chicago summer riots begin, Freeman tells his young recruits, in a final act before his inferred death, to "hit them everywhere you can [. . .]. Hit him, disappear and hit him again. [. . .] Keep gettin' up and don't back down."[10]

In addition to his use of guerilla strategy, allusions to contemporaneous revolutionary movements also align Freeman with transnational anticolonial struggles for independence: "Freeman studied the reports of the guerilla fight in Algeria, particularly as confined to urban centers; the guerilla war against the Malayan Communists; the tactics of the Viet Cong; the theories of General Vo Nyugen Giap and Mao Tse-tung."[11] Referencing the debates over militant strategy that rocked the Civil Rights Movement, Freeman dismisses the romanticism of nonviolent protesters who exhibit "all the wasted, martyred faith and courage of a people who wouldn't quit."[12] We see Freeman acting alone throughout most of the book, turning away from mass protests as he waits patiently for his moment to incite revolutionary violence. As he awaits activation, Freeman inculcates himself first into the culture of the social work agencies of Chicago, then into the CIA training class, back into the Chicago social work world and, finally, into the Cobra street gang. Like his counterparts in Vietnam and Central America, the guerilla Freeman "has a way of fading into the background."[13]

This talent for "dissembling" helps Freeman move unremarked between these very different communities. One of his CIA trainers recalls that "you can't remember his face, or what he looks like, or what he has said, even minutes after you have spoken to him."[14] Greenlee plays on the pun of the title to imply that blacks are natural "spooks." While spook has been a derogatory term for a black person since the 1940s, according to *The Caswell Dictionary of Slang*, the term originated as a reference to agents of the OSS, the World War II predecessor of the CIA, who were heavily recruited from the Yale University secret society Skull and Bones.[15] In his concept of double consciousness, Du Bois asserts a special gift of second sight for African Americans; Greenlee goes further, claiming that African Americans are gifted with the ability to see while not being seen. Like the veiled Algerian woman Fanon describes in *A Dying Colonialism*, this structural "invisibility" makes blacks better able to subvert the surveillance systems put into place to thwart rebellion.[16] In a seemingly elegant reversal, Greenlee reappropriates the term in a novel about a black person infiltrating the CIA. This irony should be read as an attempt to highlight the hypocrisy of the term and subsequently neutralize the word's derogatory connotations. By aligning an undercover black guerilla revolutionary with two elite, predominantly white institutions—the Ivy League and the CIA—the novel claims by association the cultural authority of the "Yalie" for the ethnic revolutionary.

Unlike Ellison's Invisible Man, Freeman achieves invisibility by pretending to accept racial stereotypes instead of rejecting them: "It was not difficult to conform to the image whites desired, since they did most of the work. They saw in most Negroes exactly what they most wanted to see; one need only impressionistically support the stereotype."[17] In a 1969 *Newsweek* article trumpeting the arrival of a new crop of black (and with one exception, male) writers, Greenlee said that "the book is about white faces and black masks [. . .] and is a warning that African masks have historically and traditionally served the dual function of entertaining and threatening the enemy."[18] The novel captures the prevailing sentiment that the ambivalent balancing act required by American institutional racism, or American-style colonialism, was tipping, to use Bhabha's phrase, from mimicry to menace. Greenlee's reference to Fanon also suggests that menace is the flip side of Johnson's mask. Or, in the language of Du Bois, the veil of dual consciousness was about to be rent, setting loose portrayals of a militant black consciousness that presage systemic change. Unlike the mask or double consciousness, which implies a difference between the "real" self and an assumed self, Freeman adopts a guerilla subjectivity in order to achieve revolutionary ends. The mask or veil metaphor implies a bifurcated self, but it fits less well to explain the split between the CIA Freeman, the social worker Freeman, the New York Freeman, and the guerilla Freeman. As a guerilla, Freeman has to negotiate race, class, and political differences to obscure his real purpose. For example, Freeman deceives even his childhood friend and Chicago police detective, Sergeant Dawson, eventually killing Dawson when he shows up to take Freeman into custody. As a guerilla, Freeman isn't assuming an identity in order to assimilate; he sublimates several identities in order to deceive both whites and blacks who would thwart his revolutionary intentions.

Like most revolutionary Black and Yellow Power literature, *The Spook Who Sat by the Door* has been dismissed as static, flat "propaganda," trafficking in stereotypes. Much scholarship about what Noel Schraufnagel calls "militant protest" literature dismisses it as propagandistic, simplistic, apocalyptic, sensational, stereotypical, chauvinistic "wish-fulfillment."[19] And it was. These pronouncements, however, stem as much from value judgments about the themes of social disorder, systemic change, and violent resistance fundamental to Black and Yellow Power rhetoric as from formal aesthetic criteria. Addison Gayle predicted that we would be able to evaluate Power's success only from its legacy. Now it seems only natural to us that the works of African and Asian Americans, as well as Latino and Native Americans, are produced, studied, and valued. This naturalization indicates that it may be time to evaluate the "knowledges" of blackness and yellowness that are the truest legacy of the Power period.

Schraufnagel's *From Apology to Protest: The Black American Novel* (1973) and Roger Whitlow's *Black American Literature* (1973) each deal with militant works published during the Power period, but their analyses summarize the works, using them to articulate themes of "protest" and illustrate scenes of "Armageddon." Within the formalist/political matrix, both texts lean more towards the formalist, continuing to evaluate the novels within dominant American aesthetic standards without applying even the newly articulated black aesthetic criteria. However, both critics recognize an important distinction between militant novels of the sixties and earlier periods. Unlike "apologist" militant fiction, the protagonists of this new era of militant fiction, according to Schraufnagel, are "transformed into militant revolutionaries [whose] individual rebellions are turned into coordinate insurrections."[20] Greenlee's novel constitutes the individual as an agent for cultural change and revolutionary overthrow. Freeman's guerilla subjectivity empowers him to instigate revolutionary change.

However, Sandra Hollin Flowers seems to judge the fiction of the Power period *only* according to political criteria. Her 1996 study, *African American Nationalist Literature of the 1960s: Pens of Fire*, draws heavily on sociological methods to delineate variants of nationalism operating during the Power period. She then uses this schema to evaluate how effectively a text conveys a nationalist agenda. Flowers's study covers poetry, drama, and two novels, *The Bluest Eye* and *The Spook Who Sat by the Door*. Flowers allows that prose fiction provides room for greater artistic "expression," but she dismisses prose fiction as a "retreat" from poetry and drama, "lack[ing] the vibrancy to sustain the momentum, intensity, and mutability of African American nationalist philosophy."[21] Flowers's in-depth study articulates the many strains of thought that make up the universe of black nationalist thought and politics during the Power period. Her coherent and detailed discussion brings clarity to a confusing array of shifting allegiances and practices, providing a ready methodology for applying these insights to literature. However, judging texts only according to their ideological fealty reduces literature to a drab stage for the set pieces of political thought.

Despite these critical pronouncements, Greenlee's novel was one of the most popular works of revolutionary fiction published during the Power period. An October 6 blurb in *Publishers' Weekly* predicted that the 1969 novel "should sell the best of the several recent novels on black-white confrontation."[22] Originally published by Robert Baron after initially being turned down by several publishing houses, the novel was later published in paperback by Bantam and republished in 1990 by Wayne State University Press.[23] In 1973, it was made into a motion picture. Greenlee wrote the screenplay, and along with his partner, director and producer Ivan Dixon, raised between 75 and 85 percent of the million-dollar cost of the movie.[24] In a 1971 interview, Greenlee summed up his purpose: "I was determined that I was going to write a Black book for Black people with no attempt to translate or explain or illuminate for a white audience, however sympathetic or hostile, who might not understand exactly what I was saying."[25] The popularity of Greenlee's work would seem to frustrate dismissals of revolutionary novels as inaccessible or ineffectual. Despite his rather narrow concept of audience, the novel's popularity points to a pent-up demand for extended fictional treatments of militant action.

Reviews of Greenlee's debut novel focused mainly on the social threat represented in the text, expressing an anxiety about the social threat illustrated in the novel that echoes the critical discourse that marked Fanon's initial reception in America. In a disparaging review, Kenneth Graham laments:

> I suppose propaganda novels have to be simple like this, and at their best they can achieve a lyrical intensity that *is* revolutionary. There are a few moments of such feeling in this book, and the narrative of the rioting is exciting in itself. But for the most part I can't see beyond the inhuman single-mindedness, the naïve caricatures, the reactionary love of destruction, the offense offered at every turn to what life is and what people can be. This is to write against oppression in a way that oppresses, cheapens, and tyrannizes.[26]

Paul Kiniery echoes this judgment, saying the novel is "filled with bitterness," and concluding, "I can think of no one to whom I would recommend this book. I regret that it was published."[27] Other reviews were not as blunt. David Pryce-Jones calls the novel "wish-fulfillment," saying that Greenlee's resort to violence is a part of a larger "sublimation."[28] In other words, Greenlee and his protagonist are foolish to believe that violence can ultimately bring freedom; hate can only bring hate. A review in the *Times Literary Supplement* concludes that "the writing is nothing, the warning—or threat—everything."[29] Again, many of these reviews conflate moral and aesthetic judgments in their condemnation of Greenlee. Of course, these reviewers do not belong to Greenlee's intended audience; nor do they share the revolutionary consciousness instituted by Power. In order to adequately consider the value and impact of Greenlee's novel, these critics would have to consider the text against both its aesthetic moment and its sociopolitical context.

Only *Booklist* reviews Greenlee's novel favorably, calling it "a tightly controlled, realistic first novel, with brutally honest characterization."[30] The reviewer calls Freeman "a dedicated black nationalist" who operates "under his cover as a successful man-about-town" to put in place a "plan for armed guerilla warfare" developed during Freeman's "training" as "the only Black staff member of the CIA."[31] The reviewer concludes, "Greenlee successfully portrays the authentic voice of the ghetto activist through his protagonist and will arouse sympathy and recognition in the concerned readers to whom he directs his novel."[32] The reviewer at least seems aware of how audience shapes Greenlee's text; still, he sidesteps the issue of literary merit to gush about the value of this text for "concerned readers" (i.e., liberals) turned on by militant chic. Like the others, the *Booklist* reviewer bases his reaction to the novel on ideological merit, choosing to uncritically praise the book's politics rather than risk being accused of aesthetic racism. While the reviewer pays lip service to the form of the novel, lauding the text's control and characterization, it isn't *that* good. The plot does unfurl with a minimum of reality-bending twists and turns, but most characters in the novel are caricatures; only Freeman is complex and captivating. Claiming to appreciate the honesty, realism, and "authenticity" of the text does not prevent the *Booklist* reviewer from reducing Freeman's story to a barely fictionalized, sociologically inflected dream of revolutionary rebellion.

Despite his relatively large body of work, which includes two novels, a film, a career as a television director, many short stories in journals and anthologies, and three poetry collections, critical treatment of Greenlee has been sparse. Though all discussions of his work to this point consider Greenlee within the context of racism and oppression and how he replicates the rhetoric of revolution, the value of Greenlee's work extends beyond its ability to capture the zeitgeist of the Power moment. His depiction of Dan Freeman as an agent of power capable of manipulating the oppressive social and political discourses that undergird neocolonialist American society provides a vivid fantasy of resistance that was readily taken up in popular cultural depictions of black men. Dapper Dan, the revolutionary man, resonates in blaxploitation films, in Walter Mosley's Easy Rawlins character, and in the music and images of soul singers, like Stax recording artist Isaac Hayes. Greenlee's novel provides a compelling blueprint for black male revolutionary resistance to the limiting narratives of class, race, and politics that continued to bedevil blacks after the height of the Civil Rights Movement. His depiction of Dan Freeman set the stage for blaxploitation antiheroes who drew on the tough, rugged, guerilla figure and discourses of aggressive Black masculinity to great commercial success.

Sam Greenlee's *The Spook Who Sat by the Door* explores the use of "urban uprisings" as a cover for a militant offensive to liberate the "ghetto." As in Newton, the novel reflects a shift from thinking of power as something possessed only by "the aggressor" to thinking of power as a form of social and community agency that can be used by radicalized subjects. According to Newton, freedom lies in community control over its own "destiny," in this case the always already social forces that constitute and motivate social "phenomena." His remarks point to another, power as a form of social currency by which the user can secure agency and freedom, the ability to originate social constructs, and the ability to activate those institutions and identities in the community's interests. Power, then, operates as something to be resisted on the one hand, and wielded on the other. Thus, his definition of Power requires a subject capable of resisting the power of the oppressor and exercising power in service of the "community." In Greenlee's novel, Freeman, the main character, relates to power both as an agent of the system and as a guerilla resisting the system.

A critique of the multiple systems that maintain oppression is also central to the novel. Drawing on Foucault's analysis of power as the interplay of social systems, we can understand how both black and white characters throughout the novel deploy repressive discourses of race, respectability, masculinity, and class in their attempts to contain Freeman. Foucault figures his "investigations" of power as a more bottom-up explanation of how "knowledges" and institutions are complicit in shaping a network of self-sustaining policies. His methodology aims to expose power as a process of legitimation, not just disconnected acts of domination. In this sense, powerful institutions and the social discourses they represent are "disciplinary," acting to preserve the status quo and maintain the illusion of social control.[33] This in mind, the community and aggressor that Freeman attacks are not fixed entities, because those interests can change as the interests of the community and the aggressor change. In *The Archaeology of Knowledge*, Foucault refers to the "interplay," or relationship between different competing social interests.[34] For Foucault, an effective critique of power does more than identify those who "possess" it and those who "submit" to it.[35] Power involves not only the clash of social subjects; systems of power require and create certain types of subjects at different moments. Therefore, an adequate dissection of power must explicate the many "economically advantageous and politically useful" mechanisms of control that extend across a society.[36] A critique of power must also deliver an explication of the "individuals," individual professions and knowledges, that function as the outlets by which power is retained and applied.[37] According to Foucault, "the individual is an effect of power, and at the same time, or precisely to the extent to which it is that effect, it is the element of its articulation. The individual that power has constituted is at the same time its vehicle."[38] While power protects and establishes social mechanisms, it also constitutes individuals authorized to support and sustain the system. The guerilla Freeman seeks to take advantage of this construct by acting as an authorized agent while weakening the very supports that keep dominant systems in place.

Freeman represents a very straightforward fictional adaptation of guerilla subjectivity; however, John Okada's *No-No Boy* presents a much more complicated and fraught route to revolutionary subjectivity. Like the story of Dan Freeman, the story of Kenji Kanno and Ichiro Yamada chronicled in *No-No Boy* is about the individual's response to power. Taking its title from a reference to young Japanese American men who chose not to renounce their loyalty to Japan or demonstrate their allegiance to the United States by serving in the army during World War II, the novel tells the story of Ichiro Yamada, a Nisei (second-generation, American-born of Japanese descent) "no-no boy," and Kenji, a fellow Nisei and army veteran, as they readjust to life in Seattle in the aftermath of the war. Ichiro returns from prison to jeers, slurs, and rejection from his peers and his younger brother, Taro, who turns his back on his family and runs to the army in a desperate bid to shore up his fractured identity by reaffirming his Americanness. Ichiro struggles mightily with his reasons for refusing to enter the service, bitterly blaming his mother for insisting on their Japaneseness in America in a futile and, ultimately, delusional anticipation of her family's return to Japan. He fumes:

> [T]here came a time when I was only half Japanese because one is not born in America and raised in America and taught in America and one does not speak and swear and drink and smoke and play and fight and see and hear in America among Americans in American streets and houses without becoming American and loving it. But I did not love it enough, for you were still half my mother and I was thereby still half Japanese. . . . But it is not enough to be only half an American and know that it is an empty half.[39]

This desire to distance himself from his mother and her suicidal devotion to the Japanese homeland propels Ichiro through a nightmare of recriminations, self-doubt, self-sabotage, and emotional turmoil before he finally realizes that

> [i]t wasn't his fault. Neither was it the fault of his mother, who was now dead because of a conviction which was only a dream that blew up in her face. . . . I made a mess of everything by saying no and I see now that my miserable little life is still only a part of the miserable big

world. . . . I have been guilty of a serious error. I have paid for my crime as prescribed by law. I have been forgiven and it is only right for me to feel this way or else I would not be riding unnoticed and unmolested on a bus along a street in Seattle on a gloomy, rain-soaked day.[40]

Ichiro concludes that the promise of America still holds despite the crimes against the American Japanese. He comes to realize that his "no" was partly coerced, a result of misguided fealty to his mother and the fear of fighting other Japanese; therefore, continuing to hold himself hostage to his guilt and confusion would only compound the original mistake.

While Ichiro represents the tortured Nisei id, Kenji is typically read as embodying the law-abiding superego. Together, they represent the "two extremes, the Japanese who was more American than most Americans because he had crept to the brink of death for America, and the other who was neither Japanese nor American because he had failed to recognize the gift of his birthright when recognition meant everything."[41] However, while Kenji returns from the war with "a medal, a car, a pension, even an education. Just for packing a rifle," he has also lost most of a leg and is in danger of losing his life due to a blood infection that has required two successive surgeries to amputate more and more of the limb.[42] At a time when Ichiro seems unable to think through the racial, familial, and personal forces affecting his chaotic life, Kenji, the decorated vet awaiting death, offers him insight. From his deathbed, Kenji urges Ichiro to return home and stick out the in-group and out-group opposition he's encountered: "The way I see it, they pick on you because they're vulnerable. They think just because they went and packed a rifle they're different but they aren't and they know it. They're still Japs."[43] Kenji's observation highlights the irony that torments both characters. The war and internment didn't change America's racial discourses about Japanese Americans. Instead, the experience of the war has given Kenji a "special insight" into the self-defeating hypocrisy of the system that praises him for his bravery while condemning Ichiro for his maternal loyalty.

No-No Boy is often noted for the poignant story of its "discovery" by Frank Chin and Lawson Inada, who missed meeting Okada; he had died of a heart attack a mere three months earlier. In the afterword to the 1976 University of Washington Press reissue, "In Search of John Okada," Chin recounts his feeling that "the discovery of John's 1957 novel was like a white writer feeling gloomy and alone in literary history, discovering Mark Twain."[44] He lauds the novel for its courage and its significance to the development of Asian American literary history, treating the story as a historical and sociological artifact, proof of resistance to oppression during World War II. This assessment of the text is based largely on Ichiro's character. Shirley Geok-lin Lim characterizes the novel as a "pessimistic" portrait of a character struggling for self-definition, "unable to claim either culture" and unable to create an "internal reality for himself in the face of failure of cultures to define self."[45] According to Lim, Ichiro suffers from the inability to "affirm either the Japanese or American aspects of his self, he is filled with self-contempt, hatred for his Japanese parents, loathing for the Japanese-Americans who revile him, and conflicting emotions towards white America which he recognizes has shaped him without accepting him as a native son. He is tormented by irresolution."[46] His inability to reconcile the delusional Japanese nationalism of his mother with his own decision to stand against a war for reasons he doesn't understand fuels Ichiro's self-pity and self-destructiveness. Ichiro's "internal conflict" paralyzes him, crippling his ability to illustrate resistant subjectivity.

In a 1995 consideration of the cultural and political discourses tearing at Ichiro, Jinqi Ling reads Okada's novel as a parable of the prodigal Ichiro, a protagonist struggling to "piece together his fragmented past," coming to "embrace the promise of America."[47] Ling reads *No-No Boy* as more than a broad attack on white racism. The novel represents a reaction against "the era's reigning discourse on Americanization" and Japanese American writers who capitulated to market and ideological pressures to produce literature that affirmed and celebrated "successful assimilation."[48] In the introductory essay that opens the volume, the editors of *The Big AIIIEEEEE!* memorably label Japanese American autobiography of this assimilative type "a low-maintenance, self-cleaning, self-destructive engine of white supremacy."[49] Frank Chin, in his 1989 "Come All Ye Asian American Writers of the Real and the Fake," calls these narratives part of the "Christian ... cultural extinction and behavior modification" process that erased expressions of "real" Chinese culture and replaced them with stereotypes of misogynist, comical, close-minded Chinese men who had to be eradicated for the group to achieve full assimilation.[50] These stereotypes, according to Chin, gave rise to the "fake" myths animating the fictions of Maxine

Hong Kingston and her "spawn" Amy Tan and David Hwang.[51] Ling tempers Chin's incendiary pronouncements, reading Ichiro's ambiguity as a reflection of and reaction to the limited range of narratives of resistance available to Okada within the assimilative discourses of the period. Since Okada couldn't use Ichiro to launch a full frontal attack on American oppression, he uses a number of indirect narrative strategies to convey dissent instead. According to Ling, Okada's critique of Japanese on both sides of the loyalty issue, his use of the Japanese folk figure Momatoro, and the relationship between Ichiro and Emi, a Japanese American woman whose husband abandons her to serve another stint in the army in response to her brother's well-publicized anti-internment activism are all attempts to undermine the prevailing racialist and assimilationist narratives popularized in the autobiographies that Chin rails against. Therefore, Ichiro's tortured narrative voice is not a failure. His dilemma represents an "implicit call for a breakdown of the discourse that governed the relations of Japanese Americans to the mainstream, a call that foreshadows the more explicitly confrontational strategies employed by Asian American writers in the 1970s in their attempts to negotiate their relations with the mainstream culture from relatively more empowered positions."[52] *No-No Boy*'s story represents an intervention in repressive discourses developed and deployed by both whites and Japanese during the World War II period; this resistive narrative strategy resonated with Chin and Inada, who embraced the principles of Power. Likewise, the novel resonated with discourses of self-definition, pan-ethnic identity, and empowered subjectivity called for by Power ideology.

While Ling considers Ichiro's ambiguous narrative voice a reflection of Okada's subversion of established narratives of Japanese American identity, I believe Kenji is the key to a subversive reading of the text. Most critical treatments of the novel focus on Ichiro, neglecting Kenji's role as a doppelganger, which opens up this reading of the text. Within the novel, the twinned dynamic between Kenji and Ichiro is used to rehearse the myths about Japanese American identity and community. While critics note that Okada was a veteran of World War II who served in the Pacific theater, no one has commented on the role of Kenji, the Nisei vet in the novel, in bringing Ichiro to terms with his dilemma. Kenji is a tragic figure who laments his decision to join the army and faces certain death because of his injury, but he doesn't fall prey to the same paralyzing self-doubt that grips Ichiro. Kenji, Humphrey Bogartesque lingo aside, is Ichiro's guide through the bitterness and anger left after his imprisonment. Ichiro, torn by the clichéd Asian American identity crisis, stands in stark contrast to Kenji, who has a sardonic ability to come to terms with his unintended sacrifice and impending death. Shirley Geok-lin Lim calls him "the only character who appears psychologically whole."[53]

How does Kenji achieve this wholeness in light of his ironically liminal position as a Nisei American who volunteered for service, but is facing death from his war injury? Perhaps Kenji's attitude can be attributed to the war-weary wisdom some veterans return home with. His willingness to critique his choice, his service, and his country enables Ichiro to begin his healing. Kenji's wholeness also frustrates the thematic preoccupation with internal conflict or "'identity crisis'" found in the autobiographies of Japanese American assimilation that were popular at the time.[54] Kenji's narrative voice, then, reflects a guerilla subjectivity, a Japanese American vet who did the "right" thing, according to the dominant social narratives, but who espouses a contrapuntal orientation to both nativist American and nationalist Japanese American society. Kenji tells Ichiro to see the abuse from other Nisei vets as an expression of their fear and confusion: "The guys who make it tough on you probably do so out of a misbegotten idea that maybe you're to blame because the good that they thought they were doing by getting killed and shot up doesn't amount to a pot of beans."[55] Likewise, he mocks the continued insularity of some in the Japanese American community as a reaction to internment: "They bitched and hollered when the government put them in camps and put real fences around them, but now they're doing the same damn thing to themselves."[56] In exchange for his leg and his life, Kenji seems to have gained a bitterly incisive second sight.

It is Kenji then, rather than Ichiro, who truly voices the critique of American discourses of race that spoke to the 1970s struggles for a social revolution and revised representations of Asian American life. It is Kenji who tells Ichiro to seek out social and sexual coalitions that will eventually bring about pluralism and the end of dehumanizing discourses of difference: "Go someplace where there isn't another Jap within a thousand miles. Marry a white girl or a Negro or an Italian or even a Chinese. Anything but a Japanese. After a few generations of that, you've got the thing beat. Am I making sense?"[57] Despite the fact that reverse essentialism at the heart of his admonition means that these coalitions may not last, Kenji is committed to at least imagining new modes of identity. Thus, he sends Ichiro out as a surrogate to continue the journey to self-definition that Kenji will be unable to finish.

The story is largely focalized through Ichiro, which further marginalizes Kenji's voice, but does not obscure the vital role he plays voicing resistance. When he reveals himself as a no-no boy, Ichiro notices Kenji's reaction: "There was a silence, but it wasn't uncomfortable. Ichiro could tell instantly that it did not matter to Kenji."[58] Kenji's silent acceptance soothes Ichiro's turmoil. Kenji, the former soldier, seems to embody the exact opposite fate and subjectivity embodied by Ichiro. But it is Kenji who encourages Ichiro to reject America's failed racial discourses–the racial nationalist narratives represented by Jun, Ichiro's mother, and the assimilationist narratives represented by his tormentors in the Japanese American community. It is Kenji, not Ichiro, who recognizes the potential pitfall that each of these discourses masks. Kenji convinces Ichiro that he does not have to be the victim of these failed social constructs. Instead, Kenji helps Ichiro think discursively, understanding the actions of his mother, father, brother Taro, and former friends as failed negotiations of both Japanese and American identity. Likewise, Kenji implores Ichiro to see himself as an empowered subject who can resist these past identifications and craft a subjectivity that will allow him to avoid hate and fear and develop his own relationship to his complicated heritage.

Okada uses Kenji to institute a new discourse concerning Japanese American self-definition. Ichiro can then use the insights he's gained from his friend to negotiate the complicated terrain bridged by the hyphen, the perilous route to identity represented by that slender mark. Ichiro, in the second of what seems like three endings to the novel, calls himself a "little wiser," having gained a perspective that allows him to see that "it's the same world, the same big, shiny apple with streaks of rotten brown in it. Not rotten in the center where it counts, but rotten in spots underneath the skin and a good, sharp knife can still do a lot of good."[59] With this new knowledge, Ichiro can begin to construct himself as a "knife" excising rot from American and Japanese American discourses of identity.

In the book's final ending, Ichiro "put a hand on Bull's" shoulder in the same manner that Kenji approached Ichiro ("Kenji placed a hand on his shoulder [. . .]") eight chapters earlier.[60] Bull is a vet who torments Freddy, another no-no boy. In a final fateful confrontation at the Oriental Club, Bull fights with Freddy, who leaps into his car, takes off, swerves, flips, and is killed. Bull, drunk, wounded, angry over the confrontation, and shocked by the sudden death, has his own crisis. While his cries could be interpreted as grief over his possible prosecution, Bull also seems to be expressing his frustration over the limiting and, ultimately, deadly narratives of self and community that led him to torment Freddy. Rather than "Aiiieeeee," Freddy cries, "Aggh . . . like a baby in loud, gasping, beseeching howls" voicing his "empty sorrow" and "loneliness."[61] His cries express his forlorn realization that the very narratives that led him to define manhood and selfhood through military service and bullying led to a dead end. Ichiro manages to see "a tiny bit of America . . . faint and elusive" in the tragedy, which highlights the annihilating consequences of the racializing discourses embodied in Freddy's self-destructiveness and Bull's reactionary violence.[62]

As he strolls down the alley away from the scene of Freddy's tortuous end, Ichiro also moves out of the grasp of the sirens heralding the "official voices" that have come to restore order.[63] Although Ichiro ends the story walking down the street alone, just as he entered it, this ending is meant to offer hope. The violent climactic clash of these two narratives of identity for young Nisei men institutes Ichiro's journey towards his own revolution in self-definition. Ichiro's power lies in his awareness of these narratives and his willingness to turn his back on them. By saying no to all of these discourses, Ichiro strips them of their constitutive power and institutes a new discourse of resistance that anticipates the guerilla.

Like *The Spook Who Sat by the Door* and *No-No Boy*, Alice Walker's sophomore novel, *Meridian* (1976), is preoccupied with power. While *No-No Boy* addresses the lack of narratives of resistance and *Spook* illustrates ethnic revolutionary nationalist discourses of resistance, *Meridian* critiques forms of resistance that, in their ascendancy, begin to replicate hegemonic mechanisms of oppression. By tracing Meridian's journey, we can chart the evolution of the movement from civil rights to Power, from nonviolent protest to a guerilla crusade for systemic change. Unlike previous critics, who read *Meridian* primarily as a feminist or, later, womanist critique of the Civil Rights and Black Power Movements, I believe *Meridian* is more than a mere denunciation of the treatment of women within each movement. Walker's novel represents an intervention into the discourses of representation and resistance, opening up, for both men and women, a route to guerilla subjectivity that is characterized by self-determination, radical action, and personal autonomy. The novel ends by positing an alternate form of revolutionary identity for women and men willing to take up the struggle for change.

Many early reviews of *Meridian* pick up on its preoccupation with the legacy of the Civil Rights Movement. Marge Piercy calls Meridian a "saint," lauding Walker's "fine, taut" novel for its "sharp critical sense [of] the issues of tactics and strategy in the Civil Rights Movement."[64] Virginia Marr praises the "richly affirmative novel about a Southern black woman . . . who confronts the meaning, fact, and evolution of the civil rights movement."[65] Margo Jefferson echoes this sentiment, calling *Meridian* "a novel as ambitious and complicated as the era it examines and elegizes—the '60s."[66] One of the earliest reviews sums up the initial reaction to the text, noting that the novel is "torn by the gap between the intellectual language of politics and the emotional language of people's lives."[67] While these reviews all recognize Walker's revisioning of the movement, they all place the novel within a feminist context, presaging later critical treatments.

These reviews of the novel also note the tension between the political and the personal. Early critical treatments of *Meridian* focused on the personal, reading the novel either as a primarily feminist text or as a condemnation of personal politics within the Civil Rights and Black Power Movements. Karen Stein acknowledges Walker's engagement with revolution. She argues on the one hand that the novel posits the inner struggle as the true ground for revolution; while on the other, she asserts, "Walker suggests that a primary reason for the Movement's failure was its lack of a sustained sociopolitical critique."[68] According to Stein, Walker uses the novel to rewrite "her attitudes towards '60s activism, . . . substitut[ing] for the concept of revolution the more powerful ideal of transformation."[69] While I agree that the novel forwards a new type of engagement with revolutionary principles, I don't agree that Walker is arguing that the concept of revolution is dead. The novel ends with Truman clearly acknowledging that the struggle for change will continue through a process of individual commitment pioneered by Meridian Hill. Significantly, the novel distinguishes between the need for struggle and the methods used to achieve change. By endowing Truman, the former false prophet of revolution, with Meridian's mantle, the text signals that the commitment to revolution must spring from personal conviction, not ideological fashion. Stein reads Truman early in the novel as a Black Power straw man, representing the "false promises" of "revolutionary consciousness."[70] However, the ending complicates this reading, which flattens the distinction between revolutionary nationalism and cultural nationalism that I believe the novel recognizes. Instead, I see Truman embodying the artifice and "false promises" of cultural nationalism, defined as the focus on expressions of a liberated culture before the struggle is completed. The movement's real crime is not betraying its "liberation rhetoric" by devaluing the contributions of women; the crime is substituting commodified revolutionary icons for revolutionary practice. Stein concludes that Walker counters the "death-dealing rhetoric" of female self-sacrifice, religious self-abnegation, and revolutionary self-immolation by affirming life.[71] Only by surviving can Meridian continue her struggle.

Like Stein, Susan Willis reads *Meridian* as complicating the issues at stake in revolutionary praxis. Willis places Meridian within a line of revolutionary female characters created by Walker. According to Willis, when Meridian refuses to join her college classmates in pledging to kill for the revolution she is "defin[ing] instead what will be her more difficult form of revolutionary praxis," traveling the South to confront "embedded racist and sexist practices."[72] The novel then chronicles Meridian's "process to radicalization," which results in a "radical commitment to revolutionary praxis."[73] While Willis appreciates the novel's historical milieu, she does not explicitly acknowledge Walker's articulation of a formula for revolution that would extend beyond the novel or the present moment into the future, just as the young branch extends itself from Sojourner's seemingly lifeless stump. While I agree that the novel chronicles Meridian's journey towards self-determination and her own revolutionary identity, radicalization is not an end for Meridian's journey. Instead, radicalization marks one stage in the development of Meridian's guerilla identification.

Joseph Brown goes even further in reading the novel as a spiritual journey of inner growth.[74] Steeped in the language of the black church, Brown traces Meridian's "ascent" and "immersion" in black southern folkways and systems of meanings. The journey is an integral theme in African American female fiction. According to Deborah McDowell, "[T]he Black female's journey, [. . .] though at times touching on the political and social, is basically a personal and psychological journey."[75] By applying McDowell's insight to claim space for a black female bildungsroman, the political import of Meridian's journey ends up limited to the sphere of gender. In Brown's reading, Meridian's journey teaches her to honor tradition, transforming her into a type of mystic who carries a message of life back to her people. Brown's fervent reading casts the novel as a chronicle of spiritual passage from isolation to communion with the mystical sphere, or unconscious, of African America. Reading the novel solely as a spiritual journey also ignores the libratory import of Meridian's journey. She doesn't just come into spiritual consciousness; the experience in the militant church lays the foundation for the next stage of her struggle. Reading the novel within this black feminist and spiritual context again isolates Meridian's struggle from the material conditions—the house bombing, the violence towards innocents, the demoralizing treatment by men—that compel her, and Walker, to action.

Others consider the novel more or less strictly within its historical context, reading *Meridian* alongside the events of the Civil Rights Movement and the experiences of activists. Of course, Walker's own involvement in the movement facilitates this approach. She has written extensively about her journey to self-awareness and its connections to the rise of the Civil Rights Movement. Roberta Hendrickson uses Walker's autobiographical writings to recover the lived history that informs the novel. Reading the novel through the lens of the Civil Rights Movement—"*Meridian* is a novel that affirms the Movement's vision of freedom and nonviolence, affirms blackness and African American heritage"—Hendrickson argues that Walker comes to grips with issues of gender relations, personal relationships between black women and white women, sexual relationships between black men and white women, personal and sexual relationships between black men and black women, racial identity, and the legacy of nonviolence.[76] Hendrickson concludes that the novel ultimately redefines blackness and revolution in a way that allows Walker to situate herself as a black revolutionary artist, able to sing songs of resistance to ensuing generations. Hendrickson's treatment of the novel illuminates the people and events that form historical subtext and context for the novel, bringing to life the tensions that buffered the movement from without and within. Using history to recover this heterogeneity is also key to revising our understanding of how Walker engages the principles of Power within the novel.

Norman Harris reads *Meridian* as a "Civil Rights novel" and uses the history of SNCC and the student activists who peopled the movement as a background for reading and understanding the novel's politics. Unlike others, Harris sees *Meridian* as situated at the nexus marking the twilight of the Civil Rights Movement and the consolidation of the Power moment. He also concludes that the "interplay between personal history and political activism" is integral to understanding the way forward for Meridian Hill and others. Harris reads novels of the Vietnam War, the Civil Rights Movement, and the Black Power Movement against black people's historic struggle for liberation and literacy. In the second half of his book, Harris reads Walker's *Meridian* and John McCluskey's *Look What They Done to My Song* as civil rights novels and John Killens's *The Cotillion or One Good Bull Is Half the Herd* and Ishmael Reed's *The Last Days of Louisiana Red* as Black Power novels. In addition to drawing this distinction, Harris also distinguishes between cultural nationalism and revolutionary nationalism within the novels, considering the influence of each on the development of the literature of the period. According to Harris, cultural nationalism envisions an America of "competing ethnic groups," linking advancement to the ability to organize around clearly defined, shared cultural values, in contrast to revolutionary nationalism, which uses a Marxist critique of the American class problem, casting racism as an obstacle to class struggle.[77] According to Harris, the level of racial consciousness of the situation of black people in America governs characters' responses to their political and social environments.

A heightened racial consciousness was, in the novels and in some circles at the time, equated with greater racial fealty. For some, racial consciousness is determined by the presence of and the ability to manipulate "symbols" of black cultural identity and racial solidarity.[78] Walker criticizes this tendency within "protest literature": "the superficial becomes—for a time—the deepest reality, and replaces the still waters of the collective unconscious."[79] I trace this privileging of the "symbolization of Black culture" back to cultural nationalism through the teachings of Ron Karenga, founder of the US Organization. Karenga advocated establishing parallel black organizations to counter the racist mainstream institutions. However, in the absence of a liberated society, these organizations may impede the development of a liberated consciousness. Harris, more sympathetically, argues that these novels are "shaped" by power and cites "historical understanding" and spirituality as central to navigating one's personal commitment to activism.[80] Harris's treatment of Walker uncovers a more complicated understanding of how the principles of the Civil Rights and Black Power Movements intersect in Walker's novel. His focus on the symbolic representations of black culture does not, however, leave room to consider how the characters are established as models for revolutionary behavior. While I believe historical literacy is necessary for the development of a revolutionary consciousness, it is again only one part of the journey that Meridian undertakes on her route to guerilla subjectivity.

In *Meridian*, Walker goes beyond merely critiquing the Civil Rights Movement or Black Power, suggesting another route to revolutionary social change. I understand Walker as affirming the need for revolution, not dismissing it. Walker underscores this analysis of her purpose, recounting an anecdote about an elderly civil rights activist:

> Someone said recently to an old black lady from Mississippi, whose legs had been badly mangled by local police who arrested her for "disturbing the peace," that the Civil Rights Movement was dead, and asked, since it was dead, what she thought about it. The old lady replied, hobbling out of his presence on her cane, that the Civil Rights Movement was like herself, "if it's dead, it shore ain't ready to lay down!"[81]

Walker's characterization of the Civil Rights Movement reveals various ideologies arising, gaining dominance, and being subsumed in turn like any subdominant social phenomena. In this sense, the movement cannot die. Instead it adapts to the changing social and political pressures presented by disillusioned young African Americans and recalcitrant representatives of the mainstream. In addition to capturing the ideological heterogeneity of the movement, Walker also distinguishes between "true" revolution and "play" revolution. In the chapter entitled "The Conquering Prince," Meridian, already admittedly in love with Truman, sees him standing regally in an "Ethiopian robe." But the text undercuts this majestic pan-African portrait, revealing that Truman "loved all the foreign cultures of the world, but his favorite was French."[82] Years later, Meridian greets Truman after awakening from her post–tank slaying stupor:

> "Why, Che Guevara," she said dreamily then blinked her eyes. "Truman?" [. . .] "You look like Che Guevara. Not," she began, and caught her breath, "not by accident I'm sure." She was referring to his olive-brown skin, his black eyes, and the neatly trimmed beard and mustache he'd

grown since the last time she saw him. He was also wearing a tan cotton jacket of the type worn by Chairman Mao.

"You look like a revolutionary," she said. "Are you?"

"Only if all artists are [. . .]."[83]

The revolutionary "look" that Meridian references was influenced in part by the visual aesthetic of the guerilla transmitted in newspapers like *Gidra* and *The Black Panther*. Pictures of Mao and Che Guevara frequently graced the pages of *The Black Panther*, and both papers frequently invoked Guevara's name in discussions of revolution.

In addition to this imagery, Walker also brings in the rhetoric of revolution through the language of Meridian's fellow Saxonites who hound her: "Will you kill for the revolution?" Meridian, well versed in this rhetoric, cannot bring herself to commit to violence even as she rehearses the revolutionary litany justifying action against "the pigs":

"I know I want what is best for black people . . ."
"That's what we all want!"
"I know there must be revolution . . ."
"Damn straight!"
"I know violence *is* as American as cherry pie!"
"Rap on!"
"I know nonviolence has failed . . ." [84]

Despite having internalized the rhetoric of revolutionary Black Nationalism, Meridian fails as this "type" of revolutionary because she still understands violence as a destructive force and talk as cheap. Even this "talk" can have its consequences, however. The "martyred son" of the "red-eyed" man in the militant church is killed "[f]or his talk alone"—"talk of bullets, of bombs, of revolution."[85] The destruction of Sojourner is another example of the unintended consequences of "talk" and an undisciplined violent ethos. The reactionary mob of Saxonites destroys a potent symbol of the female voice and a totem of female solidarity in a spasm of undirected anger. Thus, the narrative admits what the revolutionaries cannot, that wanton violent action is antiprogress: it leads to the death of the revolutionaries and impedes lasting, systemic change. Likewise, the tank, a symbol of violent repression that stands in Chickokema's square at the beginning of the novel, anchors the town in the past. The specter of violence is insufficient to bring about change or guard against it.

By the end, the text posits a new definition of revolution and the revolutionary. Meridian's new definition crystallizes as she attends services in a radicalized black church. Instead of a portrait of a blond-haired, blue-eyed suffering Christ above the baptismal, a stained glass window features a tall, broad-shouldered black man in a scene entitled "B. B., With Sword." Mixed in with the "amens" are shouts of "We are fed up."[86] The minister evokes the movement, channeling the tone and timbre of Martin Luther King, Jr. His message, however, overturns the conventional wisdom of some black churches, which enforced gender differences, circumscribed the lives of women, and told parishioners to bear patiently the repression of *this* world in exchange for the rewards of the next. Instead, this church advocates a new revolutionary sensibility where suffering and struggle are channeled into outrage, not defeatism and otherworldliness.

This new definition of revolution is predicated on social consciousness, radicalization, grassroots action, and a return "to the people." Undertaking this new revolution would require a guerilla sensibility. After a conversion experience, Meridian leaves the church as a disciple, prepared to embark on a new stage of her journey to revolutionary praxis. Like a guerilla, she has become a solitary agent, racially conscious and ideologically grounded, residing in the communities she serves (although "the weird gal" does have trouble blending in), and subduing her body to her struggle. The novel can, therefore, be read as a chronicle of Meridian's preparation for guerilla action.

The first step in Meridian's journey to guerilla action is becoming aware of the need for revolutionary practice. The bombing of the Freedom Riders awakens Meridian to the struggle for change. Then, she has to fail as the "type" of revolutionary huddled in the Saxon dorm room in order to be able to engage in a new form of revolution. When confronted with the incendiary rhetoric of revolution—"They needed her to kill. To say she would kill."[87]—Meridian is unable to commit to such a nihilistic act, vowing to kill for no purpose. But the death of Wile Chile radicalizes Meridian, leading her to the next step—committing to the struggle for change. By the present of the novel, isolated in her struggle and on her journey, Meridian places herself outside of time: "It was this, Meridian thought, I have not wanted to face, this is what has caused me to suffer: I am not to belong to the future. I am to be left, listening to the old music, beside the highway."[88] While Walker says that she resists labels, she does actively identify herself and her characters with a quest for real revolution, which *is always concerned with the least glamorous stuff.*"[89] This conviction leads Meridian to "go back to the people, live among them, like Civil Rights workers used to do."[90] But it is in the church that Meridian finally reaches a rapprochement with violence: "[S]he understood, finally, that the respect she owed her life was to continue, against whatever obstacles, to live it, and not to give up any particle of it without a fight to the death, preferably *not* her own. . . . [S]he made a promise to the red-eyed man herself: that yes, indeed she *would* kill, before she allowed anyone to murder his son again."[91] In this way, Meridian reserves the right to use violence as a tool to prevent injustice, even as she accepts her position singing behind the "real revolutionaries."

> But at other times her dedication to her promise came back to her strongly. She needed only to see a starving child or attempt to register a grown person who could neither read nor write. On those occasions such was her rage that she actually felt as if the rich and racist of the world should stand in fear of her, because she—though apparently weak and penniless, a little crazy and without power—was yet of a resolute and relatively fearless character, which, sufficient in its calm acceptance of its own purpose, could bring the mightiest country to its knees.[92]

When she despairs, Meridian fears that her reluctance to use violence may prevent her from moving into the future. But when she is dedicated, she understands that her commitment to change is the real revolutionary force that can overthrow an unjust system. Her commitment to change, not the threat of mayhem, is the most effective tool of revolutionary change. This new revolutionary ethos frees Meridian to move forward into the future with a guerilla subjectivity. Having resolved her inner turmoil over the use of violence and relinquished her guilt, fear, and irresolution, Meridian prepares to return to the people as an agent of change, all the while harboring her inner resolve and willingness, if circumstances justify, to kill to prevent the death of innocence or innocents.

The Spook Who Sat by the Door, No-No Boy, and *Meridian* all respond to discourses of power. Each novel should also be understood as an intervention into the discourses of revolution, resistance, and assimilation. While the themes, forms, and settings of the novels vary, each narrative preserves an expression of guerilla subjectivity. From Greenlee's infiltration of the CIA, to Kenji's subversive dismissal of his military service, to Meridian's rewriting of revolutionary strategy, each novel vividly depicts the struggle of individual characters to navigate the politics of personal and ethnic identity from a self-determined subjectivity. Dan Freeman, Ichiro Yamada, and Meridian Hill are all guerillas using guerilla tactics to survive their struggles with American style colonialism and competing ideologies of resistance to emerge with a renewed commitment to the need for systemic change in American culture. These novels become a record of their struggle. In these narratives, we see characters who, through their engagement with militant and military experience, access pan-national discourses of resistance and anti-imperialism. In each, we observe how the guerilla subjectivity develops as a result of the struggle to define self in relationship to the ideology of Power, which privileges self-determination, self-definition, and the commitment to radical social change through individual action.

CHAPTER FIVE

Promise vs. Praxis

The Legacies of Power

> We must cease once and for all to describe the effects of power in negative terms: it 'excludes', it 'represses', it 'censors', it 'abstracts', it 'masks', it 'conceals'. In fact, power produces; it produces reality; it produces domains of objects and rituals of truth. The individual and the knowledge that may be gained of him belong to this production.[1]

For a long time, this project was entitled "The Triumph of Cultural Nationalism: Asian American and African American Nationalism, Colonialism, and the Intersections of Identity Politics and Literary Study, 1967–1983." Yes, I know, long title. But that title represents my anxious attempt to encapsulate all of the political, social, and ideological dynamics I saw shaping the development of African American and Asian American representation in the literature, rhetoric, and media of the Power period. The title was also my attempt to make sense of the tangled link between the political and academic discourses of colonialism. I believed the key to understanding dismissive assessments of the Power period lay in teasing out the link between postcolonialism as political critique and as academic discourse, but the path to that explanation was in no way clear.

Because of this complex legacy, I have been asked again and again, "Why study African American literature and Asian American literature together when the history of those groups in America seems shaped by conflict and antipathy? Why talk about this guerilla? People will just perceive you as an angry young black woman who, having missed the sixties, wants to romanticize a failed revolutionary movement infamous for its misogyny and homophobia. Why a project on such angry literature when it's only bombast and rhetoric anyway? Why? Why? Why?" To various degrees of success, I have tried to answer many of these concerns within the preceding chapters. As I conclude, I will revisit the insights of each chapter, then return to Mae Henderson to reflect on what I consider the implications of my project, not as I conceived it, but as it has come to be.

Initially, this project was concerned with the legacy of power and the ways in which the iconography of Black Power has been appropriated by the "post-soul" generation to signify authentic blackness. Post-soul refers to a theory of cultural transmission, or remixing, developed by Mark Anthony Neal in the 2002 volume *Soul Babies: Black Popular Culture and the Post-Soul Aesthetic*. While Neal makes it perfectly clear that he did not coin the term—Nelson George did so in his 1992 essay collection, *Buppies, B-Boys, Baps and Bohos: Notes on Post-Soul Black Culture*—he does attempt to flesh out the concept, outlining a post-soul aesthetic, or theory of cultural production. According to Neal, this "post-soul imagination" is driven by three critical concerns: "the reconstitution of community, particularly one that is critically engaged with the cultural and political output of black communities; a rigorous form of self and communal critique; and the willingness to undermine or deconstruct the most negative symbols and stereotypes of black life via the use and distribution of those very same symbols and stereotypes."[2] Thus the post-soul is reflexive, celebrating the cultural productions of the black community while critiquing popular cultural consumerist appropriations of those same productions. It is also transformative, constituting a mode of cultural re-production that makes black culture strange and new for ensuing generations. Neal argues that the post-soul allows negotiations of familiar black cultural products, rendering them "unintelligible" to previous generations of activists and scholars, but relevant to contemporary African American youth. In this way, the post-soul functions as a mode of cultural transmission, providing an occasion for empty signifiers like disco, Malcolm X, and James Brown, cliché icons dismissed as worn out and devoid of appreciable meaning, to be imbued with new meaning and significance for later generations.

Thus, "soul" shares many of the qualities of Power and its representative subjectivity, the guerilla. Power acts as a process of transformation and transmission that informs the development of the guerilla, but also the devolution of the guerilla *from* an ideologically grounded, solitary agent, who engages in political and cultural action designed to disrupt oppressive social practices *to* a generalized antagonistic relationship towards American society signified by changes in dress, hair, naming, and other cultural practices. This declension results from the process of transmission, transformation, and reproduction, which eventually stripped the guerilla of its ideological and political specificity.

While I agree with Neal that many scholars of African American literature and culture are invested in limiting and codifying notions of race and ethnicity, his analysis does not differentiate between cultural nationalism, which gave rise to soul, blaxploitation, and Afrocentrism, and revolutionary nationalism, which was summarily dismissed and demonized because of the will to violence and the supposed failure to bring about systemic revolution. In his 2006 *Achieving Blackness*, Algernon Austin finds this a difference without distinction, arguing that cultural nationalism and revolutionary nationalism were similar in structure and scope, both seeking radical cultural change and espousing the fundamental principles of self-determination, self-defense, and self-control of community institutions, among other things. Though I believe that there was a fundamental distinction in how activists of each type pursued these goals, I agree that each strain of nationalism exhibits characteristics of the other. My hope is that this project will help reframe our understanding of revolutionary nationalism in order to intervene in the narratives of failure that shape our remembrances of Power and its antecedents, explaining the fracture and difference produced between nationalisms as a function of the unmooring of these libratory practices from their respective ideological contexts.

In a similar fashion, Manthia Diawara argues for a revised understanding of Black Studies that moves it from victim or oppression models to one that appropriates cultural studies in order to attend to the material, while at the same time embracing a paradigm of performativity. He cautions against adopting an abstract strain of cultural studies that runs the danger of evacuating political significance from categories of race and gender, just as Britishness is articulated through racial "modalities." Instead, Diawara argues for another strain of cultural studies that can be used to move beyond an "emphasis on identity politics," which he considers part of the limiting legacy of "revolutionary struggles."[3] Diawara cites black nationalism as the site for the creation of an aesthetics of "self-determination" recognizable by consumers, both black and nonblack, as "authentic" and "exotic."[4] Ultimately, Diawara advances "performance" as a paradigm for "political representation that enables the actor to occupy a different position in American society, and to interpellate the audience's approval of the new and emerging images of black people."[5] At the same time, he goes on to criticize what he calls "the black good-life society" for producing works indebted to "nationalistic black structures of feeling" that are "regressive" rather than "reflexive."[6] While I share Diawara's frustration, he seems to want it both ways, the ability to identify through performance, while also directing an audience's reception and "reading" of nonessentialist identities. This frustrating gap, praising the ability of the "black good-life society" to fulfill a hunger for "Afro-kitsch," while also criticizing its proponents and producers for being too interested in new iterations of consumable identity, is a sign that the bridge between politics and aesthetics is in need of repair. Unfortunately, Diawara's critique of black nationalism does not differentiate between the strands of ethnic nationalism that were active during the Power period. While self-determination was the ultimate goal of black and yellow nationalists, the means of determining it have more to do with the resulting "authentic" or "exotic" representations than the impulse towards greater agency in the identity formation process.

Indeed, most dismissals of Power stem from a reductive understanding of nationalism within Power ideology. Two strands of nationalism were important during this period: revolutionary nationalism and cultural nationalism.[7] Revolutionary nationalism, promulgated by Huey Newton, whom I consider the chief theorist of the Black Panthers, is based on a socialist dialectical critique of oppression that envisions African Americans and other Americans of color as the foundation for a vanguard that could head up a multiethnic revolutionary coalition dedicated to overturning the American system. Cultural nationalism, best articulated by Maulana Karenga and his US Organization, stressed the development of independent cultural institutions over militant posturing. Looking to Pan-African anticolonialist struggles, cultural nationalists developed an African-inspired belief system that would allow for the development of a liberated consciousness and culture even within the American colonial system. Revolutionary nationalism looked outward, believing that a coalition would have to consist of radical people of many backgrounds (including whites), while cultural nationalism turned inward, believing that the community's energy should focus on shoring up cultural institutions, rather than looking to an uncertain uprising to spark social change. Revolutionary nationalism and cultural nationalism, therefore, envision the route to self-determination in different ways; nonetheless, both point toward radical social change.

For each, the process of achieving self-determination would be revolution. Both revolutionary nationalists and cultural nationalists understood revolution as the process of overthrowing the American racialist system. Revolution then would address the political, artistic, scholastic, and cultural mechanisms of that system. Revolutionary nationalists, drawing on Frantz Fanon's anticolonialist prescription, understood militant struggle as the surest way to overthrow a colonial system and achieve a postcolonial society. In the American context, struggle would entail both political and militant resistance. While the arts also had a role in this struggle, offering up representations of resistance that could radicalize people of color and transmit the principles of revolution, they should not distract from the focus on revolutionary politics. On the other hand, cultural nationalism figured struggle as the effort to establish independent community institutions. According to the tenets of cultural nationalism, these institutions would accomplish revolution through the proliferation of liberated cultural forms. The arts would offer up representations of blackness or yellowness that could then be embraced by the community.

As a result of this cultural nationalist/revolutionary nationalist paradigm, art and literature from the Power period have long been judged according to ideological standards. Most of these assessments considered only how effectively a work advocated for and embodied the principles of revolution. Instead, my investigation of the guerilla aesthetic asks, how does a literary text depict the individual struggle to make sense of and adhere to Power's principles of revolutionary change? Unlike Houston Baker's "Blues" trope, the guerilla is not intended as an explanation of the entire African American or Asian American literary tradition.[8] I see the guerilla as an American adaptation of a global form, a figure that participates in a global discourse of liberation without being totally determined by the global nature of that discourse. By reinstituting an understanding of how these texts were shaped by competing political and social discourses of identity and subjectivity, resistance and revolution, our analysis can extend beyond mere rhetoric to an analysis of how each narrative re-visions the ongoing struggle for liberation.

Just as each text presents a different story of revolution, Black and Yellow Power represent distinct, though related, adaptations of Fanonian anticolonialism in the American context. This shared critique is but one irruption of a transnational AfroAsian discourse of resistance that facilitated cooperation in the struggle to combat oppression at home and abroad.[9] Just as Martin Luther King, Jr., imported the concept of nonviolent resistance from Ghandi's anticolonialist activism against the British occupation of India, black nationalists embraced the struggles of Chinese and Vietnamese socialist revolutionaries and the rhetoric and teachings of Mao to formulate their brand of militancy. In turn, the Black Power ideology crafted by Newton, Cleaver, and others influenced the growth and development of the Asian American Movement and Yellow Power ideology. Young Asian American activists observed Black Power's development as they sought to create their own movement to confront and correct the specifics of Asian American oppression. Understanding anticolonialism as the basis for activism situates the struggle against America's colonial system within shared critiques of similar oppressive systems, while still allowing for local strategies of resistance. As Fanon observed, once the oppressed becomes aware of the effects of colonialism on his life, he would be compelled to overthrow it. The compulsion to freedom, therefore, knows no difference.

In a 1996 special edition of *Callaloo,* Henderson surveys the landscapes of the then emerging field of Black Cultural Studies, laying the foundation for a new methodology for studying black popular culture. While optimistic about the promise of this new field, Henderson warns that an unreflective move towards cultural studies would result in a dangerous dilution of the founding principles of Black Studies in particular and, by implication, Ethnic Studies in general. Like Henderson, I know full well that Black Studies has a complicated legacy, and I agree with her warning against swallowing Black British Cultural Studies whole without attending to the specifics of African American and, in this case, Asian American culture. Henderson goes on to express dismay at "young" critics who dismiss the Black Power moment because of its "essentialism," overlooking a potentially rich source for cultural studies theory. Indeed, as I look back on my project, I see that I am attempting to apply an Ethnic Cultural Studies–inflected lens to the Power moment in an effort to separate the later critiques of Power posturing from its underlying libratory principles. This method, I hope, illuminates the many forces operating on the moment.

Additionally, juxtaposing the African American and Asian American traditions highlights the process of racialization whereby social and ethnic minorities are marginalized and othered. Recognizing the elasticity of this process also throws light on the space that lies between alterity and "difference." In "Two Kinds of Other and Their Consequences," Tim Dean uses a critique of Charles Spinosa and Hubert L. Dreyfus's article "Two Kinds of Antiessentialism and Their Consequences" to restore Lacan's original conception of the "Other" as "not simply language understood as a system of signs or signifiers but also the ontological consequences of linguistic subjectivity."[10] According to Dean, the muddying of "Other" has had the consequence of conflating Otherness with difference and alterity with othering in the service of "celebrating diversity."[11] Rather than make "Otherness" palatable, Dean argues that "the big Other" must be properly understood as embodying an irreducibly antagonistic relationship with the Subject. Therefore, acknowledging how Otherness is instituted between, among, and within so-called minority groups prevents moves to cast difference as novelty, illuminating the array of cultural, political, and linguistic strategies used to enforce and resist difference within the American racial system. Dean concludes that unhooking Otherness from difference would facilitate "cross-dwelling," or antiessentialist pluralism. Complicating the Power period and paralleling Asian American and African American literary traditions during this period also participates in an antiessentialist project by illuminating the array of responses to Power's call for self-definition and self-determination as specific responses to racism in America's social and political systems.

I began with a consideration of the meanings of colonialism, a consideration of how African American and Asian American activists initially adapted the concept of colonialism and how this adaptation led to the consolidation of a "guerilla" figure and aesthetic. My project has been concerned with power: how it was defined, resisted, and critiqued by black and Asian American ethnic revolutionary nationalist activists, media, and scholars. For activists, power was tied to the politics of representation—how people of color were constituted by the American social and political system. In the media, power functions as a ready metaphor for the revolutionary critique of American institutionalized racism, deployed by Black and Yellow Power and embodied in the editorials and images in *The Black Panther* and *Gidra*. In academia, power functions as both access to the legitimating functions of the university and as a critical stance dedicated to bringing the study of African American and Asian American culture into the academy and using the power of the university to benefit those communities. In the literature, the guerilla aesthetic represents an intervention into the discourses of resistance, assimilation, and revolution. From Greenlee's infiltration of the CIA to Kenji's subversive dismissal of his military service to Meridian's rewriting of revolutionary strategy, the novels I've discussed also depict the struggle of individual characters to navigate the politics of personal and ethnic identity. Dan Freeman, Ichiro Yamada, and Meridian Hill use guerilla tactics to reconcile their individual struggles with their motives for revolutionary action, but only Ichiro and Meridian emerge with a renewed commitment to the need for systemic change in American society. Ichiro and Meridian are able to avoid the guerilla's violent end by revising revolution. By understanding violence as a tool for revolution, not the end of revolution, Ichiro and Meridian became a new "type" of revolutionary.

Ultimately, "Power" is about the ability to control the representations of black and yellow people in order to exercise self-determination on behalf of a community created through struggle. In the wake of "backlashes" against Muslim Americans, gays, and antiwar activists, the words of Langston Hughes's 1967 poem seem even more prescient.

>   Mister Backlash, Mister Backlash,
>   Just who do you think I am?
>   You raise my taxes, freeze my wages,
>   Send my son to Vietnam.
>   . . . .
>   But the world is big,
>   Big and bright and round—
>   And it's full of folks like me who are
>   Black, Yellow, Beige, and Brown.
>
>   Mister Backlash, Mister Backlash,
>   What do you think I got to lose?
>   . . . .
>   You're the one
>   Will have the blues.
>   Not me—
>   Wait and see![12]

The anonymous narrator of Hughes's poem seems poised to take up Foucault's admonition that we move beyond negative characterizations of power as a force to be deployed against the marginalized and unruly, and recognize the constitutive nature of power. While Foucault's statement addresses power's ability to determine the individual and his or her reality from without and within, his formulation seems to offer the promise of subjectivity, even within the limits of discipline. This promise also informs the dual message communicated in the narrator's lament. One day, the narrator predicts, Mister Backlash will feel the deconstructive effects of the power he has exploited for so long. In a similar fashion, the guerilla, even with feet of clay, provides the continuing promise of radical change, resistance, and revolution for a world full of folks, "Black, Yellow, Beige, and Brown."

NOTES

Introduction

1. Laura Pulido, *Black, Brown, Yellow and Left: Radical Activism in Los Angeles* (Berkeley: U of California P, 2006) and Daryl Maeda, "Black Panthers, Red Guards, and Chinamen: Constructing Asian American Identity through Performing Blackness, 1969–1972," *American Quarterly* 57.4 (2005): 1079–1103.

2. Vijay Prashad, *Everybody Was Kung Fu Fighting: Afro-Asian Connections and the Myth of Cultural Purity* (Boston: Beacon P, 2002), xii.

3. One indicator of the strength of this metaphor is the surprising number of mentions of "movements" that borrowed or signified upon the name. A review of newspapers in the Alternative Press Collection at the University of California at Santa Barbara revealed mentions of Gay Power, Pussy Power, White Power (a radical leftist version dedicated to building revolutionary coalitions), and Girl Power, as well as the more familiar Red, Yellow, and Brown Power.

4. Robin D. G. Kelley and Betsy Esch, "Black Like Mao: Red China and Black Revolution," in *Afro Asia: Revolutionary Political and Cultural Connections between African Americans and Asian Americans*, ed. Fred Ho and Bill Mullen (Durham, NC: Duke U P, 2008), 100.

5. Stokely Carmichael and Charles Hamilton, *Black Power: The Politics of Liberation in America* (New York: Vintage Books, 1967), 47.

6. Mae Henderson, "'Where, by the Way, Is This Train Going?': A Case for Black (Cultural) Studies." *Callaloo* 19.1 (1996): 60–67.

7. Henderson, 63. For more on Black Studies assessments of British Cultural Studies, see Manthia Diawara, "Cultural Studies/Black Studies," in *Borders, Boundaries, and Frames: Essays in Cultural Criticism and Cultural Studies*, ed. Mae G. Henderson (New York: Routledge, 1995), 202–211, and Houston Baker et al., eds., *Black British Cultural Studies: A Reader* (Chicago: U of Chicago P, 1996).

8. Henderson, 63.

9. For assessments of Asian American studies, see Gary Okihiro et al., *Reflections on Shattered Windows: Promises and Prospects for Asian American Studies* (Pullman, WA: Washington S U P, 1988); Shirley Hune et al., *Asian Americans: Comparative and Global Perspectives* (Pullman, WA: Washington S U P, 1991); Gail M. Nomura, *Frontiers of Asian American Studies: Writing, Research*

and Commentary (Pullman, WA: Washington S U P, 1989); Peter Kiang, "Asian American Studies: Moving into the Third Decade," in *Gidra: Twentieth Anniversary Edition* (Los Angeles: Gidra, 1989); and Lisa Lowe, "Canon, Institutionalization, Identity: Contradictions for Asian American Studies," in *The Ethnic Canon: Histories, Institutions, and Interventions* (Minneapolis: U of Minnesota P, 1995). For assessments of African American Studies, see Houston Baker, "Discovering America: Generational Shifts, Afro-American Literary Criticism, and the Study of Expressive Culture," in *Blues, Ideology and Afro-American Literature* (Chicago: U of Chicago P, 1984), 64–112.

10. Angadipuram Appadorai, *The Bandung Conference* (New Delhi: The Indian Council of World Affairs, 1955).

11. Ibid., 28.

12. Grace Lee Boggs, *Living for Change: An Autobiography* (Minneapolis: U of Minnesota P, 1998). This book chronicles the lives of Boggs and her husband, James "Jimmy" Boggs.

13. Carolyn Skaug, "Black Studies," in *Crisis at San Francisco State* (San Francisco: Insight, 1969), 21–23.

14. For more on AfroAsian Studies, see Bill Mullen's *Afro-Orientalism* (2004); Vijay Prashad, *Everybody Was Kung Fu Fighting* (2002); Daniel Kim, *Writing Manhood in Black and Yellow: Ralph Ellison, Frank Chin, and the Literary Politics of Identity* (2005); and Laura Pulido, *Black, Brown, Yellow, and Left* (2006). See also anthologies such as *AfroAsian Encounters: Culture, History, Politics* (2006), edited by Heike Raphael-Hernandez and Shannon Steen, and *Afro Asia: Revolutionary Political and Cultural Connections Between African Americans and Asian Americans* (2008), edited by Fred Ho and Bill Mullen.

15. James E. Smethurst, *The Black Arts Movement: Literary Nationalism in the 1960s and 1970s* (Chapel Hill: U of North Carolina P, 2005), 4.

16. See, among others, Calvin Hernton, "The Sexual Mountain and Black Women Writers," *Black American Literature Forum* 18.4 (1984): 139–145; Combahee River Collective, "A Black Feminist Statement," in *This Bridge Called My Back: Writings by Radical Women of Color*, ed. Cherríe Moraga and Gloria Anzaldúa (New York: Kitchen Table: Women of Color P, 1981), 210–218; and bell hooks, *Talking Back: Thinking Feminist, Thinking Black* (Boston, MA: South End P, 1989).

17. See, among others, Anthony Appiah, "The Uncompleted Argument: Du Bois and the Illusion of Race," in *"Race," Writing, and Difference*, ed. Henry Louis Gates, Jr. (Chicago: U of Chicago P, 1986), 21–37; Homi Bhabha, "Locations of Culture" and "The Postcolonial and the Postmodern: The Question of Agency," in *The Location of Culture* (New York: Routledge, 1994), 1–27, 245–282;

and Michele Wallace, *Black Macho and the Myth of the Superwoman* (New York: Dial P, 1979).

18. Baker's take on the Black Aesthetic is perhaps most compactly given in "On the Criticism of Black American Literature: One View of the Black Aesthetic," in *Reading Black: Essays in the Criticism of African, Caribbean, and Black American Literature* (Ithaca, NY: Cornell U P, 1976).

19. For a seminal study of the NAACP's role in the making of the Civil Rights Movement, see Patricia Sullivan, *Lift Every Voice: The NAACP and the Making of the Civil Rights Movement* (New York: The New Press, 2009). This reappraisal places pressure on the critical assumption that Black Power constitutes a radical break from the nonviolent, integrationist imperatives of the Civil Rights Movement.

20. Smethurst, 15.

21. Dubey, 2, 4.

22. Pulido, 21.

23. Maeda, 1081–1082.

24. Kwame Anthony Appiah, *In My Father's House: Africa in the Philosophy of Culture* (New York: Oxford U P, 1992), 149.

25. Sara Suleri, *Meatless Days* (Chicago: U of Chicago P, 1989), 105. She elaborates on a similar link between the subaltern woman and the postmodern in "Woman Skin Deep: Feminism and the Postcolonial Condition," *Critical Inquiry* 18 (Su 1992): 756–69.

26. Appiah, 139.

27. Abdul JanMohamed, "Worldliness-Without-World, Homelessness-as-Home: Toward a Definition of the Specular Border Intellectual," in *Edward Said: A Critical Reader*, ed. Michael Spinker (Cambridge, MA: Blackwell, 1992), 96–120.

28. Hortense Spillers, "Mama's Baby, Papa's Maybe," *Diacritics: A Review of Contemporary Criticism* 17.2 (1987): 67.

29. Maulana Karenga, *Introduction to Black Studies* (Inglewood, CA: Kawaida, 1982); Addison Gayle, Jr., *Black Expression: Essays By and About Black Americans in the Creative Arts* (New York: Weybright and Tally, 1969) and *The Black Aesthetic* (Garden City, NY: Anchor Books, 1972); and Larry Neal, "The Black Arts Movement," *Tulane Drama Review* 12.4 (Su 1968): 29–39.

30. Bobby Seale, *Seize the Time: The Story of the Black Panther Party and Huey P. Newton* (New York: Random House, 1970), 179.

31. William Wei, *The Asian American Movement* (Philadelphia: Temple UP, 1993), 102.

32. Ibid., 103.

33. Ibid., 105.

34. Lisa Lowe, "Heterogeneity, Hybridity, Multiplicity: Making Asian American Difference," in *Immigrant Acts: On Asian American Cultural Politics* (Durham, NC: Duke U P, 1996), 60–83; and Paul R. Spickard, "What Must I Be? Asian America and the Question of Multiethnic Identity," in *Asian American Studies: A Reader*, eds. Jean Yu-wen Shen Wu and Min Song (New Brunswick, NJ: Rutgers U P, 2000).

35. Richard Barksdale and Keneth Kinnamon, eds., *Black Writers of America* (New York: Macmillan, 1972), 34.

36. S. X. Goudie, "Theory, Practice and the Intellectual: A Conversation with Abdul R. JanMohamed," *Jouvert* 1.2 (1997): para 46.

37. For more on the critical conundrum in African American literary studies, see Sandra Adell, "The Crisis in Black American Literary Criticism and the Postmodern Cures of Houston A. Baker, Jr. and Henry Louis Gates, Jr.," in *African American Literary Theory: A Reader*, ed. Winston Napier (New York: New York U P, 2000), 523–539.

Chapter One

1. Frantz Fanon, *Black Skin, White Masks* (New York: Grove P, 1967), 14.

2. Ibid., 11.

3. Peniel E. Joseph, *Waiting 'til the Midnight Hour: A Narrative History of Black Power in America* (New York: Holt, 2006), 209.

4. James Forman, *The Making of Black Revolutionaries* (New York: Macmillan, 1972), xii.

5. Irene Gendzier, *Frantz Fanon: A Critical Study* (New York: Pantheon, 1973), 156, 161.

6. Ibid., 36; Alice Cherki, *Frantz Fanon: A Portrait*, trans. Nadia Benabid (Ithaca, NY: Cornell U P, 2006), 196–197.

7. Information about the publication dates of Fanon's works seems to be muddled because of the multiple translations and reprints. My chronology of his American editions was compiled using information from several biographies and reference works: Peter Geismer, *Fanon*; Alice Cherki, *Frantz Fanon: A Portrait*; Aristide Zolberg, "Frantz Fanon: A Gospel for the Damned"; *Book Review Index: A Master Cumulation, 1965–1984*; and *Book Review Digest 1965, 1967, and 1968*.

8. Gendzier, 262–263.

9. William Buchanan, ed., *Combined Retrospective Index to Book Reviews in Scholarly Journals, 1886–1974* (Arlington, VA: Carrollton P, 1980), 16; Stanley

Schindler, ed., *Combined Retrospective Index to Book Reviews in Scholarly Journals, 1886–1974* (Woodbridge, CT: Research Pub, 1983), 94; Gary Tarbert and Barbara Beach, *Book Review Index: A Master Cumulation, 1965–1984* (Detroit: Gayle Research, 1985), 1609.

10. Frantz Fanon, *The Wretched of the Earth*, trans. Constance Farrington (New York: Grove P, 1963), back cover.

11. "Prisoner of Hate," *Time*, 30 April 1965: 114.

12. "The Neurosis of Colonialism," *The Nation*, 21 June 1965: 675.

13. Emile Capouya, "Time to Turn a Tide of Violence," *Saturday Review*, 24 April 1965: 34.

14. Irene Gendzier, "Frantz Fanon: In Search of Justice," *The Middle East Journal* 20.4 (1966): 534.

15. Ibid., 544.

16. Ibid., 534.

17. Calvin Sinnette, "The Nature of Revolution," *Freedomways: A Quarterly Review of the Negro Freedom Movement* 4.3 (1964): 446.

18. Ibid.

19. Russ Stetler, "The Works of Frantz Fanon," *Bulletin: University of Chicago Students for a Democratic Society Newsletter*, 8 April 1966: 4. Rpt. *Liberation USA*.

20. Fanon, *The Wretched of the Earth*, 190.

21. Ibid., 33.

22. Ibid., 130.

23. Ibid., 170.

24. Ibid., 32.

25. Saul Maloff, "Vicious Circle," *Newsweek*, 24 April 1967: 100–102.

26. Kwame Ture (formerly Stokely Carmichael) and Charles V. Hamilton, *Black Power: The Politics of Liberation in America* (1967; New York: Vintage, 1992), 5.

27. Ibid.

28. Ibid., 46.

29. Ibid., 5.

30. Similarly, Goldberg in "In/Visibility and Super/Vision: Fanon and Racial Formation," examines tropes of invisibility and visibility in Fanon to argue for invisibility as a strategy for resistance, a way to escape "supervision" for black intellectuals. Theo Goldberg, *Racial Subjects* (New York: Routledge, 1997), 79–108.

31. Carmichael and Hamilton, 44.

32. Maxwell Geismar, "Introduction," Eldridge Cleaver, *Soul on Ice* (New York: Ramparts P, 1967), 9.

33. Cleaver, *Soul on Ice*, 64.

34. "Letter to [unreadable]", Eldridge Cleaver Papers, BANC MSS 91/213 c, The Bancroft Library, University of California, Berkeley.

35. Eldridge Cleaver, *Post-Prison Writings and Speeches*, ed. Robert Scheer (New York: Random House, 1969), 61.

36. Cleaver, *Soul on Ice*, 66.

37. Ibid., 67.

38. Ibid., 125.

39. Ibid., 116.

40. Ibid., 117.

41. Ibid., 118–119.

42. Warren Furutani, "The Warren Report 1990," in *Asian Americans: The Movement and the Moment*, ed. Steve Louie and Glenn K. Omatsu (Los Angeles: UCLA Asian American Studies Center P, 2001), 65.

43. Examples: "A Note to Black Nationalists," editorial, *Gidra* [Los Angeles], Nov. 1969: 13; "Asians Support Panthers," editorial, *Gidra* [Los Angeles], May 1970: 4.

44. Amy Uyematsu, "The Emergence of Yellow Power in America," *Gidra* [Los Angeles] Oct. 1969: 8.

45. Ibid., 8–9.

46. Ibid., 10.

47. David Hsin-Fu Wand, ed., *Asian American Heritage: An Anthology of Prose and Poetry* (New York: Washington Square P, 1974), 21.

48. Ibid.

49. Larry Kubota, "Yellow Power," *Gidra* [Los Angeles], 10 Oct. 1973: 3.

50. Ibid., 4.

51. Uyematsu, 10.

52. Franklin Odo, Preface, *Roots: An Asian American Reader*, ed. Amy Takachi et al. (Los Angeles: Continental Graphics, 1971), ix.

53. Ibid.

54. Kubota, 3.

55. Michael Omi and Howard Winant, *Racial Formation in the United States: From the 1960s to the 1980s* (New York: Routledge and Kegan Paul, 1986).

56. For William Petersen's original definition of this phenomenon, see "Success Story, Japanese American Style," *New York Times Magazine*, 20 Jan. 1966: 20. For more about the legacy of this issue, see Frank Wu, *Yellow: Race in America Beyond Black and White* (New York: Basic, 2002).

57. Keith Osajima, "Asian Americans as the Model Minority: An Analysis of the Popular Press Image in the 1960s and the 1980s," in *Reflections on Shattered Windows: Promises and Prospects for Asian American Studies*, ed. Gary Y. Okihiro et al. (Pullman: Washington State U P, 1988), 166.

58. Ibid., 165.

59. Uyematsu, 8.

60. Ibid., 10.

61. Osajima, 167.

62. Uyematsu, 10.

63. Daniel Okimoto, *American in Disguise* (1970; New York: Walker/Weatherhill, 1971), 5.

64. Ibid., 147.

65. Fanon, *Black Skin, White Masks*, 232.

66. Okimoto, 206.

67. Henry Louis Gates, Jr., "Critical Fanonism," *Critical Inquiry* 17: 3 (1991): 458.

68. Ibid.

69. Diana Fuss, *Identification Papers* (New York: Routledge, 1995).

70. Gates, 469.

71. Ibid., 470.

72. Cedric Robinson, "The Appropriation of Frantz Fanon," *Race & Class* 35.1 (1993): 87.

73. For more on Fanon's slipperiness examined through a Creole context, see Francoise Verges, "Creole Skin, Black Mask: Fanon and Disavowal," *Critical Inquiry* 23 (1997.)

74. Posnock, 325–326.

75. Fanon, *The Wretched of the Earth*, 73.

76. Ibid., 190.

77. Carmichael and Hamilton, 34.

78. Judith Butler, *The Psychic Life of Power: Theories in Subjection* (Palo Alto, CA: Stanford U P, 1997).

79. Cleaver, *Post-Prison Writings and Speeches,* 18.

80. Cleaver, *Soul on Ice*, 90–91.

81. Cleaver, *Post-Prison Writings and Speeches*, 20.

82. Ibid.

83. Cleaver, *Soul on Ice,* 123.

84. Ibid., 121.

85. King, 86.

86. Cleaver, "The Black Man's Stake in Vietnam," in *Soul on Ice*, 121–127.

87. Deanna Lee, "Interview with Bobby Seale," *Gidra* [Los Angeles], June/July 1970: 14.

88. Ibid.

89. Cleaver, *Soul on Ice*, 75.

90. Ibid.

91. Martin Luther King, Jr., *Where Do We Go from Here: Chaos or Community?* (Boston: Beacon P, 1968), 55.

92. Ibid., 66.

93. In his comprehensive work *The Black Arts Movement: Literary Nationalism in the 1960s and 1970s*, James Smethurst touches on the relationship between the Black Power Movement and the Asian American Movement. Smethurst does not mention Yellow Power, but he does acknowledge the existence of a derivative Asian American activism that he attributes more to "post civil rights movement nationalism" than any previous "civil rights activities and organizations" (288).

94. Hortense Spillers, "Mamma's Baby, Papa's Maybe," *Diacritics: A Review of Contemporary Criticism* 17.2 (1987): 67.

95. Carolyn Marie Cusick, "Fanon's Black Skin, White Masks on Race Consciousness," *AmeriQuests* 4.1 (2007): 11.

96. Carmichael and Hamilton, 179.

97. Ibid., 55.

98. Ibid., 39.

Chapter 2

1. See Edmund T. Gordon, "Cultural Politics of Black Masculinity," *Transforming Anthropology* 6.1–2 (1997): 36–53; Maurice Wallace, *Constructing the Black Masculine* (Durham, NC: Duke U P, 2002); William L. Van DeBurg, *Hoodlums: Black Villains and Social Bandits in American Life* (Chicago: U of Chicago P, 2004).

2. W. E. B. Du Bois, "Tribute," *The Black Panther* [Berkeley] 4 Jan. 1969: 17.

3. W. E. B. Du Bois, *The Souls of Black Folk* (1903; New York: Signet, 1969), 54.

4. See also Walter Laquer, ed., *The Guerilla Reader: A Historical Anthology* (New York: New American Library, 1977); Robert Moss, *Urban Guerillas: The New Face of Political Violence* (London: Temple Smith, 1972); William McNaughton, ed. and trans., *Guerrilla War* (Oberlin, OH: Crane P, 1970); Mao Tse-tung, *On Practice: On the Relation Between Knowledge and Practice—Between Knowing and Doing* (Peking: Foreign Languages P, 1958); Charles W. Thayer, *Guerilla* (New York: Harper and Row, 1963); John Ellis, *A Short History of Guerilla War-*

fare (New York: St. Martin's P, 1976); Mao Tse-tung, *Selected Military Writings of Mao Tse-tung* (Peking: Foreign Languages P, 1963).

5. Arthur Frazier, "A Note to Black Nationalists," *Gidra*, Nov. 1969: 13.

6. Du Bois, *The Souls of Black Folk*, 45.

7. Stuart Hall, "The Spectacle of the Other," in *Representations: Cultural Representations and Signifying Practices*, ed. Stuart Hall (London; Thousand Oaks, CA: Sage, 1997).

8. Fanon, *Black Skin, White Masks*, 109.

9. Louis Althusser, *Lenin and Philosophy and Other Essays,* trans. Ben Brewster (New York: Monthly Review P, 1971), 73.

10. Ibid., 174.

11. "Guerra," *Concise Oxford Spanish Dictionary*, 1995 ed.

12. "Guérilla," *Concise Oxford French Dictionary*, 1995 ed.

13. "Guerilla," 1989 ed., Oxford English Dictionary online, 2 May 2003, http://dictionary.oed.com/cgi/entry/00099964.

14. Robert Taber, *War of the Flea: A Study of Guerilla Warfare Theory and Practice* (New York: Lyle Stuart, 1965), 156.

15. "Guerra."

16. "Guerilla."

17. Taber, 12.

18. Ibid., 152.

19. "The Nature of Guerilla Warfare," *The Black Panther* [Berkeley], 20 April 1969: 20.

20. Mao Tse-tung, *On Guerilla Warfare*, trans. Samuel B. Griffith (New York: Frederick A. Praeger, 1961).

21. Cleaver, *Post-Prison Writings and Speeches*, 37.

22. Mao, 53.

23. Ibid., 54.

24. Ibid., 92.

25. Ibid., 88.

26. Ibid.

27. In 1972, the Party Program and Platform were changed to more accurately reflect the evolution of Panther ideology from a purely nationalist socialism to a Marxist-Leninist approach opposed to imperialism, capitalism, and exploitators of any color. Points 6 and 10 were deleted and 3, 7, 8, and 9 were changed to reflect the broader nature of the socialist struggle.

28. "October 1966 Black Panther Party Platform and Program," *The Black Panther* [Berkeley], 4 Jan. 1969: 21.

29. Ibid.

30. Bobby Seale, *Seize the Time: The Story of the Black Panther Party and Huey P. Newton* (New York: Random House, 1970), 63.

31. "October 1966 Black Panther Party Platform and Program," 21.

32. Harries-Clinchy Peterson, *Che Guevara on Guerilla Warfare* (New York: Frederick A. Praeger, 1961), 33.

33. Taber, 7.

34. Ibid., 154.

35. Peterson, 32.

36. Ibid., 9.

37. Ibid., 43.

38. Regis Debray, *Revolution in the Revolution?: Armed Struggle and Political Struggle in Latin America* (New York: Monthly Review P, 1967), 47.

39. Weusi, "For Black Guerillas," *Soulbook* 2 (1969), 183.

40. Ibid., 186.

41. Taber, 14.

42. Ibid.

43. Cleaver, *Soul on Ice*, 147.

44. Ibid., 146.

45. Bobby Seale recounts the definition of a "freak" as defined by Huey Newton as the people that "get enjoyment by watching what he's [the geek, or a social outcast] doing *because he has to*"(my emphasis). Seale, *Seize the Time*, 184.

46. Alan Nishiro, "The Oriental as a Middleman Minority," *Gidra*, May 1969: 3.

47. Ibid.

48. Elaine H. Kim, *Asian American Literature: An Introduction to the Writings and Their Social Context* (Philadelphia: Temple U P, 1982), 173.

49. Jeffrey Paul Chan and Frank Chin, "Racist Love," in Richard Kostelanetz, ed., *Seeing through Schuck* (New York: Ballentine Books, 1972). Qtd. in Elaine H. Kim, *Asian American Literature: An Introduction to the Writings and Their Social* Context (Philadelphia: Temple U P, 1982), 179.

50. Daryl J. Maeda, "Black Panthers, Red Guards, and Chinamen: Constructing Asian American Identity through Performing Blackness, 1969–1972," *American Quarterly* 57.4 (2005): 1079–1103.

51. "October 1966 Black Panther Party Platform and Program," 21.

52. Seale, *Seize the Time*, 115.

53. "We Want All Black Men to Be Exempt from Military Service," cartoon, *The Black Panther* [Berkeley], 4 May 1968: 9.

54. Bobby Seale, "Black Soldiers as Revolutionaries to Overthrow the Ruling Class," *The Black Panther* [Berkeley], 20 Sept. 1969: 2.

55. "Editorial Statement," *The Black Panther* [Berkeley], 2 Feb. 1969: 5.

56. Christian A. Davenport, "Reading the 'Voice of the Vanguard': A Content Analysis of The Black Panther Intercommunal News Service, 1969–1973," in *The Black Panther Party Reconsidered*, ed. Charles E. Jones (Baltimore: Black Classics P, 1998), 195.

57. Ibid., 115.

58. Nelson Nagai, "I Come from a Yellow Seed," in *Asian Americans: The Movement and the Moment*, ed. Steve Louie and Glenn K. Omatsu (Los Angeles: UCLA Asian American Studies Center P, 2001), 255.

59. Yen Le Espiritu, *Asian American Panethnicity: Bridging Institutions and Identities* (Philadelphia: Temple U P, 1992), 38.

60. Emory Douglas, "In Revolution One Wins, or One Dies." *The Black Panther*, 27 Apr. 1969: back cover.

61. I use the term "otherwordly" to denote a theological orientation that implies that all injuries and injustices would be resolved in the coming world under Christ. Early in the Civil Rights Movement, many religious leaders discouraged active resistance because "the battle is not ours, but the Lord's." Liberatory theology countered this view and endorsed demonstrations citing Christ as the ultimate example of a revolutionary. See also C. Eric Lincoln and Lawrence Mamiya, *The Black Church in the African American Experience* (Durham: Duke U P, 1990).

62. Larry Kubota, "Yellow Power," *Gidra* [Los Angeles], 10 Oct. 1973: 3.

63. Taber, 171.

64. Ibid.

65. Ibid.

66. Frantz Fanon, *A Dying Colonialism*, trans. Haakon Chevalier (New York: Grove P, 1965), 6.

67. Althusser, 167.

68. Ibid., 165.

69. Ibid., 11.

70. Ibid.

71. Ibid., 170.

72. Judith Butler, *The Psychic Life of Power: Theories in Subjection* (Stanford, CA: Stanford U P, 1997), 2.

73. Homi Bhabha, "Signs Taken for Wonders," in *"Race," Writing, and Difference*, ed. H. L. Gates, Jr. (Chicago: U of Chicago P, 1986), 163–184.

74. The events of 9/11/01 are also examples of how ideology can lead to

violence. While I would not want to endorse the violence of the 9/11 hijackers, it would be disingenuous to deny that the figure of the guerilla, as I conceive of it, could encompass figures like them. Indeed, the 9/11 hijackers considered their strike a blow against a symbol of their understanding of America and the evil it represented in their ideology. This uncomfortable juxtaposition with the hijackers also highlights what I consider the fatal flaw in the guerilla subjectivity. If the guerilla's purpose is to struggle, then he has to engage in ever-greater all-encompassing struggles in order to remain coherent.

75. Phillip Brian Harper, "Nationalism and Social Division in Black Arts Poetry of the 1960s," in *African American Literary Theory: A Reader*, ed. Winston Napier (New York: New York U P, 2000), 464.

Chapter 3

1. Abdul JanMohamed, "Worldliness Without World, Homelessness as Home," 96–120.

2. Fabio Rojas, *From Black Power to Black Studies: How a Radical Social Movement Became an Academic Discipline* (Baltimore: Johns Hopkins U P, 2007), 44.

3. Robert Dale Parker, "Material Choices: American Fictions, the Classroom, and the Post-Canon," *American Literary History* 5 (1993): 92.

4. Sandra Hollin Flowers, *African American Nationalist Literature of the 1960s: Pens of Fire* (New York: Garland, 1996) 131. Flowers asserts that novel-length fiction was the least preferred medium for nationalist writers, because the length of time it took to write and publish a book would hamper an author's ability to respond to current events. I would argue that, first, the period of consideration for nationalistic fiction should be extended well beyond the 1960s. Second, the definition of nationalistic fiction should be extended to include any work that deals with the issues of radical ethnic politics. Even black authors like Alice Walker, Toni Morrison, and Ishmael Reed show nationalist concerns and attempts to negotiate racial identity, even as they critique the Black Power project.

5. Gary Y. Okihiro, "Education for Hegemony, Education for Liberation," *Ethnic Studies: Vol. I—Cross Cultural, Asian and Afro-American Studies* (New York: Markus Wiener, 1989), 5.

6. Yuri Kochiyama, "'Because Movement Work Is Contagious': Reflections of Yuri Kochiyama," *Gidra: Twentieth Anniversary Edition* (Los Angles: Gidra, 1989), 4.

7. Okihiro, 5.

8. Asian American Political Alliance, "To All Asian Students," in *Asian*

Americans: The Movement and the Moment, ed. Steve Louie and Glenn Omatsu (Los Angeles: UCLA Asian American Studies Center P, 2001), 187–189.

9. Richard Gambino, *A Guide to Ethnic Studies Programs in American Colleges, Universities and Schools* (New York: Rockefeller Foundation, 1975).

10. Henry Louis Gates, Jr. *Loose Canons: Notes on the Culture Wars* (New York: Oxford U P, 1992), 21, 32.

11. Ibid., 76.

12. Michael Bérubé, *Marginal Forces/Cultural Centers: Tolson, Pynchon, and the Politics of the Canon* (Ithaca, NY: Cornell U P, 1992), 52. He articulates these modes of representation as being employed by Melvin Tolson and Thomas Pynchon in their constructions of "the agents and institutions of cultural reproduction" (52).

13. Paul Lauter, "Race and Gender in the Shaping of the American Literary Canon: A Case Study from the Twenties," in *Feminist Criticism and Social Change: Sex, Class, and Race in Literature and Culture*, ed. Judith Newton and Deborah Rosenfelt (New York: Methuen, 1985), 109.

14. Ibid., 23.

15. Ibid., 26.

16. Ibid., 19.

17. Ibid., 28.

18. Ibid.

19. Paul Lauter, "The Literatures of America: A Comparative Discipline," in *Redefining American Literary History*, ed. A. LaVonne Brown Ruoff and Jerry W. Ward (New York: MLA, 1990), 22.

20. John Guillory, "Canonical and Non-Canonical: A Critique of the Current Debate," ELH 54.3 (1987): 483.

21. Ibid., 494.

22. Ibid., 486.

23. Ibid., 483.

24. Homi K. Bhabha, *The Location of Culture* (New York: Routledge, 1994), 51.

25. Stuart Hall, "The Spectacle of the Other," in *Representation: Cultural Representations and Signifying Practices*, ed. Stuart Hall (Thousand Oaks, CA: Sage, 1997), 225–238.

26. David Palumbo-Liu, "The Ethnic as 'Post-': Reading *Reading the Literatures of Asian America*," *American Literary History*, 1 (1995): 161.

27. Lisa Lowe, *Immigrant Acts* (Durham: Duke U P, 1996), 52.

28. Ibid., 56.

29. Amiri Baraka, Foreword, in *Black Fire: An Anthology of Afro-American Writing*, ed. Amiri Baraka and Larry Neal (New York: William Morrow, 1968), xvii.

30. Larry Neal, "And Shine Swam On," in *Black Fire: An Anthology of Afro-American Writing*, ed. Baraka and Neal, 638.

31. Baraka, xvii.

32. Ibid., xvii.

33. Neal, 649–650.

34. Ibid., 648–649.

35. Ibid., 655.

36. Ahmed Al Hamisi and Harun Kofi Wangara, eds., *Black Arts: An Anthology of Black Creations* (Detroit: Black Arts, 1969).

37. Keorapetse Kgositsile, Introduction, in *Black Arts: An Anthology of Black Creations*, ed. Ahmed Al Hamisi and Harun Kofi Wangara (Detroit: Black Arts, 1969), 15.

38. Ibid.

39. Ibid., 16.

40. Ibid.

41. James A. Emanuel and Theodore L. Gross, eds., *Dark Symphony: Negro Literature in America* (New York: Macmillan, 1971), ix–x.

42. Ibid., 2.

43. Ibid.

44. Richard Barksdale and Keneth Kinnamon, eds., *Black Writers of America* (New York: Macmillan, 1972), xi.

45. Ibid., 34.

46. Ibid., xi.

47. Ibid.

48. William Adams, *Afro-American Authors* (Boston: Houghton Mifflin, 1972), 2.

49. Ibid., 2–3.

50. Jeffrey Paul Chan et al., eds., *AIIIEEEEE!: An Anthology of Asian-Amercan Writers* (Washington, D. C.: Howard U P, 1974), viii.

51. Ibid., xxxvi.

52. Ibid., viii–ix.

53. Ibid., xvi.

54. M. M. Bakhtin, "Discourse in the Novel," in *The Dialogic Imagination*, ed. Michael Holquist (Austin: U of Texas P, 1981), 291.

55. Ibid.

56. Shirley Geok-lin Lim, "The Ambivalent American: Asian American Literature on the Cusp," in *Reading the Literatures of Asian America*, ed. Shirley Geok-lin Lim and Amy Ling (Philadelphia: Temple U P, 1992), 23.

57. Elaine Kim, *Asian American Literature: An Introduction to the Writings and Their Social Contexts* (Philadelphia: Temple U P, 1982), xv.

58. Ibid., xi–xii.

59. Ishmael Reed, "Crushing the Mutiny," *MELUS* 3.2 (1976): 10–12.

60. Ishmael Reed, "Introduction, I," *Yardbird* 1 (1972), xix.

61. Ishmael Reed, "Integration or Cultural Exchange," *Yardbird* 5 (1976), 3.

62. Ishmael Reed, Preface, in *Yardbird Lives!*, ed. Ishmael Reed and Al Young (New York: Grove P, 1978), 14.

63. Ishmael Reed, "Back Cover," *Yardbird* 3 (1974), back cover.

64. Frank Chin and Shawn Hsu Wong, "Introduction to Yardbird Publishing #3," *Yardbird* 3 (1974): vii.

65. Ibid., iv.

66. Ibid., iv,v.

67. Frank Chin, Afterword, *MELUS* 3.2 (1976): 16.

68. Jeffrey F. L. Partridge and Shawn Wong, "Aiiieeeee! and the Asian American Literary Movement: A Conversation with Shawn Wong," *MELUS* 29.3/4 (2004): 94.

69. Frank Chin and Shawn Wong, "Introduction to Yardbird Reader #3," vi.

70. Ibid., iv.

71. Jeffrey Paul Chan and Frank Chin, "Racist Love," in *Seeing through Schuck*, ed. Richard Kostelanetz (New York: Ballentine Books, 1972). Qtd. in Elaine H. Kim, *Asian American Literature: An Introduction to the Writings and Their Social Context* (Philadelphia: Temple U P, 1982), 179.

72. Chan and Chin, 178.

73. Daniel Y. Kim, *Writing Manhood in Black and Yellow: Ralph Ellison, Frank Chin and the Literary Politics of Identity* (Stanford, CA: Stanford U P, 2005), 207.

74. Ibid., 207.

75. Werner Soller, "A Critique of Pure Pluralism," in *Reconstructing American Literary History*, ed. Sacvan Bercovitch (Cambridge, MA: Harvard U P, 1986), 275.

76. Harold H. Kolb, Jr., "Defining the Canon," in *Redefining American Literary History*, ed. A LaVonne Brown Ruoff and Jerry W. Ward (New York: MLA, 1990), 39.

Chapter 4

1. Larry Neal, "Black Art and Black Liberation," in *The Black Revolution: An Ebony Special Issue* (Chicago: Johnson, 1970), 31–54.

2. Huey Newton, "Statement," *The Black Panther* [Berkeley], 10 April 1971: 2.

3. Huey Newton, "Black Capitalism Re-Analyzed," *The Black Panther* [Berkeley], 5 June 1971: 9.

4. Larry Neal, "The Black Arts Movement," in *Norton Anthology of African American Literature*, ed. Henry Louis Gates, Jr., and Nellie Y. McKay (New York: Norton, 1997), 1960.

5. Ibid., 1960.

6. Ibid., 1961.

7. Haki R. Madhubuti, "The Long Reality," in *Norton Anthology of African American Literature*, ed. Gates, Jr., and McKay, 1979.

8. Houston Baker describes a trope as "the type of image or model that is always present in accounts of culture and cultural productions." Houston Baker, *Blues, Ideology, and Afro-American Literature: A Vernacular Theory* (Chicago: The University of Chicago P, 1984), 9.

9. Greenlee, 28.

10. Ibid., 247.

11. Ibid., 61.

12. Ibid., 64.

13. Ibid., 28.

14. Ibid.

15. "Spook," *The Cassell Dictionary of Slang*, ed. Jonathan Green (London: Cassell, 1998).

16. Frantz Fanon, *A Dying Colonialism,* trans. Haakon Chevalier (1959; New York: Grove P, 1965).

17. Greenlee, 32.

18. Robert A. Gross, "The Black Novelists: 'Our Turn,'" *Newsweek*, 16 June 1969: 98.

19. As opposed to "apologist protest" literature. Schraufnagel distinguishes between an outwardly directed literature of justification and an inwardly directed literature of instruction depicting deliberate action. Noel Schraufnagel, *From Apology to Protest: The Black American Novel* (Deland, FL: Everett/Edwards, 1973); David Pryce-Jones, "First Novels," *Punch*, 30 April 1969: 657.

20. Schraufnagel, 171.

21. Sandra Hollin Flowers, *African American Nationalist Literature of the 1960s: Pens of Fire* (New York: Garland, 1996), 145.

22. "The Spook Who Sat by the Door," review of *The Spook Who Sat by the Door* by Sam Greenlee, *Publishers' Weekly*, 6 Oct. 1969: 50.

23. Gross, 98.

24. Lottie Joiner, "After 30 Years, A Controversial Film Re-Emerges," *Crisis* (Nov./Dec. 2003): 41. In the 1971 "Rappin' with Sam Greenlee" article, Greenlee talks about his desire to do a film because "since their invention, they've been one of the most important means of perpetuating the white supremacy myth." (In the same article, he dismisses writing for TV—"because it is a fantasy medium and fantasy is not my bag"—but went on to enjoy a long career in directing for TV shows like *The Waltons* and *Magnum, P.I.*)

25. Walter Burrell, "An Interview: Rappin' with Sam Greenlee," *Black World* 20.9 (July 1971): 43.

26. Kenneth Graham, "Dandies and the Deluge," *The Listener*, 20 March 1969: 396.

27. Paul Kiniery, review of *The Spook Who Sat by the Door* by Sam Greenlee, *Best Sellers*, 15 Nov. 1969: 324–325.

28. David Pryce-Jones, "First Novels," *Punch*, 30 April 1969: 657.

29. Review of *The Spook Who Sat by the Door* by Sam Greenlee, *Times Literary Supplement*, 4 March 1969: 372.

30. Review of *The Spook Who Sat by the Door* by Sam Greenlee, *Booklist*, 15 Dec. 1969: 494.

31. Ibid.

32. Ibid.

33. Michel Foucault, "Two Lectures: Lecture One: 7 January 1976," *Power/Knowledge: Selected Interviews and Other Writings, 1972–1977* (1977; New York: Pantheon, 1981), 105.

34. Michel Foucault, *The Archaeology of Knowledge and the Discourse on Language*, trans. A. M. Sheridan Smith (New York: Pantheon, 1972).

35. Foucault, "Two Lectures," 98.

36. Ibid., 99, 101.

37. Ibid., 98.

38. Ibid.

39. John Okada, *No-No Boy* (1957; Seattle: U of Washington P, 1976), 15–16.

40. Ibid., 229–232.

41. Ibid., 73.

42. Ibid., 60.

43. Ibid., 163.

44. Ibid., 254.

45. Shirley Geok-Lin Lim, "Twelve Asian American Writers: In Search of Self-Definition," *MELUS* 13:1–2 (1986): 63.

46. Ibid.

47. Jinqi Ling, "Race, Power, and Cultural Politics in John Okada's *No-No Boy*," *American Literature* 67.2 (1995): 360.

48. Ibid., 361.

49. Jeffrey Paul Chan et al., *The Big AIIIEEEEE!: An Anthology of Chinese American and Japanese American Literature* (New York: Meridian, 1991), xiv.

50. Frank Chin, "Come All Ye Asian American Writers of the Real and the Fake," in *The Big AIIIEEEEE!: An Anthology of Chinese American and Japanese American Literature*, 18.

51. Ibid., 11.

52. Ling, 363–364.

53. Lim, 63.

54. Chin, 14.

55. Okada, 163.

56. Ibid., 164.

57. Ibid.

58. Ibid., 62.

59. Ibid., 232.

60. Ibid., 250.

61. Ibid.

62. Ibid., 251.

63. Ibid., 250.

64. Marge Piercy, review of *Meridian* by Alice Walker, *The New York Times Book Review*, 23 May 1976: 5.

65. Virginia Marr, review of *Meridian* by Alice Walker, *Library Journal*, 1 May 1976: 1145.

66. Margo Jefferson, review of *Meridian* by Alice Walker, *Newsweek*, 31 May 1976: 71.

67. Ibid.

68. Karen Stein, "*Meridian*: Alice Walker's Critique of Revolution," *Black American Literature Forum* 20.1/2 (Sp–Su 1986): 131.

69. Ibid., 129.

70. Ibid., 136.

71. Ibid., 141.

72. Susan Willis, *Specifying: Black Women Writing the American Experience* (Madison: U of Wisconsin P, 1987), 116.

73. Ibid., 120, 111.

74. Joseph Brown, "'All Saints Should Walk Away': The Mystical Pilgrimage of Meridian," *Callaloo* 12 (1989): 321–331.

75. Deborah E. McDowell, "New Directions for Black Feminist Criticism," *Black American Literature Forum* 14:4 (1980): 157.

76. Roberta Hendrickson, "Remembering the Dream: Alice Walker, *Meridian*, and the Civil Rights Movement," *MELUS* 24:3 (1999): 111–128.

77. Norman Harris, *Connecting Times: The Sixties in Afro-American Fiction* (Jackson: U P of Mississippi, 1988) 92.

78. Ibid., 93.

79. John O'Brien, "Alice Walker: An Interview," in *Alice Walker: Critical Perspectives Past and Present*, ed. Henry Louis Gates, Jr., and K. Anthony Appiah (New York: Amistad, 1993), 339.

80. Harris, 95–96.

81. Alice Walker, "The Civil Rights Movement: What Good Was It?" in *In Search of Our Mothers' Gardens* (1967; New York: Harcourt Brace Jovanovich, 1983), 119–120.

82. Alice Walker, *Meridian* (New York: Washington Square P, 1976), 99.

83. Ibid., 24.

84. Ibid., 27.

85. Ibid., 196.

86. Ibid.

87. Ibid., 30.

88. Ibid., 201.

89. Alice Walker, "Duties of the Black Revolutionary Artist," in *In Search of Our Mothers' Gardens*, 135.

90. Walker, *Meridian* 31.

91. Ibid., 200.

92. Ibid., 201.

Chapter 5

1. Michel Foucault, *Discipline and Punish: The Birth of the Prison* (1977; New York: Pantheon, 1979), 194.

2. Mark Anthony Neal, *Soul Babies: Black Popular Culture and the Post-Soul Aesthetic* (New York: Routledge, 2002), 120.

3. Manthia Diawara, "Cultural Studies/Black Studies," in *Borders, Boundaries, and Frames: Essays in Cultural Criticism and Cultural Studies,* ed. Mae G. Henderson (New York: Routledge, 1995), 204.

4. Ibid., 210, 207.

5. Ibid., 210.

6. Ibid.

7. Algernon Austin, *Achieving Blackness: Race, Black Nationalism, and Afrocentrism in the Twentieth Century* (New York: New York U P, 2006).

8. Houston Baker, *Blues, Ideology, and Afro-American Literature: A Vernacular Theory* (Chicago: U of Chicago P, 1984).

9. Ross visits the idea of "borrowing" strategies from other political movements. According to Ross, the white homosexual community sought "to establish a permanent viable, open culture virtually from scratch against the grain of oppression and obscurity the long history of African American culture had to provide a valuable resource for a homosexual consciousness in search of ways to consolidate and mobilize a fragmented, distorted, hidden protoculture." Ross argues that the white homosexual community appropriated the civil rights strategies of African Americans and succeeded in creating a powerful political identity where blacks couldn't. This was due in part to the voluntary nature of the homosexual identity for the upwardly mobile white middle-class community that Ross describes. Marlon B. Ross, "Some Glances of the Black Fag," *African American Literary Theory*, ed. Winston Napier (New York: New York U P, 2002), 498–522.

10. Tim Dean, "Two Kinds of Other and Their Consequences," *Critical Inquiry* 23.4 (1997): 919.

11. Ibid., 912.

12. Langston Hughes, *The Panther and the Lash: Poems of Our Times* (New York: Knopf, 1967).

BIBLIOGRAPHY

Adams, William. *Afro-American Authors*. Boston: Houghton Mifflin, 1972.

Adell, Sandra. "The Crisis in Black American Literary Criticism and the Postmodern Cures of Houston A. Baker, Jr. and Henry Louis Gates, Jr." In *African American Literary Theory: A Reader*, edited by Winston Napier. New York: New York U P, 1992.

Alhamisi, Ahmed, and Harun Kofi Wangara, eds. *Black Arts: An Anthology of Black Creations*. Detroit: Black Arts P, 1969.

Althusser, Louis. *Lenin and Philosophy and Other Essays*. Translated by Ben Brewster. New York: Monthly Review P, 1971.

Appadorai, Angadipuram. *The Bandung Conference*. New Delhi: The Indian Council of World Affairs, 1955.

Appiah, K. Anthony. "The Uncompleted Argument: Du Bois and the Illusion of Race." In *"Race," Writing, and Difference*, edited by Henry Louis Gates, Jr. Chicago: U of Chicago P, 1986.

———. *In My Father's House: Africa in the Philosophy of Culture*. New York: Oxford U P, 1992.

Asian American Political Alliance. "To All Asian Students." In *Asian Americans: The Movement and the Moment*, edited by Steve Louie and Glenn K. Omatsu. Los Angeles: UCLA Asian American Studies Center P, 2001.

Austin, Algernon. *Achieving Blackness: Race, Black Nationalism, and Afrocentrism in the Twentieth Century*. New York: New York U P, 2006.

Baker, Houston A., Jr. *Blues, Ideology, and Afro-American Literature: A Vernacular Theory*. Chicago: U of Chicago P, 1984.

———, ed. *Three American Literatures: Essays in Chicano, Native American, and Asian-American Literature for Teachers of American Literature*. New York: MLA, 1982.

Baker, Houston A., Jr., and Patricia Redmond, eds. *Afro-American Literary Study in the 1990s*. Chicago: U of Chicago P, 1989.

Bakhtin, M. M. "Discourse in the Novel." In *The Dialogic Imagination*, edited by Michael Holquist. Austin: U of Texas P, 1981.

Baraka, Amiri. *Blues People: The Negro Experience in White America and the Music that Developed from It*. New York: Morrow Quill, 1963.

Baraka, Amiri, and Larry Neal, eds. *Black Fire: An Anthology of Afro-American Writing*. New York: William Morrow, 1968.

Barksdale, Richard K. *Praisesong of Survival: Lectures and Essays, 1957–89*. Urbana: U of Illinois P, 1992.

Barksdale, Richard, and Keneth Kinnamon, eds. *Black Writers of America*. New York: Macmillan, 1972.

Bercovitch, Sacvan, ed. *Reconstructing American Literary History*. Cambridge, MA: Harvard U P, 1986.

Bérubé, Michael. *Marginal Forces/Cultural Centers: Tolson, Pynchon, and the Politics of the Canon*. Ithaca: Cornell U P, 1992.

Bhabha, Homi K. *The Location of Culture*. New York: Routledge, 1994.

———. "Signs Taken for Wonders." In *"Race," Writing, and Difference*, edited by Henry Louis Gates, Jr. Chicago: U of Chicago P, 1986.

Boggs, Grace Lee. *Living for Change: An Autobiography*. Minneapolis: U of Minnesota P, 1998.

Bontemps, Arna, ed. *American Negro Poetry*. New York: Hill and Wang, 1963.

Brawley, Benjamin, ed. *Early Negro American Writers*. Chapel Hill: U of North Carolina P, 1935.

Brown, Joseph. "'All Saints Should Walk Away': The Mystical Pilgrimage of Meridian." *Callaloo* 12 (Spring 1989): 310–320.

Buchanan, William, ed. *Combined Retrospective Index to Book Reviews in Scholarly Journals, 1886–1974*. Arlington, VA: Carrollton P, 1980.

Burrell, Walter. "An Interview: Rappin' with Sam Greenlee." *Black World* 20 (1971): 42–47.

Butler, Judith. *Gender Trouble: Feminism and the Subversion of Identity*. New York: Routledge, 1990.

———. *The Psychic Life of Power: Theories in Subjection*. Stanford: Stanford U P, 1997.

Capouya, Emile. "Time to Turn a Tide of Violence." *Saturday Review*, 24 April 1965: 34.

Cartoon. *The Black Panther*. 4 January 1969: 8.

Cartoon. *The Black Panther*. 7 June 1969: 18.

Cartoon. *The Black Panther*. 20 September 1969: 2.

Cartoon. *Gidra*. April 1970: 9.

Cartoon. *Gidra*. May 1971: front cover.

Carmichael, Stokely. *Stokely Speaks: Black Power to Pan-Africanism*. 1965; New York: Random House, 1971.

Carmichael, Stokely, and Charles Hamilton. *Black Power: The Politics of Liberation in America*. New York: Vintage Books, 1967.

Chan, Jeffery Paul et al., eds. *AIIIEEEEE!: An Anthology of Asian-American Writers*. Washington, D. C.: Howard U P, 1974.

———. *The Big AIIIEEEEE!: An Anthology of Chinese American and Japanese American Literature*. New York: Meridian, 1991.

Chan, Jeffrey Paul, and Frank Chin. "Racist Love." In *Seeing through Schuck*, edited by Richard Kostelanetz. New York: Ballentine Books, 1972. Qtd. in Elaine H. Kim, *Asian American Literature: An Introduction to the Writings and Their Social Context*. Philadelphia: Temple U P, 1982.

Cherki, Alice. *Frantz Fanon: A Portrait*. Translated by Nadia Benabid. Ithaca, NY: Cornell U P, 2006.

Cheung, King-Kok, ed. *An Interethnic Companion to Asian American Literature*. New York: Oxford U P, 1997.

Chin, Frank. "Come All Ye Asian American Writers of the Real and the Fake." In *The Big AIIIEEEEE!: An Anthology of Chinese American and Japanese American Literature*, edited by Jeffrey Paul Chan et al. New York: Meridian, 1991.

———. "Afterword." *MELUS* 3.2 (1976): 16.

———, and Shawn Wong. "Introduction to Yardbird Reader #3," *Yardbird* 3 (1974): vi.

Cleaver, Eldridge. "Letter to [unreadable]." Eldridge Cleaver Papers, BANC MSS 91/213 c, The Bancroft Library, University of California, Berkeley.

———. *Post-Prison Writings and Speeches*. Edited by Robert Scheer. New York: Ramparts P, 1969.

———. *Soul on Ice*. New York: Ramparts, 1967.

Cruse, Harold. *The Crisis of the Black Intellectual*. New York: William Morrow and Co., 1967.

Cusick, Carolyn Marie. "Fanon's Black Skin, White Masks on Race Consciousness." *AmeriQuests* 4.1 (2007): 11.

Davenport, Christian A. "Reading the 'Voice of the Vanguard': A Content Analysis of The Black Panther Intercommunal News Service, 1969–1973." In *The Black Panther Party Reconsidered*, edited by Charles E. Jones. Baltimore: Black Classics P, 1998.

Dean, Tim. "Two Kinds of Other and Their Consequences." *Critical Inquiry* 23.4 (1997): 910–920.

Debray, Regis. *Revolution in the Revolution?: Armed Struggle and Political Struggle in Latin America*. New York: MR Press, 1967.

Diawara, Manthia. "Cultural Studies/Black Studies." In *Borders, Boundaries, and Frames: Essays in Cultural Criticism and Cultural Studies*, edited by Mae G. Henderson. New York: Routledge, 1995.

Di Pietro, Robert J., and Edward Ifkovic, eds. *Ethnic Perspectives in American Literature: Selected Essays on the European Contribution*. New York: Modern Language Association, 1983.

Douglas, Emory. "In Revolution One Wins, or One Dies." Cartoon. *The Black Panther.* 27 April 1969: back cover.

Du Bois, W. E. B. *The Souls of Black Folk.* 1903. New York: Signet, 1969.

———. "Tribute." *The Black Panther.* 4 Jan. 1969: 17.

"Editorial Statement." *The Black Panther.* 2 Feb. 1969: 5.

Edwards, Audrey. "Blackpower." *Vibe Magazine* (Sept 2002): 188.

Ellis, John. *A Short History of Guerilla Warfare.* New York: St. Martin's P, 1976.

Emanuel, James A., and Theodore L. Gross, eds. *Dark Symphony: Negro Literature in America.* New York: Macmillan, 1971.

Espiritu, Yen Le. *Asian American Panethnicity: Bridging Institutions and Identities.* Philadelphia: Temple U P, 1992.

Fanon, Frantz. *Black Skin, White Masks.* New York: Grove P, 1967.

———. *A Dying Colonialism.* Translated by Haakon Chevalier. 1959; New York: Grove P, 1965.

———. *Toward the African Revolution.* Translated by Haakon Chevalier. 1964; New York: Grove P, 1967.

———. *The Wretched of the Earth.* Translated by Constance Farrington. New York: Grove P, 1963.

Flowers, Sandra Hollin. *African American Nationalist Literature of the 1960s: Pens of Fire.* New York: Garland P, 1996.

Forman, James. *The Making of Black Revolutionaries.* New York: Macmillan, 1972.

Foucault, Michel. "Two Lectures: Lecture One: 7 January 1976." *Power/Knowledge: Selected Interviews and Other Writings, 1972–1977.* 1977; New York: Pantheon, 1981.

———. *The Archaeology of Knowledge & the Discourse on Language.* Translated by A. M. Sheridan Smith. 1969; New York: Pantheon, 1972.

———. *Discipline and Punish: The Birth of the Prison.* 1977; New York: Pantheon, 1979.

Frazier, Arthur. "A Note to Black Nationalists." *Gidra.* Nov. 1969:13.

Furutani, Warren. "The Warren Report 1990." In *Asian Americans: The Movement and the Moment,* edited by Steve Louie and Glenn K. Omatsu. Los Angeles: UCLA Asian American Studies Center P, 2001.

Fuss, Diana. *Identification Papers.* New York: Routledge, 1995.

Gambino, Richard. *A Guide to Ethnic Studies Programs in American Colleges, Universities and Schools.* New York: The Rockefeller Foundation, 1975.

Gates, Henry Louis, Jr. "Canon-Formation, Literary History, and the Afro-American Tradition: From the Seen to the Told." In *Afro-American Literary*

Study in the 1990s, edited by Houston A. Baker, Jr., and Patricia Redmond. Chicago: U of Chicago P, 1989.

———. "Critical Fanonism." *Critical Inquiry* 17:3: 457–470.

———. *Loose Canons: Notes on the Culture Wars*. New York: Oxford U P, 1992.

——— et al., eds. *The Norton Anthology of African American Literature*. New York: W. W. Norton and Co., 1997.

———. "Whose Canon Is It, Anyway." In *Debating P. C.: The Controversy Over Political Correctness on College Campuses*, edited by Paul Berman. New York: Laurel, 1992.

Gayle, Addison, Jr. *The Black Aesthetic*. Garden City, NY: Anchor Books, 1972.

———. *Black Expression: Essays By and About Black Americans in the Creative Arts*. New York: Weybright and Tally, 1969.

Geismar, Peter. *Fanon*. New York: Dial P, 1971.

Gendzier, Irene. *Frantz Fanon: A Portrait*. Translated by Nadia Benabid. Ithaca, NY: Cornell U P, 2006.

———. "Frantz Fanon: In Search of Justice." *The Middle East Journal* 20.4 (1966): 534.

Goldberg, Theo. *Racial Subjects*. New York: Routledge, 1997.

Gordon, Edmund T. "Cultural Politics of Black Masculinity." *Transforming Anthropology* 6.1–2 (1997): 36–53.

Goudie, S. X. "Theory, Practice and the Intellectual: A Conversation with Abdul R. JanMohamed." *Jouvert* 1.2 (1997): para 46.

Graham, Kenneth. "Dandies and the Deluge." *The Listener*. 20 March 1969: 396.

Greenlee, Sam. *The Spook Who Sat by the Door*. 1969; Detroit: Wayne S U P, 1990.

Gross, Robert A. "The Black Novelists: 'Our Turn.'" *Newsweek*. 16 June 1969: 98.

"Guerilla." *Oxford English Dictionary Online*. 2nd ed. April 2003. http://www.oed.com.

"Guérilla." *Concise Oxford French Dictionary*, 1995 ed.

"Guerre." *Oxford English Dictionary Online*. 2nd ed. April 2003. http://www.oed.com.

Guillory, John. "Canonical and Non-Canonical: A Critique of the Current Debate." *ELH* 54.3 (1987): 483–526.

———. *Cultural Capital*. Chicago: U Chicago P, 1993.

Hagedorn, Jessica. *Charlie Chan Is Dead: An Anthology of Contemporary Asian American Fiction*. New York: Penguin, 1993.

Hall, Stuart. "The Spectacle of the Other." In *Representation: Cultural Repre-

sentations and Signifying Practices, edited by Stuart Hall. Thousand Oaks, CA: Sage, 1997.

Hamisi, Ahmed Al, and Harun Kofi Wangara, eds. *Black Arts: An Anthology of Black Creations*. Detroit: Black Arts Pub., 1969.

Harper, Phillip Brian. *Framing the Margins: The Social Logic of Postmodern Culture*. New York: Oxford U P, 1994.

———. "Nationalism and Social Division in Black Arts Poetry of the 1960s." *Critical Inquiry* 19.2 (1993): 234–255.

Harris, Norman. *Connecting Times: The Sixties in Afro-American Fiction*. Jackson: U P of Mississippi, 1988.

Haslam, Gerald W. "The Subtle Thread: Asian-American Literature." *Arizona Quarterly* 25 (1969): 197–208.

Heath, G. Louis, ed. *Off the Pigs: The History and Literature of the Black Panther Party*. Metuchen, NJ: Scarecrow P, 1976.

Henderson, Mae. "'Where, by the Way, Is This Train Going?': A Case for Black (Cultural) Studies." *Callaloo* 19.1 (1996): 60–67.

Hendrickson, Roberta. "Remembering the Dream: Alice Walker, *Meridian*, and the Civil Rights Movement." *MELUS* 24:3 (Autumn 1999): 111–128.

Hernton, Calvin C. *The Sexual Mountain and Black Women Writers*. New York: Doubleday, 1987.

Hill, Patricia Liggins et al., eds. *Call and Response: The Riverside Anthology of the African American Literary Tradition*. New York: Houghton Mifflin Co., 1998.

Hong, Maria, ed. *Growing Up Asian American: An Anthology*. New York: William Morrow and Co., 1993.

hooks, bell. *Talking Back: Thinking Feminist, Thinking Black*. Boston, MA: South End P, 1989.

Hsaing, Bob. "Growing Up in Turmoil: Thoughts on the Asian American Movement."In *Asian Americans: The Movement and the Moment*, edited by Steve Louie and Glenn K. Omatsu. Los Angeles: UCLA Asian American Studies Center P, 2001.

Hughes, Langston. "The Backlash Blues." *The Panther and the Lash*. New York: Knopf, 1967.

Hull, Gloria et al. "Toward a Black Feminist Criticism." In *All the Women Are White, All the Blacks Are Men, But Some of Us Are Brave: Black Women's Studies*. Old Westbury, New York: The Feminist P, 1979.

Hune, Shirley et al. *Asian Americans: Comparative and Global Perspectives*. Pullman, WA: Washington S U P, 1991.

Inge, M. Thomas. "Artistic Merit and Ethnic Literature." *MELUS* 3.1 (1976): 6–7.

JanMohamed, Abdul R. "The Economy of Manichean Allegory: The Function of Racial Difference in Colonialist Literature." In *"Race," Writing, and Difference*, edited by Henry Louis Gates, Jr. Chicago: U of Chicago P, 1986.

———. "Worldliness-Without-World, Homelessness-as-Home: Toward a Definition of the Specular Border Intellectual." In *Edward Said: A Critical Reader*, edited by Michael Spinker. Cambridge, MA: Blackwell, 1992.

JanMohamed, Abdul R., and David Lloyd, eds. *The Nature and Context of Minority Discourse*. New York: Oxford U P, 1990.

Jefferson, Marge. Untitled *Newsweek* review, 31 May 1976, 71.

Johnson, Charles S., ed. *Ebony and Topaz*. 1927. Freeport, New York: Books for Libraries P, 1971.

Joiner, Lottie. "After 30 Years, A Controversial Film Re-Emerges." *Crisis* (Nov./Dec. 2003): 41.

Jones, Charles. "Reconsidering Panther History: The Untold Story." In *The Black Panther Party Reconsidered*, edited by Charles Jones. Baltimore: Black Classic P, 1998.

Karenga, Maulana. *Introduction to Black Studies*. Inglewood, CA: Kawaida, 1982.

Kelley, Robin D. G. *Freedom Dreams: The Black Radical Imagination*. Boston: Beacon P, 2002.

Kelley, Robin D. G., and Betsy Esch. "Black Like Mao: Red China and Black Revolution." In *Afro Asia: Revolutionary Political and Cultural Connections between African Americans and Asian Americans*, edited by Fred Ho and Bill Mullen. Durham, NC: Duke U P, 2008.

Kelly, Ernece B., ed. *Searching for America*. Urbana: National Council of Teachers of English, 1972.

Kgositsile, Keorapetse. "Introduction." In *Black Arts: An Anthology of Black Creations*, edited by Ahmed Al Hamisi and Harun Kofi Wangara. Detroit: Black Arts Pub., 1969.

Kiang, Peter. "Asian American Studies: Moving into the Third Decade." In *Gidra: Twentieth Anniversary Edition*. Los Angeles: Gidra, 1989.

Kim, Daniel Y. *Writing Manhood in Black and Yellow: Ralph Ellison, Frank Chin and the Literary Politics of Identity*. Stanford, CA: Stanford U P, 2005.

Kim, Elaine. *Asian American Literature: An Introduction to the Writings and Their Social Contexts*. Philadelphia: Temple U P, 1982.

King, Martin Luther, Jr. *Where Do We Go from Here: Chaos or Community?* Boston: Beacon P, 1968.

Kiniery, Paul. "Rev. of *The Spook Who Sat by the Door*." *Best Sellers*, 15 Nov. 1969: 324–325.

Kochiyama, Yuri. "'Because Movement Work is Contagious': Reflections of Yuri Kochiyama." *Gidra: Twentieth Anniversary Edition*. Los Angeles: Gidra, 1989.

Kolb, Harold H., Jr. "Defining the Canon." In *Redefining American Literary History*, edited by A. LaVonne Brown Ruoff and Jerry W. Ward. New York: Modern Language Association, 1990.

Kopley, Richard, ed. *Prospects for the Study of American Literature: A Guide for Scholars and Students*. New York: New York U P, 1997.

Koshy, Susan. "The Fiction of Asian American Literature." *The Yale Journal of Criticism* 9 (1996): 315–346.

Kubota, Larry. "Yellow Power." *Gidra* [Los Angeles], 10 Oct. 1973: 3.

Laquer, Walter, ed. *The Guerilla Reader: A Historical Anthology*. New York: New American Library, 1977.

Lauter, Paul. "The Literatures of America: A Comparative Discipline." In *Redefining American Literary History*, edited by A. LaVonne Brown Ruoff and Jerry W. Ward. New York: Modern Language Association, 1990.

———. "Race and Gender in the Shaping of the American Literary Canon: A Case Study from the Twenties." In *Feminist Criticism and Social Change: Sex, Class and Race in Literature and Culture*, edited by Judith Newton and Deborah Rosenfelt. New York: Methuen, 1985.

———, ed. *Reconstructing American Literature: Courses, Syllabi, Issues*. New York: Feminist P, 1983.

Lee, Deanna. "Interview with Bobby Seale." *Gidra* [Los Angeles], June/July 1970: 14.

Lim, Elaine. *Asian American Literature: An Introduction to the Writings and Their Social Contexts*. Philadelphia: Temple U P, 1982.

Lim, Shirley Geok-lin. "The Ambivalent American: Asian American Literature on the Cusp." In *Reading the Literatures of Asian America*, edited by Shirley Geok-lin Lim and Amy Ling. Philadelphia: Temple U P, 1992.

———. "Twelve Asian American Writers: In Search of Self-Definition." *MELUS* 13: 1–2 (Sp-Su 1986): 57–77.

Lim, Shirley Geok-lin, and Amy Ling, eds. *Reading the Literatures of Asian America*. Philadelphia: Temple U P, 1992.

Lincoln, C. Eric, and Lawrence Mamiya. *The Black Church in the African American Experience*. Durham: Duke U P, 1990.

Ling, Jinqi. "Race, Power, and Cultural Politics in John Okada's *No-No Boy*." *American Literature* 67.2 (June 1995): 360.

Locke, Alain, ed. *The New Negro*. 1925; New York: Atheneum, 1968.

Lowe, Lisa. *Immigrant Acts*. Durham: Duke U P, 1996.

——. "Canon, Institutionalization, Identity: Contradictions for Asian American Studies." In *The Ethnic Canon: Histories, Institutions, and Interventions*, edited by David Palumbo-Liu. Minneapolis: U of Minnesota P, 1995.

Madhubuti, Haki R. "The Long Reality." In *The Norton Anthology of African American Literature*, 2nd ed., edited by Henry L. Gates et al. New York: Norton, 2002.

Maeda, Daryl J. "Black Panthers, Red Guards, and Chinamen: Constructing Asian American Identity through Performing Blackness, 1969–1972." *American Quarterly* 57:4 (2005): 1079–1103.

Maitino, John R., and David R. Peck, eds. *Teaching American Ethnic Literatures: Nineteen Essays*. Albuquerque: U of New Mexico P, 1996.

Maloff, Saul. "Vicious Circle." *Newsweek*, 24 April 1967: 100–102.

Marr, Virginia. "Untitled Review of *Meridian*." *Library Journal* (1 May 1976): 1145.

McDowell, Deborah E. "New Directions for Black Feminist Criticism." *Black American Literature Forum*, 14:4 (Winter 1980): 157.

McNaughton, William, ed. and trans. *Guerrilla War*. Oberlin, OH: Crane P, 1970.

Miller, Ruth, ed. *Blackamerican Literature, 1760–Present*. Beverly Hills: Glencoe Press, 1971.

Moraga, Cherríe, and Gloria Anzaldúa, eds. *This Bridge Called My Back: Writings by Radical Women of Color*. New York: Kitchen Table: Women of Color P, 1981.

Moss, Robert. *Urban Guerillas: The New Face of Political Violence*. London: Temple Smith, 1972.

Mullen, Bill. *Afro-Orientalism*. Minneapolis: U of Minnesota P, 2004.

Nagai, Nelson. "I Come from a Yellow Seed." In *Asian Americans: The Movement and the Moment*, edited by Steve Louie and Glenn K. Omatsu. Los Angeles: UCLA Asian American Studies Center P, 2001.

"The Nature of Guerilla Warfare." *The Black Panther* [Berkeley], 20 April 1969: 20.

Neal, Larry. "And Shine Swam On." In *Black Fire: An Anthology of Afro-American Writing*, edited by Amiri Baraka and Larry Neal. New York: William Morrow, 1968.

——. "Black Art and Black Liberation." In *The Black Revolution: An Ebony Special Issue*. Chicago: Johnson, 1970.

——. "The Black Arts Movement." In *Norton Anthology of African American Literature*, edited by Henry Louis Gates, Jr., and Nellie Y. McKay. New York: Norton, 1960.

Neal, Mark Anthony. *Soul Babies: Black Popular Culture and the Post-Soul Aesthetic*. New York: Routledge, 2002.

"The Neurosis of Colonialism." *The Nation*. 21 June 1965: 675.

Newton, Huey. "Black Capitalism Re-Analyzed." *The Black Panther* [Berkeley]. 5 June 1971: 9.

———. "The Correct Handling of Revolution." *The Black Panther* [Berkeley]. 20 April 1969: 3.

———. "Statement." *The Black Panther* [Berkeley]. 10 April 1971: 2.

Nishio, Alan. "The Oriental as a Middleman Minority." *Gidra* [Los Angeles]. May 1969: 3.

Nomura, Gail M. *Frontiers of Asian American Studies: Writing, Research and Commentary*. Pullman, WA: Washington S U P, 1989.

O'Brien, John. "Alice Walker: An Interview." In *Alice Walker: Critical Perspectives Past and Present*, edited by Henry Louis Gates, Jr., and K. Anthony Appiah. New York: Amistad, 1993.

"October 1966 Black Panther Party Platform and Program." *The Black Panther*. 4 Jan. 1969: 21.

Odo, Franklin. "Preface." In *Roots: An Asian American Reader*, edited by Amy Takachi et al. Los Angeles: Continental Graphics, 1971.

Ogbar, Jeffrey O. G. *Black Power: Radical Politics and African American Identity*. Baltimore: Johns Hopkins U P, 2004.

Okada, John. *No-No Boy*. 1957; Seattle: U of Washington P, 1976.

Okihiro, Gary Y. "Education for Hegemony, Education for Liberation." *Ethnic Studies: Vol. I—Cross Cultural, Asian and Afro-American Studies*. New York: Markus Wiener Pub., 1989.

Okihiro, Gary Y. et al. *Reflections on Shattered Windows: Promises and Prospects for Asian American Studies*. Pullman, WA: Washington S U P, 1988.

Okimoto, Daniel. *American in Disguise*. 1970; New York: Walker/Weatherhill, 1971.

Olaniyan, Tejumola. "African American Critical Discourse and the Invention of Cultural Identities." *African American Review* 26.4 (1992): 533–545.

Omi, Michael, and Howard Winant. *Racial Formation in the United States: From the 1960s to the 1980s*. New York: Routledge and Kegan Paul, 1986.

Osajima, Keith. "Asian Americans as the Model Minority: An Analysis of the Popular Press Image in the 1960s and the 1980s." In *Reflections on Shattered Windows: Promises and Prospects for Asian Americans Studies*, edited by Gary Y. Okihiro et al. Pullman, WA: Washington State U P, 1988.

Palumbo-Liu, David. Introduction. *The Ethnic Canon: Histories, Institutions, and Interventions*. Minneapolis: U of Minnesota P, 1995.

———. "The Ethnic as 'Post-': Reading *Reading the Literatures of Asian America*." *American Literary History* 7 (1995): 161–168.
Parker, Robert Dale. "Material Choices: American Fictions, the Classroom, and the Post-Canon." *American Literary History* 5 (1993): 89–100.
Partridge, Jeffrey F. L., and Shawn Wong. "Aiiieeeee! and the Asian American Literary Movement: A Conversation with Shawn Wong." *MELUS* 29.3/4 (2004): 94.
Peterson, Harries-Clinchy. *Che Guevara on Guerrilla Warfare*. New York: Frederick Praeger, 1961.
Peterson, William. "Success Story, Japanese American Style." *New York Times Magazine*, 20 Jan. 1966: 20.
Piercy, Marge. "Review of *Meridian*." *The New York Times Book Review*, 23 May 1976: 5.
Prashad, Vijay. *Everybody Was King Fu Fighting: Afro-Asian Connections and the Myth of Cultural Purity*. Boston: Beacon P, 2002.
"Prisoner of Hate." *Time*, 30 April 1965: 114.
Pryce-Jones, David. "First Novels." *Punch*. 30 April 1969: 657.
Pulido, Laura. *Black, Brown, Yellow, and Left: Radical Activism in Los Angeles*. Berkeley: U of California P, 2006.
Quinn, Arthur Hobson, ed. *The Literature of the American People: An Historical and Critical Survey*. New York: Appleton-Century-Crofts, Inc., 1951.
Reed, Ishmael. Foreword. In *Literary Mosaic Series: Asian American Literature*, edited by Shawn Wong. New York: Harper Collins, 1996.
———. "Back Cover." *Yardbird* 3 (1974) back cover.
———. "Crushing the Mutiny." *MELUS* 3.2 (1976):10–12.
———. "Integration or Cultural Exchange." *Yardbird* 5 (1976): 3.
———. "Introduction, I." *Yardbird* 1 (1972): xix.
———. "Preface." In *Yardbird Lives!*, edited by Ishmael Reed and Al Young New York: Grove P, 1978.
Review of *The Spook Who Sat by the Door* by Sam Greenlee. *Times Literary Supplement*, 4 March 1969: 372.
Review of *The Spook Who Sat by the Door* by Sam Greenlee. *Booklist*, 15 Dec. 1969: 494.
Robinson, Cedric. "The Appropriation of Frantz Fanon." *Race & Class* 35.1 (1993): 87.
Rojas, Fabio. *From Black Power to Black Studies: How a Radical Social Movement Became an Academic Discipline*. Baltimore: Johns Hopkins U P, 2007.
Rose, Tricia. *Black Noise: Rap Music and Black Culture in Contemporary America*. Hanover: Wesleyan P, 1996.

Ross, Marlon B. "Some Glances of the Black Fag." In *African American Literary Theory*, edited by Winston Napier. New York: New York U P, 2002.

Ruoff, A. LaVonne Brown, and Jerry W. Ward, Jr., eds. *Redefining American Literary History*. New York: The Modern Language Association of America, 1990.

Rustin, Bayard. "Means to an End: Strategy and Tactics." In *The Black Revolt and Democratic Politics*, edited by Sondra Silverman. Lexington, MA: D. C. Heath and Co., 1970.

Schindler, Stanley, ed. *Combined Retrospective Index to Book Reviews in Scholarly Journals, 1886–1974*. Woodbridge, CT: Research Pub., 1983.

Schraufnagel, Noel. *From Apology to Protest: The Black American Novel*. DeLand, FL: Everett/Edwards, Inc., 1973.

Seale, Bobby. "Black Soldiers as Revolutionaries to Overthrow the Ruling Class." *The Black Panther* [Berkeley]. 20 Sept. 1969: 2.

———. *Seize the Time: The Story of the Black Panther Party and Huey P. Newton*. New York: Random House, 1970.

Singh, Nikhil Pal. "The Black Panthers and the 'Undeveloped Country' of the Left." In *The Black Panther Party Reconsidered*, edited by Charles E. Jones. Baltimore: Black Classic P, 1998.

Sinnette, Calvin. "The Nature of Revolution." *Freedomways: A Quarterly Review of the Negro Freedom Movement* 4.3 (1964): 446.

Skaug, Carolyn. "Black Studies." In *Crisis at San Franciso State*. San Francisco: Insight, 1969.

Smethurst, James E. *The Black Arts Movement: Literary Nationalism in the 1960s and 1970s*. Chapel Hill: U of North Carolina P, 2005.

Smithson, Isaiah, and Nancy Ruff, eds. *English Studies/Culture Studies: Institutionalizing Dissent*. Urbana: U of Illinois P, 1994.

Sollers, Werner. "A Critique of Pure Pluralism." In *Reconstructing American Literary History*, edited by Sacvan Bercovitch. Cambridge, MA: Harvard U P, 1986.

Spickford, Paul R. "What Must I Be? Asian America and the Question of Multiethnic Identity." In *Asian American Studies: A Reader*, edited by Jean Yuwen Shen Wu and Min Song. New Brunswick, NJ: Rutgers U P, 2000.

Spillers, Hortense. "Mama's Baby, Papa's Maybe: An American Grammar Book." *Diacritics* 17.2 (1987): 67.

"Spook." *The Cassell Dictionary of Slang*, edited by Jonathan Green. London: Cassell, 1998.

"The Spook Who Sat by the Door." *Publishers' Weekly*. 6 Oct. 1969: 50.

Stein, Karen. "Meridian: Alice Walker's Critique of Revolution." *Black American Literature Forum* 20.1/2 (Sp–Su 1986): 131.

Stetler, Russ. "The Works of Frantz Fanon." *Bulletin: University of Chicago Students for a Democratic Society Newsletter*. 8 April 1966. Rpt. *Liberation USA*.

Suleri, Sara. "Woman Skin Deep: Feminism and the Postcolonial Condition." *Critical Inquiry* 18 (Su 1992): 756–769.

Taber, Robert. *War of the Flea: A Study of Guerilla Warfare Theory and Practice*. New York: Lyle Stuart, 1965.

Tarbert, Gary, and Barbara Beach. *Book Review Index: A Master Cumulation, 1965–1984*. Detroit: Gayle Research, 1985.

Thayer, Charles W. *Guerilla*. New York: Harper and Row, 1963.

Tse-tung, Mao. *On Guerilla Warfare*. Translated by Samuel B. Griffith. New York: Frederick Praeger, 1961.

———. *On Practice: On the Relation Between Knowledge and Practice—Between Knowing and Doing*. Peking: Foreign Languages P, 1958.

———. *Selected Military Writings of Mao Tse-tung*. Peking: Foreign Languages P, 1963.

Uyematsu, Amy. "The Emergence of Yellow Power in America." *Gidra* [Los Angeles]. Oct. 1969: 10.

Van DeBurg, William L. *Hoodlums: Black Villains and Social Bandits in American Life*. Chicago: U of Chicago P, 2004.

Verges, Francoise. "Creole Skin, Black Mask: Fanon and Disavowal," *Critical Inquiry* 23.3 (1997): 578–595.

Vickers, George. *The Formation of the New Left: The Early Years*. Lexington, MA: Lexington Books, 1975.

Walker, Alice. *In Search of Our Mothers' Gardens*. 1967; New York: Harcourt Brace Jovanovich, 1983.

———. *Meridian*. New York: Washington Square P, 1976.

Wallace, Maurice. *Constructing the Black Masculine*. Durham, NC: Duke U P, 2002.

Wallace, Michele. *Black Macho and the Myth of the Superwoman*. New York: Dial P, 1979.

Wand, David Hsin-Fu, ed. *Asian American Heritage: An Anthology of Prose and Poetry*. New York: Washington Square P, 1974.

"We Want All Black Men to Be Exempt from Military Service." Cartoon. *The Black Panther*. 4 May 1968: 9.

Wei, William. *The Asian American Movement*. Philadelphia: Temple U P, 1993.

Weusi. "for black guerillas." *Soulbook* 2:3 (1967): 183.

Williams, Raymond. *Culture*. London: Fontana, 1981.

Willis, Susan. *Specifying: Black Women Writing the American Experience*. Madison: U of Wisconsin P, 1987.

Wong, Shawn. *Asian American Literature: A Brief Introduction and Anthology*. New York: Longman, 1996.

Wu, Frank. *Yellow: Race in America Beyond Black and White*. New York: Basic, 2002.

Yep, Laurence, ed. *American Dragons: Twenty-Five Asian American Voices*. New York: Harper Collins Publishers, 1993.

Zolberg, Aristide R. "Frantz Fanon: A Gospel for the Damned." *Encounter* 27.5 (1966).

INDEX

Afro-American Authors, 100
AIIIEEEEE!!!: An Anthology of Asian American Writers, 18, 84, 102–6, 108–10
anthologies, 18–19, 37, 82–113
anticolonialism, 15–16, 18, 24, 27, 29–30, 32–33, 36, 43, 44, 47, 50–52, 84, 97, 147–48
Aoki, Richard, 8
Asian American identity, 23, 38–40, 104
Asian American Literatures, 88
Asian American Movement, 17, 35, 85, 106

Baker, Houston, 147
Big AIIIEEEEE!, The, 129
Black Arts: An Anthology of Black Creations, 18, 84, 96–98, 100, 105
Black Arts Movement, 9–10, 16, 85, 88, 96, 99, 105–6, 114–15
Black Fire: An Anthology of Afro-American Writing, 18, 84, 96, 98, 100, 105, 110
"black Maoism," 4
Black Panther, The, newspaper, 16–17, 35, 54, 69, 71–76, 81, 82, 139, 149
Black Panther Party, 7, 8, 9, 23, 32, 49, 58, 60–62, 69–72, 78, 82
Black Power, 4–8, 9–11, 16, 23, 31, 32, 33, 35, 36, 41, 49–50, 67, 76–78, 79–80, 85, 114, 117, 133–38, 144, 148. *See also* self-defense; self-definition; self-determination

Black Power: The Politics of Liberation, 5, 29–32, 42, 46
Black Writers of America, 99–100
blackness, 5, 8, 15, 16, 19, 20, 69, 80, 84, 89, 101, 111, 116–17, 122, 136, 144, 147
Boggs, Grace Lee, 8

California, 17; Berkeley, 71, 106, 112; Oakland, 8; San Francisco, 34
Call and Response: The Riverside Anthology of the African American Literary Tradition, 106
canon, canonicity, canonization, 18, 23, 82, 83, 84, 88–94, 99, 102–4, 109, 113
Carmichael, Stokely, 5–7, 30–31, 36, 38, 46, 48–50, 52, 65, 79
Chan, Jeffrey Paul, 16, 69, 103, 108, 111
Chin, Frank, 16, 18–19, 68–69, 84, 103, 106–14, 118, 128–30
Civil Rights Movement, 8, 17, 22, 28, 30–31, 76, 115, 120, 125, 134, 136–38
Cleaver, Eldridge, 31–34, 46–50, 58, 66–68, 100, 101, 111, 148. *See also Soul on Ice*
colonialism, 7, 15–16, 17, 21–23, 25, 26, 27–31, 33, 34, 36, 37, 39, 40, 42–45, 46, 51, 54, 71, 81, 84, 86, 148–49
conference of non-aligned countries (Bandung), 3, 8

consciousness: black, 5, 6, 29, 32, 96; black, colonized/decolonized, 8, 26–29, 31, 44–47, 50, 65, 146; "double consciousness," 55, 120–21; revolutionary, 15, 16–17, 20, 32, 67–71, 77–78, 96, 124, 135, 138; yellow, 36–37, 40–41, 109
cultural nationalism, 12, 17, 19, 55, 84, 105, 106, 111, 135, 137, 143–47

Dark Symphony: Negro Literature in America, 98, 105
Debray, Regis, 51, 54–55, 64–66, 74, 119
decolonization, 24, 27–32, 44–45, 50, 56, 84
dialectical materialism, 51, 116
"dissembling," 120
Douglas, Emory, 16, 72

Elaine, Kim, 68–69, 104–5
ethnic studies, 9, 12, 18–19, 82–87, 92–93, 106, 112, 148

Fanon, Frantz, 5, 7, 15, 21–22, 44, 49, 147; biography, 27; *Black Skin, White Masks*, 21, 24–25, 27, 29–32, 40–42, 50–51, 66, 83; *Studies in a Dying Colonialism*, 21, 24; *Toward the African Revolution*, 24; *The Wretched of the Earth*, 21, 24–32 44, 46, 49, 50

Gates, Henry Louis, 42–44, 86, 89
Gidra, 16–17, 34–35, 48, 54, 68, 71–74, 77, 81, 82, 139, 149
gorilla, 53, 66, 68, 70

Greenlee, Sam, 19, 115, 125; *The Spook Who Sat By the Door*, 115, 119, 122–26, 133, 141

guerilla, 5, 7, 14–20, 46, 51–59, 62–70, 73–74, 78–81, 82, 85, 88, 106, 111–13, 115–22, 124–27, 131, 133, 135, 138–42, 143–45, 147, 149, 150, 151
Guevara, Che, 4, 6, 51, 54, 55, 62–65, 111, 119, 138–39

Harlem Renaissance, 7, 10, 88, 98, 99
Hughes, Langston, 100, 101, 114, 150

identity, 4, 9, 12, 15, 16, 18–23, 29, 30, 33, 35, 36, 38–52, 54, 56, 57, 68–69, 71, 72, 78, 80–81, 82, 83, 87, 93, 94, 95, 98, 100, 101, 102, 103–5, 107, 109, 111, 113, 115–17, 119, 122, 127, 130–37, 142, 143, 145–47, 150
ideology, 4, 5, 6–7, 8, 11, 14–15, 18, 20, 22, 28, 30, 37, 45, 49, 50, 52, 53, 55, 56, 58, 63, 69–74, 78, 79–81, 84, 85, 89, 90, 96, 98, 105, 116, 130, 142, 146, 148
illustrations, 70, 73, 75, 76, 77
internal colony paradigm, 7, 15; American style colonialism, 142

JanMohamed, Abdul, 15, 20, 42, 82

Karenga, Maulana, 16, 137, 146
King, Martin Luther, 23, 47, 49, 140, 148
Kingston, Maxine Hong, 16, 18, 130
Kochiyama, Yuri, 8

Lim, Shirley Geok-Lin, 104, 129, 131
"long Civil Rights Movement," 10–11

masculinity, 26, 47, 53, 67–69, 111, 125–26, 133
model minority, 13, 37–42, 69, 81
Mullen, Bill, 31; *Afro-Orientalism*, 3

National Liberation Front (South Vietnamese), 73, 74, 111
Neal, Larry, 16, 96, 118
Newton, Huey, 16, 23, 52, 58, 60–63, 72, 74, 116–17, 125, 146, 148
Norton Anthology of African American Literature, 105

Okada, John, 19, 108, 115, 127–28; *No No Boy*, 115, 127–33, 141
Okihiro, Gary, 85
Okimoto, Daniel, 36, 40; *American in Disguise*, 36, 40, 41

postcolonial, 7, 12–15, 21, 94
"post-soul," 144
Prashad, Vijay, 3, 4; *Everybody Was Kung Fu Fighting*, 3, 4, 154

Reading the Literature of Asian America, 105
Reed, Ishmael, 16, 19, 84, 106, 112, 137
representation, 6, 7, 14, 33, 40–41, 54–55, 79–81, 88–89, 93–94, 101, 104, 117
resistance, 9, 10, 12, 14–15, 18, 19, 48, 50, 51–52, 54, 67, 79, 80, 82, 110–11, 115, 117, 119, 122, 125, 129, 130, 132, 133, 136, 142, 147–48, 150, 151
revolution, 16–19, 25–26, 30, 33, 47, 50, 55, 58, 62–66, 72–74, 81, 87, 112, 115, 118, 131, 134–36, 138–42, 145, 147, 150–51; Algerian, 26, 44
revolutionary aesthetic, 6–7, 16, 57, 71, 97–98, 105–8, 109–12, 115, 139
revolutionary identity, 16, 47, 53–81, 115, 133–35
revolutionary ideology, 38, 43, 55, 58, 69–70, 73, 78, 96, 110, 118
revolutionary nationalism, 19, 106, 135, 137, 145–46
revolutionary rhetoric, 14, 18, 24, 32–34, 35, 51, 55, 64, 67–69, 111, 117, 122, 125, 135, 139–40
revolutionary struggle, 6, 53, 55, 59, 62, 106

San Francisco State College, 9, 24, 35, 72, 82–83
Seale, Bobby, 17, 48, 60–61, 70, 72
Seize the Time, 60
self-defense, 6, 22, 68, 145
self-definition, 6, 41, 52, 54, 72, 85, 97, 103, 110, 115, 117–18, 129, 130, 132–33, 142, 149
self-determination, 5, 6, 16, 30, 32, 37, 39, 41, 46, 52, 60, 68, 72, 80, 87, 97, 103, 105, 110, 115, 117, 134, 135, 142
Smethurst, James, 10, 11
Soul on Ice, 31–33, 40, 41, 42, 48, 66. *See also* Cleaver, Eldridge
"struggle," 7, 17, 22, 25, 26, 28, 30, 36, 38, 43. *See also* resistance

Index 189

subjectivity, 5, 7, 9, 14–15, 18–21, 26,
38, 41, 44–46, 51, 52, 53, 55, 56,
57, 63, 73, 78, 80, 82, 95, 106, 110,
112, 115–22, 127, 130, 132, 134, 138,
141, 142, 144, 147–48, 151

Third World College Strike (San
Francisco State), 9, 24, 35, 72,
82–83, 86
Tse-tung, Mao, 4, 6, 54, 55, 58–59,
61–63, 111, 119, 120, 139, 148

University of California at Berkeley,
24, 35, 72, 106

Vietnam, 9, 14, 16, 33–35, 47–49, 115,
119, 120, 137, 150

Walker, Alice, 19, 115, 133; *Meridian*,
115, 133–42, 150

Yardbird Journal, 19, 84, 107–11
Yellow Power, 3, 5, 15–20, 22, 25, 28,
34–41, 45, 47, 48, 50, 51, 66, 69,
72, 77–80, 83, 114, 117, 119, 122,
147–49